Prisons and the Process of Justice

A672286
8/5

Prisons and the Process of Justice

The Reductionist Challenge

Andrew Rutherford

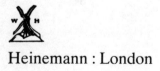

Heinemann : London

William Heinemann Ltd
10 Upper Grosvenor Street, London W1X 9PA
LONDON   MELBOURNE   TORONTO
JOHANNESBURG   AUCKLAND

First published 1984
© A. Rutherford 1984

0 434 91770 2

Printed in England by
Mackays of Chatham Ltd

Preface

The number of persons held in prison in Britain and the United States doubled between 1950 and 1980. The prison systems of these and some other western countries remain set on a relentless expansionist course. Far from protecting citizens from crime, the massive growth of incarceration undermines the essential values which distinguish free and authoritarian societies. Prison systems are expanding despite expenditure cuts on schools, hospitals and social services. Indeed, imprisonment has emerged as a growth industry even in periods of economic stagnation, and some prison systems are geared up to redoubling their size over the coming decades.

To break the expansionist mould requires the recognition that prison populations are the consequence of policy choices concerning the scope and direction of criminal justice. The alternative policy direction, to reduce substantially the apparatus of imprisonment, has to confront the strategic complexities of controlling decision-making throughout the criminal justice process. Experience from several countries, however, suggests that these difficulties are not insurmountable.

This book is addressed to people working throughout the criminal justice process, to students who seek to understand what is going on and, primarily, to concerned citizens to whom criminal justice activities are ultimately accountable. A real and sustained change of direction requires, above all, an informed and sceptical view of prisons and the process of justice by the public and their political representatives. This book is intended to contribute to the emerging scepticism.

Andrew Rutherford

For my parents,
Mark and Gwen Rutherford

Contents

Acknowledgements

The impetus for this book derives from twenty years of working in or around prison systems. I joined the English prison system as an assistant governor in the early 1960s, but after involvement in regimes focused on social work techniques, I became doubtful whether rehabilitative efforts could ever offset the damaging impact of custody. A twenty-one month furlough in the United States, under the auspices of the Commonwealth Fund of New York, encouraged me to explore ways by which prisoners might themselves attempt to make some sense of captivity. Based for most of this time with Donald Cressey at the University of California in Santa Barbara, I was able to see something of prison systems throughout the United States, from Mississippi penal cotton plantations to guided group interaction in New Jersey.

Three final years in the English prison system were concerned primarily with new forms of organizational arrangements which might encourage useful links with the urban areas to which the young men would be returning. My dismay at this time was two-fold. Despite the valiant efforts of staff and prisoners, known then as 'borstal trainees', the numbers returning swiftly to custody remained as high as ever. In addition, I was disappointed by the lack of progress in developing replacements to the use of custody, and in the expansionist direction of the prison bureaucracy.

On resigning from the prison system in 1973, I worked in the United States for six years. As a Fellow of the Crime and Justice programme at the Academy for Contemporary Problems in Columbus, Ohio, I worked closely with a small group of prison system administrators and academics from across the United States, and was impressed by the possibilities open to administrators to act upon a reductionist agenda. One member of this remarkable group was Jerome Miller, who had effectively shut down most institutions for delinquent youth in Massachusetts. After some time at the University of Minnesota and Yale Law School, my final period in the United States was concerned with directing a large-scale study of American prisons and jails. The research, ordered by Congress in 1977, was a response to the massive escalation in prison population size experienced by many state prison systems. The study's findings demonstrated that there are policy options to yet further prison construction. I am grateful to the many persons associated with this research project, and to other friends and colleagues in the United States.

Since returning to England, I have learned much about criminal justice policy issues in the course of discussions with colleagues and students at the University of Southampton. The deepening crisis of the English prison system has been the topic of numerous meetings with criminal justice practitioners, and in particular, I should acknowledge the insights gained from a group of prison officials and academics convened from time to time by Vivien Stern at NACRO. The problems facing the English prison system are not unique and there is much to be learned from practice elsewhere. With David Ward, of the University of Minnesota, I have carried out a cross-national study of prison policy and practice. The findings from this study, to be published by the National Institute of Corrections in Washington D.C., have been drawn upon throughout this book. My thanks are due to Phyllis Modley of the National Institute of Corrections, Irvin Waller of the University of Ottowa, Dato Steenhuis of the Dutch Ministry of Justice, Johannes Feest of the University of Bremum, Eckart Kuhlhorn of the University of Stockholm, Shinichi Tsuchiya of the Japanese Ministry of Justice, Rod Morgan of the University of Bath and David Ward, Herman Milligan and Constance Osterbaan-Milligan of the University of Minnesota.

I want to thank Diana Marshallsay and Joan Hoyle of the University of Southampton Library, Christine Hardwick for preparation of the index, Mark Rutherford for his assiduous proof reading and suggestions regarding literary style, and Fatima Mitchell, Janine Alsford, Suzanne Gillespie and Loraine Birch for typing the manuscript through its various stages. Finally, my gratitude is due to Martin Wright, Arthur de Frisching, Ken Pease, and especially to Judith Rutherford, each of whom suggested improvements to the manuscript.

Part One

Introduction

1 The New Gaol Fever

In his account of gaol fever, William A. Guy quoted Lord Bacon's testimony:

'The most pernicious infection, next to the plague, is the stress of the jail, when prisoners have been long, and close and nastily kept; whereof we have had in our time experienced twice or thrice, when both the judges that sat upon the jail, and numbers of those that attended the business or were present, sickened upon it, and died.'

Professor Guy found that outbreaks of gaol fever had, 'on many occasions, made the legal service of the State a service of danger; but the mischief did not end there; it interfered with the due course of justice by the terror it inspired'.[1] Gaol fever, which was almost certainly typhus, remained prevalent until the end of the eighteenth century. Because it could not be confined within the prison, it was the cause of terror far beyond the prison walls. This terror was used by some early prison reformers, such as the indefatigable chronicler, John Howard, to broaden the constituency for improving conditions endured by persons in prison.

A new and virulent gaol fever is now endemic in many societies, including some which set high store on democratic values and aspirations. Imprisonment is being used more extensively and the apparatus of the prison system being greatly expanded despite, in some instances, stated government policy that parsimony should guide decisions to impose custody. The new gaol fever has every appearance of being beyond political control. Like its eighteenth century predecessor, it may be curbed only when it is widely recognized that the uses made of imprisonment and the conditions within modern prison systems have consequences which transcend the experience endured by persons who become society's prisoners. The scope and administration of criminal law is a measure of the weight given by any society to humanitarian values including liberty. Prison systems are the deep-end of the process of criminal justice. As the prison system expands the ultimate values of democratic society are threatened.

The most visible symptom of the new gaol fever is grossly overcrowded conditions with two, three or more persons being crammed into cells

designed for single occupation. One Home Secretary, and therefore responsible for the English prison system,[2] described his most pressing and
dangerous problem as being 'the chronic crisis of overcrowding in our
prisons which threatens to undermine our criminal justice system and its
contribution to maintaining law and order in society.'[3] The reality of
overcrowded conditions of English prisons in the 1980s is described in
graphic detail by official reports.

The Chief Inspector of Prisons wrote in 1982:

'If any reader unfamiliar with the prison system finds it difficult to picture
the squalor in which many inmates of local prisons are expected to spend
their sentence, let him imagine finding himself obliged to stay in an hotel so
overbooked that he has to share his room with two complete strangers. The
room itself is so cramped that there is little space for his clothes or personal
possessions, and if he wants to walk up and down, the other occupants must
first lie on their beds. Worse, the hotel management insists that guests
remain in their rooms for all but an hour or so a day and must take their
meals there. As a result, the atmosphere rapidly becomes fetid, especially
since neither the reader nor his room mates have been able to take a bath
for some days. But not only is there no basin or bath available, there is
no lavatory either, and the reader and his companions are faced with the
prospect of relying for the foreseeable future upon chamber pots thought-
fully provided by the management. If the reader does not conclude that
such an experience lasting several days would be degrading and brutalizing,
he is being less than honest with himself, how much worse would it be after
several weeks?'[4]

In several American prisons systems, conditions are so bad that prisoners
have successfully litigated under the Fifth Amendent of the Constitution
which outlaws cruel and unusual punishment. In 1980 a federal court found
that overcrowding in the Texas State prison system,

'. . . exercises a malignant effect on all aspects of inmate life . . . Crowded
two or three to a cell or in closely packed dormitories inmates sleep with
the knowledge that they can be molested or assaulted by their fellows at
any time. Their incremental exposure to disease and infection from other
inmates in such narrow confinement cannot be avoided. They must urinate
and defecate, unscreened, in the presence of others.'[5]

In many prison systems, the abysmal conditions are considerably worse
than they were a century or more ago. The deterioration in prison conditions is paradoxical in at least three respects: it has occurred despite the
investment of massive resources into prison systems (in England at a rate
greater than that of public expenditure generally); despite considerable
efforts to extend the range of non-custodial punishments for the courts;
and despite exhortations by government and commissions to sentencers to
be more selective in their use of custody. The established rhetoric is that
prison is a scarce resource and should be used as a last resort. As is often

the case in penal practice, the rhetoric bears little resemblance to the reality. The core of the new gaol fever is indiscriminate use of imprisonment which is both cause and consequence of relentless expansion of all aspects of the prison system.

That the new gaol fever is now pathogenic in some countries and jurisdictions, but absent in others is of crucial importance, suggesting that there is much scope for cross-national learning. There are pitfalls to be avoided in making inferences based on comparing criminal justice practice from one country to another. In particular, cultural traditions, the degree of social homogeneity and differing economic forces have to be taken into consideration. But comparisons across countries or jurisdictions do highlight viable policy choices which otherwise remain obscured. By the early 1980s in the United States and in England, prison populations had established new record high levels. In the United States there are over one half million persons held in prisons and jails, almost twice the number held in 1950. In England, prison population size more than doubled over the same period to surpass 45,000. Prison personnel and the number of cells also experienced rapid growth.

Yet the construction of new prisons has failed both to reduce overcrowding or to replace dilapidated institutions. New prisons exist alongside legacies from the last century. Grossly overcrowded prisons exist in England and many parts of the United States but are unknown in parts of western Europe. A disturbing question arising from the policy quagmire is whether the prison population expansion has been, in part, prompted by the massive investment of resources.

Many prison systems are set upon an expanding course for the remainder of the century. In the United States a Justice Department committee has urged that 2,000 million dollars be made available by the federal government to states for new prison construction.[6] Two years earlier, in 1978, a national study of prisons and jails estimated that to resolve the discrepancy between reported physical capacity and providing the existing prison population with unshared cellular accommodation would cost between 8 and 10,000 million dollars. The study concluded: '. . . even allowing for a wide margin of error, the costs of maintaining 1978 population levels and meeting minimum floor space standards, will far exceed the resources of many state and local corrections systems.'[7]

An inquiry in the United Kingdom, chaired by Mr Justice May, reached the extraordinary conclusion in 1979, despite evidence to the contrary, that the prison systems of England and Wales, Scotland and Northern Ireland have been starved of resources and that, '. . . there is no alternative but to inject much larger resources into UK prisons than has hitherto been decided'.[8] The May Committee concluded that to provide adequate physical accommodation for the 42,000 prisoners held in 1979 would require capital expenditure of £720 million. Although expenditure on these levels is unlikely to be undertaken on either side of the Atlantic official estimates of required spending assume further expansion, or at best a standstill of prison system size. The restraints on public expenditure imposed by the necessities of national economies are opportune if they prompt urgent reassessments to be made as to the direction of penal practice. The central theme of this book is that prison populations are not delivered by a providential stork, but, like the prison systems of which they are a part, are determined by criminal justice policy and practice.

Prison Systems for All Seasons

That a long-standing purpose of imprisonment is to provide punishment is made clear in Ralph Pugh's study of prisons in the English Middle Ages.[9] But there are non-punitive functions of prisons as well, and in the case of some prison systems, these are of considerable importance. Given the esoteric literature on purposes of imprisonment and theories of punishment, there is a tendency to overlook the prison system's more traditional tasks of remand and enforcement. Most, but not all, prison systems provide remand facilities for the courts, holding persons who are either unconvicted or convicted but awaiting sentence. In most European prison systems about one in five of the prison population are of remand status, although because of the relatively short periods of time involved, remand prisoners account for larger proportions of the total throughput of persons. An exception is the Netherlands, where one result of successful stategies reducing the sentenced prison population is that more than half the total prison population are unsentenced persons.

In the United States most state prison systems hold only sentenced prisoners, usually for terms of one year or more, and it is with the local jail system that the remand function is paramount. The federal prison system provides both functions in addition to a more generic warehousing role. For example, following the exodus of refugees from Cuba to the United States in 1980, it was noticed that some of these persons had criminal records and had been released from prison by the Castro government to take advantage of the welcome extended by the Carter administration. Consequently, some 1,500 Cubans were held by the federal prison system while the United States government decided what to do with them. This episode illustrates the multifarious purposes to which a prison system may be put.

In 1982 an English prison governor declared he had no wish to manage a 'penal dustbin'. The household analogy of dustbin is perhaps less instructive than that of the attic, serving the function of storage pending decisions as to disposal. As with the attic, one function of the prison system is to delay or circumvent tough decisions. Remove the easy resort to the prison system and then, but only then, alternative modes of action come to be considered. The very presence of the prison system discourages constructive thinking and action around alternatives. This is, for example, the fate of homeless petty offenders who end up in prison because of decisions based on personal and home circumstances rather than seriousness of offence.

A related function of the prison system has to do with enforcement of non-custodial criminal penalties and civil sanctions. The English prison system, for example, has traditionally been much involved with the business of fine enforcement. Prior to 1914 almost half of all sentenced persons entering the English prison system were sent there as fine defaulters, and in 1981, fine defaulters still accounted for one quarter of sentenced receptions.[10] An ingredient of any reductionist strategy is the loosening of links between the prison system and non-custodial sanctions.

Finally, links between imprisonment and the civil legal process must not be overlooked. Contemporary prison systems are the deep-end of the criminal rather than the civil legal process, but this has not always been the case. Towards the end of the eighteenth century, John Howard estimated that three out of every five persons in English prisons were civil prisoners.[11] The increasing resort to the imprisonment of debtors in the eighteenth century became a major cause of prison overcrowding. Legislation enacted during the first seventy years of the nineteenth century drastically reduced the extent to which the prison system was used to deal with debtors.[12] In the early 1980s civil prisoners account for around one per cent of the average daily English prison population, most of whom were defaulters of maintenance payments ordered by the civil courts.[13]

Since the end of the eighteenth century, the prison system has served primarily as a sanction on conviction for a criminal offence. As use of the death penalty and physical mutilation waned and criminal codes were enacted on the European continent and in America, the punishment role of the prison was enhanced. In England, and to a lesser extent in France, this development was delayed by the practice of transporting some sentenced offenders to distant colonies. However, significant as transportation was in England during the eighteenth and early nineteenth century, there was probably never a time when it was used more frequently than imprisonment.[14] By the mid-nineteenth century, there was an annual prison intake in excess of 160,000 persons.[15]

With the establishment of imprisonment as the most important punishment, the task of holding persons in custody came to be regarded in more ambitious and complex terms. As the French historian Michel Foucault notes, the inherent focus of punishment shifted from the body to the soul. Foucault observes that once the prison had arrived at the end of the eighteenth century, it was difficult to recall what had preceded it or to imagine what it might be replaced with: 'It seemed to have no alternative, as if carried along by the very movement of history . . . it is the detestable solution which one seems unable to do without.'[16]

The prison literature deals more extensively with utilitarian purposes than with normative issues which arise in considering imprisonment. The effectiveness of prison as a means of dealing with crime and other social problems has been called into question since at least the mid-eighteenth century. Henry Fielding, writing on houses of correction in 1750, warned: '. . . whatever these houses were designed to be, or whatever they at first were, the fact is, that they are at present, in general, no other than schools of vice, seminaries of idleness, and common bearers of nastiness and disease.'[17]

Four utilitarian purposes are usually identified and two of these, rehabilitation and individual deterrence, can be considered together. Purposes of rehabilitation and individual deterrence have the same intended outcome, namely the non-return to crime of the offender. The recidivism measure is identical for a detention centre with a para-military routine and the prison which attempts to develop a regime based upon the model of the therapeutic community. The notion of the prison as an instrument of rehabilitation has been an important factor in its survival.

David Rothman's history of early American prisons shows that by 1820 the viability of the entire prison system was in doubt. There were serious problems regarding the control of prisoners and concern as to prisons being schools of crime and places of moral contamination. However, within fifteen years the American penitentiary provided a resurgence of confidence in penal isolation and achieved national acclaim and international study.[18] Spanning the Atlantic, a heated debate raged as to whether reformative benefits of the prison might best be secured through the 'separate system', solitary confinement without contact with other prisoners, or through the 'silent system', association with others at work although in total silence. Reformers lined up on both sides of the controversy expressing opinions with dogmatic passion. From a contemporary standpoint the debate seems oddly irrelevant, but it did serve to divert attention from the institution of imprisonment itself.

From the end of the nineteenth century the mainstream of criminological theory attempted to locate crime causation factors within the individual. The positivist tradition remained dominant until the early 1970s, providing credence to rehabilitative activities inside and outside the prison. As the quality of research into the effectiveness of rehabilitative methods improved, so claims of success faded. Reviews of the research literature in the United States and Europe pointed to the same general conclusion: persons who participate in treatment programmes are neither more nor less likely to commit further offences than non-participants.[19] In particular, Robert Martinson's article 'What Works?', published in 1974, made a considerable impact in the United States, contributing to the downfall of the so-called medical model of dealing with offenders. A rather similar result occurred in England with the publication in 1976 of a Home Office study, *The Effectiveness of Sentencing.*[20]

These studies have had two important implications for the prison system. Firstly, an insistence has emerged that persons should not be sent to prison for the purpose of rehabilitation. Secondly, there is a recognition that even if non-custodial alternatives are not more effective in terms of recidivism they are generally less expensive and almost certainly less intrusive and damaging. The rehabilitative ideal, as it was dubbed by Francis Allen in an influential critique published in 1959,[21] has demonstrated enormous resilience, and it is possible that it will recover lost ground, even to the point of again providing respectability for the prison system.[22] For the 1980s, however, it is other utilitarian purposes which are in the ascendant.

General deterrence refers not only to the threat of punishment but also to the effect of criminal law on behaviour of actions taken at earlier stages of the criminal justice process, such as those taken by the police. Claims are sometimes made that exemplary prison sentences have had a general deterrent effect. These claims, however, remain at the anecdotal level, and most studies are inconclusive as to the efficacy of general deterrent measures. One review of the deterrence literature has concluded: 'A theory for predicting deterrence is impossible without a theory of the generation of attitudes towards laws and offences and a theory of the communication of threats. Such theories are not available and no scientific basis exists for a general policy of deterrence.'[23] Notions of deterrence regularly underline demands for 'getting tough' on crime as is the case regarding the third utilitarian purpose, incapacitation.

Incapacitation refers to the notion that by applying a penal sanction the offender is prevented from committing further offences. Unlike other utilitarian punishment purposes, incapacitation usually implies imprisonment, although in some societies it also suggests the death penalty and various forms of physical mutilation. In the United States, since the mid-1970s incapacitation has emerged as the most potent rationale for imprisonment. Hardline 'law and order' proponents often advocate general deterrence and incapacitation in the same breath. This position, however, involves assumptions about criminality which are contradictory. On the one hand, underlying the notion of general deterrence, the assumption is that the supply of offenders in any given society is elastic. With severe penalties, it is held, the number of offenders declines, whereas any relaxation of law enforcement encourages people to turn to crime. On the other hand, the assumption underlying the notion of incapacitation is that there is an inelastic supply of offenders. With efficient identification and prediction of offenders, society can be protected by long-term incarceration.[24]

The champions of incapacitation as a rationale for imprisonment generally ignore violence and other crime within the prison. The official statistics portray a high level of assaults within prison systems and these almost certainly greatly under-estimate the real situation. The fear of violence is greater in most prisons than in the community generally. Unless the view is taken that persons entering the prison system have forfeited all claims on safety from attack, events which occur within the prison system must be included in the incapacitation equation.

The point of controversy which has most often arisen in the incapacitation debate has had to do with whether or not future violent and dangerous offending can be predicted. Norval Morris attempted to lay the notion of dangerousness to rest. 'The concept of dangerousness is so plastic and vague – its implementation so imprecise – that it would do little to reduce either the present excessive use of imprisonment or social injury from violent crime.'[25] In England the dangerousness debate was rekindled in the early 1980s with the publication of *Dangerousness and Criminal Justice*, the report of a working party which recommended a new 'protective sentence' for the minority of exceptional, high-risk offenders who cause grave harm.[26] The Floud report has been much criticized,[27] and its general thrust was hardly consistent with the conclusion reached by a Home Office study the preceding year. 'The infrequency of really serious crimes of violence, their apparently generally random quality and the rarity of anything like a genuinely "dangerous type" offers little encouragement for a policy which aims to reduce assaults by selective incapacitation of those with violent records.'[28] The Floud Committee fell into the trap of believing that if the issue of really dangerous persons can be disposed of, sanctions for less serious offenders can then be scaled down. There is little reason to believe that the notion of dangerousness will shed its plasticity and every reason to fear that severe protective sentences will tighten rather than loosen the ratchet quality of the overall penalty structure.

Support for notions of incapacitation which goes beyond offenders deemed to be dangerous has come most often, but not exclusively, from conservative commentators on criminal justice. Extracts from a book by James Q. Wilson, the conservative political scientist, were published in the *New York Times Magazine* under the heading 'Lock 'Em Up and Other Thoughts on Crime'. Wilson, who was later appointed by the Reagan administration to a federal task force on violent crime, argued, 'Wicked people exist. Nothing avails but to set them apart from innocent people.'[29] However, support for incapacitation as a rationale for imprisonment has not only come from the political Right. Ironically, the notion of incapacitation was endorsed by the liberal Committee for the Study of Incarceration as an additional rationale to just deserts for the use of imprisonment. 'The incapacitative effect can be achieved, moreover, without need to rely on predictions of individual dangerousness. Incarceration can be prescribed as the only authorized severe punishment – so that all offenders convicted of sufficiently serious crime would be confined, irrespective of the likelihood of their returning to crime.'[30]

The Committee at least acknowledged problematic aspects of incapacitation policy, namely, that imprisonment may simply shift the location of some crime from general community to prison, that the criminogenic influences of the prison may increase the likelihood of further offending and the political risk that the incapacitation net will be widely cast. Such qualms do not appear to have worried Michael Sherman and Gordon Hawkins in their abrasive endorsement of selective incapacitation as the central purpose of imprisonment. 'If the non-violent offenders were not imprisoned, a great deal of correctional capacity would become available for longer stays for violent offenders now incarcerated, or to lock up many violent criminals who now go free.'[31] This simplistic proposal ignores the ways by which discretion is exercised in the early stages of the criminal justice process. In practice, incapacitation is anything but selective as is amply demonstrated by the history of preventative detention in England and the sexual psychopath laws in the United States.

The advocates of incapacitation, selective or general, attempt to dodge the predicament, posed by Lewis Carroll's White Queen, of punishing people for crimes they have not yet committed.

'What sort of things do you remember best?' Alice ventured to ask.

'Oh, things that happened the week after next,' the Queen replied in a careless tone. 'For instance, now,' she went on, sticking a large piece of plaster on her finger as she spoke, 'there's the King's Messenger. He's in prison now, being punished: and the trial doesn't even begin till next Wednesday: and of course the crime comes last of all.'

'Suppose he never commits the crime,' said Alice.

'That would be all the better, wouldn't it?' the Queen said, as she bound the plaster round her finger with a bit of ribbon.

Alice felt there was no denying that. 'Of course it would be all the better,' she said: 'but it wouldn't be all the better his being punished'.

'You're wrong there, at any rate,' said the Queen. 'Were you ever punished?'

'Only for faults', said Alice.

'And you were all the better for it, I know!' the Queen said triumphantly.

'Yes, but then I had done the things I was punished for', said Alice: 'that makes all the difference.'

'But if you hadn't done them', the Queen said, 'that would have been better still; better, and better, and better!' Her voice went higher with each 'better,' till it got quite to a squeak at last.

Alice was just beginning to say 'There's a mistake somewhere –,' when the Queen began screaming, so loud that she had to leave the sentence unfinished.[32]

Most literature on prisons and the justice process focuses on questions of effectiveness with reference to the utilitarian purposes of rehabilitation, deterrence and incapacitation. The range of punishments has been insufficiently considered from a values standpoint. Even the so-called justice model of punishment, which arose largely as a reaction to the excesses of treatment ideology, has almost exclusively been concerned with fairness in the distribution of punishment rather than with the intrinsic nature of available punishments. The point was put well by D. J. Galligan in a critique of the justice model: 'The obsession with fair treatment within a penalty system, whatever it happens to be, rather than concern about the penalty system is a tragic mistake. It is easier and more politic to reform distribution than the system itself, but to pursue the one without the other is largely misplaced.'[33] In broad terms, punishments can fairly easily be differentiated according to severity. For example, there is likely to be consensus that the death penalty is a more severe punishment than imprisonment, even when confinement for life is envisaged.[34] Similarly, few people would dissent from the general proposition that imprisonment is more severe than penalties not involving custody. The comprehensive scaling of penalties requires regard to both qualitative and quantitative considerations, but this task, perhaps because of its complexities, has largely been ignored by criminologistis and legislators.[35]

It is instructive to compare approaches to imprisonment with the death penalty. A crucial aspect of the case against the death penalty is that it differs qualitatively from other types of punishment. In an elegant essay, Charles Black developed an argument against the death penalty in the context of the inevitability of mistake in the course of criminal justice. Black, writing in the early 1970s and before a new spate of executions got underway in the United States, held that 'death *is* different, that it is irrevocable in quite a distinct sense from the general irrevocability of all happenings. If a mistake of any kind is discovered, it is too late. In every way and for every purpose, it is too late'.[36] Black holds that the death penalty should be rejected because of the arbitrary and fallible nature of decision-making within the criminal justice process. This line of reasoning clearly has implications, as Black notes, for other criminal penalties and in particular for imprisonment. The criminal justice process is comprised, as described in the next chapter, of a set of decisions characterized by discretion which is inevitably uneven and often unfair in application. Charles Black persuasively concludes that this feature of criminal justice is sufficient to outlaw use of the death penalty. While an extension of this thesis does not amount to the complete rejection of the prison system, it does much to reinforce the view that very sparing use be made of custody.

Imprisonment is qualitatively different from punishments which do not involve custody. Four features of imprisonment, in particular, account for its uniqueness. First, imprisonment is irrevocable in a sense that does not apply to non-custodial punishment. Although without the obvious finality of the death penalty, time spent in prison cannot be restored. In cases of imprisonment of persons later found to be innocent, while financial compensation may be available, time itself cannot be repaid. Time spent in prison, as prisoners' calendars invariably testify, is typically regarded as time lost from life.

The second central feature of imprisonment is the denial of basic freedoms of choice. These areas of choice are of such commonplace nature that they are easily overlooked. As Bernard Shaw counselled, to understand imprisonment one first has to understand freedom.[37] Such basic choices encompass a wide range of everyday life, and represent the stamp of individuality. A former prisoner and first offender, Peter Wildeblood, who spent a year in English prisons in the mid-1950s, noted the all-embracing impact of the prison: 'The purpose, or at least the effect, of sentencing a man to prison is to strip him of everything he has – of the possessions, the attitudes of mind that go to make up a distinguishable human personality.'[38] Of paramount importance is freedom to choose companions and associates. Most people, to use English prison parlance, who are 'on the out', are able to choose with whom they live and work. Such choices, if they exist within the prison system, exist within very narrow bounds. The absence of choice in this area has a double-edged quality. The prisoner, separated from family and friends is at the same time being thrust into company which he or she may dislike intensely.

Even where efforts have been made to 'normalize' the prison experience, these inherent consequences of imprisonment remain. As argued in Chapter 5, 'normalization' is a misnomer in the context of imprisonment, and at best, it refers to modest and tenuous efforts to humanize the prison. Measures such as access to a telephone, conjugal visits or frequent furloughs, while not unimportant, hardly substitute for family and social life. Contemporary penal rhetoric stresses that imprisonment should not go beyond removal of those rights which are essential to effect custody. In reality, imprisonment means stepping into another world. An English prison system official once noted that young prisoners returning by coach from a football game would sing until they reached the institution, when the chorus stopped and 'they paused to put on their institutional faces'. Use of phrases such as 'deadening routine' or the 'The Tombs' reguarly evoke imagery of death in the context of the prison. Life in prison is neither life nor death but doing time.

The third crucial feature of imprisonment is the impact upon the prisoner's family. Prison imposes a stigma and burden upon the family which goes far beyond that of conviction in court. Being in prison, for family members, is a continual reminder of the court's judgment. The impact of imprisonment may involve consequences as severe as break-up of the family through divorce or children being removed from their homes. Even with respect to relatively short periods of custody, family members are likely to experience considerable distress, arising from the shame of prison and the difficulties involved in keeping in touch. In particular, visits to the prison impose emotional and physical strain. Pauline Morris found that many prisoners' wives reported that their children had no idea their father was in prison, but she went on to comment: 'Bearing in mind that many children can read simple words by the age of five, and since the word 'PRISON' in capital letters is written outside the entrance to each establishment, it seems unlikely that so many children are in fact, wholly ignorant. The effect of this pretence is two-fold; children have to repress their feelings about their father, and at the same time to support the mother when she invents reasons for his absence.'[39]

The stigma of having been inside prison is the fourth feature of imprisonment and may last a lifetime. The personal consequences of penal incarceration often close social, educational and employment opportunities. The scars of imprisonment take different forms. For some, the horror and the shame of penal incarceration remain many years after release. Jimmy Boyle, who described himself as a professional criminal for whom prison was just a hazard of life, has written: 'The fact is prison eats your insides out and ties your stomach in knots, leaving your heart very heavy. All this takes place when you are alone, but it wouldn't be the done thing to let this be seen by other people.'[40] For others, prison induces dependency on institutional life, providing a more predictable environment than the outside world. Many persons in prison, as in other closed institutions, are socially and emotionally crippled by years of institutional life. The condition of being a 'state-raised convict' is vividly described by Jack Henry Abbott. 'As a boy in reform school, he is punished for being a little boy. In prison, he is punished for trying to be a man . . . He is treated as an adolescent in prison . . . At age 37 I am barely a precocious child. My passions are those of a boy.'[41] Many prisoners are ambivalent about their dependence on the prison; others are resigned to be part of the shuffling mass conforming to prison routine.

Imprisonment should be separate from and not overlap with other forms of punishment. The gap which divides the prison from alternative punishments might be termed the custodial threshold. It is one of the ironies of penal policy that two apparently liberalizing steps can threaten to undermine the custodial threshold. Only brief mention is required here as both are discussed in subsequent chapters. First, there are attempts to reduce the appearance of custody by means such as the 'half-way house', weekend or other variations on intermittent custody. Second, there is the danger that very short custodial sentences will appear less severe than other punishments. It appears from the few empirical efforts at scaling penalties, that this is likely to occur.[42] The pains of imprisonment remain, although these may be reduced, even when custody is imposed for very short periods or takes a mitigated form.

The absence of basic principles concerning the use of imprisonment is at the root of the crisis facing many prison systems. Legislatures have created an extensive apparatus for dealing with crime but have rarely paused to consider either underlying purposes or overall design. This reluctance to articulate principles is exemplified by the absence of a coherent juris-prudence of sentencing. In particular, the decision to imprison has been left to the vagaries of individual discretion and the influences of local tradition. The task of fashioning a jurisprudence of the decision to imprison has only just begun, with the common starting point that prison only be used when any other punishment would depreciate the seriousness of the offence.[43]

The reality which characterizes many prison systems is that, far from being the last resort, imprisonment is used as an early resort. These prisons systems primarily hold persons for offences not involving violence, as shown in Table 1.1.

Table 1.1

Most serious offence of sentenced prison population in England,
West Germany, Sweden and Japan

	Percentage of total sentenced prison population		
	Violence	*Property*	*Other*
England (1981)	29	56	14*
W. Germany (1978)	23	55	22
Sweden (1979)	18	35	47
Japan (1978)	24	53	22

Violence = homicide, rape and other sex offences, assaults, robbery
Property = burglary, fraud/tax evasion, larceny
Other = alcohol, drugs, driving, other offences
* includes cases where no offence was recorded

Source: forthcoming report on cross-national prison policy and practice. Hereafter referred to as cross-national study.

A more detailed profile of the English prison population in terms of offence type is presented in Table 1.2. It can be seen that the percentage of persons received into the prison system sentenced for offences of violence, including sexual offences and robbery, is about half that of the standing population.

The paucity of detailed information regarding the composition of prison populations is remarkable. The only survey to be undertaken in England was a small sample of sentenced prisoners in the south-east region in 1972 which found that 30 per cent were sentenced for petty or minor offences. The researchers developed four criteria for divertability from the prison system – no serious offence against the person, no intent of making considerable gain from crime, no large sums acquired by crime and no obvious competence in planning. The study found that one third of the sample met each of the four criteria.[44]

Table 1.2

Offence composition of English prison population, 1981
(sentenced persons including fine defaulters as percentage of total sentenced population and receptions)

	Sentenced population on 30/6/81	Sentenced receptions during 1981
Violence	18 ⎫	13 ⎫
Sexual	4 ⎬ 29	1 ⎬ 17
Robbery	7 ⎭	3 ⎭
Theft	26	33
Burglary	30	26
Other	15*	24
Total	100(N = 36,669)	100(N = 88,110)

* includes 3.4 per cent where no offence was recorded

Source: abstracted from *Prison Statistics 1981*.

One of the most striking features of many prison populations is their relative youth. A survey undertaken of federal and state prison systems in the United States in 1978 revealed that 40 per cent were aged under 25.[45] In England in 1981, 50 per cent of the sentenced prison population were aged under 25 and 30 per cent were under 21. The increasingly youthful composition of persons entering the English prison system is illustrated below in Table 1.3

Table 1.3

Receptions of persons under sentence (including fine defaulters)
by the English prison system, 1951–81

	Aged Under 21		Total Receptions		Under 21 year olds as
	Total	Index (1951 = 100)	Total	Index (1951 = 100)	percentage of total receptions under sentence
1951	3,232	100	36,164	100	8.9
1961	9,275	286	46,618	128	19.8
1971	19,846	614	60,427	157	32.8
1981	32,892	1,018	88,100	243	37.3

Source: data abstracted from relevant volumes of annual reports of Prison Department and Prison Statistics

People in prison tend to be from the lowest social and economic groups. This is hardly surprising given the greater extent to which the misbehaviour of disadvantaged persons is criminalized and penalized. Prisoners are sometimes stereotyped by their keepers with such low status terminology as 'animals' or 'sleazy scumbags'. In earlier times a commentator on criminal justice had this to say: 'These filthy and unprofitable generation, this refuse and off-scouring of the world, must be purged away by the hand of the magistrate.'[46]

It is not part of the reductionist argument that there is no place for the prison in contemporary society, and that the prison should follow the death penalty, at least in those parts of the world where capital punishment has been abolished, into the pages of history. Prison is likely to remain the 'detestable solution' into the foreseeable future, but, it is argued here, should be restricted to the business of serious crime. Only when used as a last resort does the prison serve a function which is useful and legitimate. This general conclusion is shared by several explorers of contemporary prison systems. Norval Morris in *The Future of Imprisonment*, while propounding a parsimonious use of prison, offered 'an optimistic view of the future of imprisonment in which the prison retains an important residual role in the criminal justice system'.[47] The Committee for the Study of Incarceration agreed that the prison had to be retained despite, 'our acute awareness of the inhumanity of present conditions, our sense of the inability of courts or administrative agencies to effect meaningful changes in the quality of prison life, and the strongly-felt desire on the part of at least some members of the committee to be done with this horrendous system once and for all. . . .'[48] John Irwin, sociologist and champion of prisoners' rights, concurred in his review of the American prison scene, 'I defend prisons because they are the only feasible punishment for serious crime'.[49] The thesis of this book is not for the abolition of prisons but for drastic paring. Expansionist prison systems are fuelled by expectations that custody is readily available. If prison is to be a last resort it must be regarded as a scarce resource.

Prison systems pursuing an expansionist course are in the company of nations and jurisdictions hardly noted, in Winston Churchill's words, for 'constant heart-searching by all charged with the duty of punishment'. To redirect prison system policy in a reductionist direction gives rise to many challenges. More is involved than curtailing the pressures which favour growth. Expansionism must be replaced by reductionist policy that endorses three basic steps. The first step is acknowledgement that policy choices are available, as is demonstrated by developments in countries such as Japan and the Netherlands. The second step requires targeting new low levels for prison usage and population size. The third step is mustering the political will to pursue the reductionist course across difficult terrain. The nature of the obstacles to be encountered will vary from one country to another, and reductionist strategies need to be fashioned to meet local circumstances. This book is, therefore, intended to serve less as a chart than as a compass.

References

1 William A. Guy, *Public Health, A Popular Introduction to Sanitary Science*, London: Henry Renshaw, 1870, pp. 166–77.

2 References here and throughout the text to 'England' means England and Wales. Scotland and Northern Ireland have separately administered prison systems. In 1981 the Scottish prison system had an average daily prison population of 4,500, representing a prison population rate per 100,000 inhabitants of 90, very similar to that of England. See *Prisons in Scotland, Report for 1981*, Edinburgh: HMSO 1982. Useful material on prisons in Scotland is contained in Mike Fitzgerald and Joe Sim, *British Prisons*, Oxford: Blackwell 1979. See also *Report of Committee of Inquiry into United Kingdom Prison Services* (chairman Mr Justice May), Cmnd 7673, London: HMSO 1979, for review of prison problems in Scotland and Northern Ireland.

3 William Whitelaw, unpublished speech to Leicestershire magistrates, 13 February 1981.

4 *Report of H.M. Chief Inspector of Prisons for England and Wales, 1981*, Cmnd 8532, 1982, pp. 18–19.

5 *Ruiz* v *Estelle*, 503 F.Supp. 1277 (E.D. Tex., 1980).

6 *Attorney General's Task Force on Violent Crime, Final Report*, U.S. Department of Justice, Washington D.C., 1981, p. xiii.

7 National Institute of Justice, *American Prisons and Jails*, Volume III, *Conditions and Costs of Confinement*. National Institute of Justice, Washington D.C.: Government Printing Office, 1981, p. 125.

8 This estimate included £180m to replace 5,500 cells resulting from the installation of integral sanitation, and further £300m for the provision of 8,500 places in order to eliminate cell-sharing. See *Report of the Inquiry into the United Kingdom Prison Services*, op. cit., note 2, pp. 143–4.

9 Ralph B. Pugh, *Imprisonment in Medieval England*, Cambridge: Cambridge University Press, 1968, esp. pp. 26–47.

10 *Prison Statistics for England and Wales, 1981*, Cmnd 8654, London: HMSO, 1982, p. 22.

11 John Howard, *The State of the Prisons*, London: Dent 1929, p.17.

12 For a review of this legislation see Seán McConville, *A History of English Prison Administration*, vol. I, London: Routledge & Kegan Paul, 1981, pp. 341–7.

13 See generally, Geoff Wilkins, *Making Them Pay*, London: NACRO, 1979; also M. D. A. Freeman and Christina M. Lyon 'The Imprisonment of Maintenance Defaulters', *Howard Journal*, **20**, 1981, pp. 15–28. There was, however, in 1982 a suggestion to reintroduce imprisonment for debt. See *Insolvency Law and Practice*, Report of the Review Committee (Chairman, Sir K. Cork), Cmnd 8558, 1982, para. 264.

14 See e.g. Leon Radzinowcicz, *A History of English Criminal Law and its Administration from 1750*, vol. 1, London: Stevens and Sons, 1948, p. 160.

15 Henry Mayhew, *The Criminal Prisons of London and Scenes of Prison Life*, London: Griffin, Bohn, 1862, p. 84.

16 Michel Foucault, *Discipline and Punish: The Birth of the Prison*, New York: Vintage Books, 1979, p. 232.

17 Henry Fielding, 'An Enquiry into the Causes of the Late Increases in Robbers' 1751, cited by Leon Radzinowicz, *A History of English Criminal Law and its Administration, from 1750*, vol. I, *The Movement for Reform, London*: Stevens and Stevens, 1948, pp. 409–10. See also John Howard, op. cit., note 11, p. 8.

18 David J. Rothman, *The Discovery of the Asylum, Social Order and Disorder in the New Republic*, Boston and Toronto: Little Brown, 1971, pp. 93–4.

19 See e.g. W. C. Bailey, 'Correctional Outcome: an evaluation of 100 Reports', *Journal of Criminal Law, Criminology and Police Science*, **57**, 1966, pp. 153–60; J. Robison and G. Smith, 'The effectiveness of correctional programmes', *Crime and Delinquency* **17**, 1971, pp. 67–80; Robert Martinson, 'What Works? questions and answers about prison reform'. *The Public Interest*, Spring, 1974, pp. 22–54.

20 S. R. Brody, *The Effectiveness of Sentencing – a review of the literature*, Home Office Research Study No. 35, London: HMSO, 1976.
21 Francis A. Allen, *The Borderland of Criminal Justice: Essays in Law and Criminology*, Chicago: University of Chicago Press, 1964.
22 In 1979 the May Committee attempted to introduce the phrase 'positive custody' to the rich and fertile area of penal rhetoric. May Report, op. cit., note 2, pp. 67–73.
23 Deryck Beyleveld, 'Deterrence Research as a Basis for Deterrence Policies', *Howard Journal*, **18**, 1979, p. 146; see also Deryck Beyleveld 'Identifying, Explaining and Predicting Deterrence'. *British Journal of Criminology*, **19**, 1979, pp. 205–224; Franklin E. Zimring and Gordon J. Hawkins, *Deterrence: The Legal Threat in Crime Control*, Chicago: University of Chicago Press, 1973; Johannes Andenaes, *Punishment and Deterrence*, Ann Arbor: University of Michigan Press, 1976.
24 That contradictory assumptions might underline general deterrence and incapacitation was raised by Bruce Ackerman at a seminar held in 1977 for Yale Law Faculty led by James Q. Wilson of Harvard University.
25 Norval Morris, *The Future of Imprisonment*, Chicago: University of Chicago Press, 1974, p. 62.
26 Jean Floud and Warren Young, *Dangerousness and Criminal Justice*, London: Heinemann, 1981. The working party defined 'grave harm' as 'death, serious bodily injury; serious sexual assaults; severe or prolonged pain or mental stress; loss of or damage to property which causes severe personal hardship; damage to the environment which has a severely adverse effect on public health or safety; serious damage to the security of the State'. ibid, p. 154.
27 See e.g. Leon Radzinowicz and Roger Hood, 'Dangerousness and Criminal Justice: a few reflections'. *Criminal Law Review* 1981, pp. 756–61; A. E. Bottoms and Roger Brownsword, 'The Dangerousness Debate after the Floud Report'. *British Journal of Criminology* **22**, 1982, pp. 229–254, one of several articles in a special number on dangerousness.
28 Stephen Brody and Roger Tarling, *Taking Offenders out of Circulation*, Home Office Research Study No. 64, London: HMSO, 1980.
29 James Q. Wilson, *Thinking About Crime*, New York: Basic Books, 1975, p. 235. Wilson's article appeared in *The New York Times Magazine*, March 9, 1975.
30 Andrew von Hirsch, *Doing Justice: The Choice of Punishments*, New York: Hill and Wang, 1976, pp. 112–13.
31 Michael Sherman and Gordon Hawkins, *Imprisonment in America, Choosing the Future*, Chicago: University of Chicago Press, 1981, p. 111.
32 Lewis Carroll, *Through the Looking Glass*, New York: Random House, 1946, pp. 73–4.
33 D. J. Galligan, 'Guidelines and Just Deserts: A Critique of Recent Trends in Sentencing Reform'. *Criminal Law Review* 1981, p. 307. Similarly, Nils Christie has written of, 'the overwhelming interest shown in neo-classical literature in the control of pain delivery, rather than in the pain itself. To regulate pain becomes more important – more in the centre of public and scholarly attention – than to use pain. Regulation of pain becomes so important that the necessity of inflicting pain is more or less taken for granted'. Nils Christie, *Limits to Pain*, Oxford: Martin Robertson, 1982, p. 49.
34 This general proposition holds despite exceptional cases where individuals opt for death rather than exhausting the appeal process.
35 As Leslie Sebba has commented. '. . . the sophisticated research and intense energy that have been expanded in improving upon the legislature's categorisation of offences by means of the seriousness of offence studies . . . have not been matched by any similar attempt to scale penalties'. Leslie Sebba, 'Some Explorations in the Scaling of Penalties', *Journal of Research in Crime and Delinquency*, 1978, p. 253. Sebba reported empirical work in this area with college students, ibid, pp. 257–62; see also V. L. Hamilton and L. Rotkin, 'Interpreting the Eighth Amendment: Perceived Seriousness of Crime and Severity of Punishment' in H. A. Bedau and C. M. Pierie (eds.), *Capital Punishment in the United States*, New York: AMS Press, 1976.
36 Charles L. Black, Jr. *Capital Punishment: The Inevitability of Caprice and Mistake*, New York: W. W. Norton, 1974, p. 32. It might be noted that in 1983 there were over 1,100 persons on 'death row' in the United States.

37 George Bernard Shaw, preface to Sidney and Beatrice Webb, *English Prisons Under Local Government*, London: Longmans, Green, 1922, p. xxiii.

38 Peter Wildeblood, *Against the Law*, Harmondsworth: Penguin, 1957, p. 116.

39 Pauline Morris. *Prisoners and their Families*, London: George Allen and Unwin, 1965, p. 114; see generally, Howard League for Penal Reform, *Losing Touch, Restrictions on Prisoners' Outside Contacts*, Working Party Report, London, 1979.

40 Jimmy Boyle, *A Sense of Freedom*, London: Pan, 1977, p. 107.

41 Jack Henry Abbott, *In the Belly of the Beast: Letters from Prison*, New York: Village Books, 1982, pp. 14–15. On state-raised youths, John Irwin wrote, 'The world view of these youths is distorted, stunted or incoherent. To a great extent, the youth prison is their only world, and they think almost entirely in the categories of this world. They tend not to be able to see beyond the walls. They do conceive of the streets, but only from the perspective of the prison.' John Irwin, *The Felon*, Englewood Cliffs, N. J.: Prentice-Hall, 1970, p. 29.

42 Leslie Sebba, for example, found that college students rated a fine of $250 more severely than one month imprisonment. There are difficulties in interpreting findings of this sort, however, Sebba also found that the students rated a fine of $50,000 as being more severe than five years imprisonment. Sebba, op. cit., note 35, p. 259; public opinion polls have not gone beyond a very general differentiation of offences. See e.g. Stephen Shaw, *The People's Justice*, Prison Reform Trust, London, pp. 17–19.

43 Norval Morris regards imprisonment as the least restrictive punishment when any other punishment would depreciate the seriousness of the offence. Morris's other two criteria for deciding to imprison are those of general deterrence and as a means of dealing with cases where lesser sanctions have frequently or recently been imposed for earlier offences. Norval Morris, op. cit. note 25, pp. 77–80; see also von Hirsch, op. cit. note 30, p. 110.

44 'A Survey of the South East Prison Population', *Home Office Research Unit Bulletin*, No. 5, 1978, pp. 12–24. The profile of the south east prison population was based on a ten per cent sample in prison on 2.2.1972, and consisted of 771 sentenced prisoners, excluding 40 life sentenced prisoners. See also Susan Fairhead and Tony F. Marshall, 'Dealing with the Petty Persistent Offender' in *The Petty Persistent Offender*, proceedings of a Seminar held at NACRO, London: NACRO, 1979, pp. 1–9. For a useful discussion of the policy implications of this study see A. E. Bottoms and William McWilliams, 'A Non-Treatment Paradigm for Probation Practice', *British Journal of Social Work*, **9**, 1979, pp. 179–181.

45 *American Prisons and Jails*, vol. 2, op. cit., note 7, pp. 121–2.

46 Cited by Seán McConville, op. cit., note 12., p. 46.

47 Norval Morris, op. cit., note 25, p. 12.

48 William Gaylin and David J. Rothman in introduction to von Hirsch, op. cit. note 30, p. xxxv.

49 John Irwin, *Prisons in Turmoil*, Boston and Toronto: Little Brown, 1980, p. 239.

2 From Great Expectations to Bleak House

The prison system is the ultimate expression of the entire criminal justice process. The size and composition of the prison population, the throughput of prisoners, the level of resources invested and the determination of policy priorities all reflect broader concerns which arise in the administration of criminal law. The expansionist tendencies of many contemporary prison systems are, in large part, a consequence of expectations of what can be achieved through criminal law. Prison policy choices must necessarily take account of the criminal justice process, but these choices are not always as restricted as is presumed by the traditional and reactive stance of policy-makers. To view the size of the prison system as the inevitable consequence of decisions made at earlier stages of the criminal justice process obscures the extent to which different aspects of the criminal justice process might be changed.

The scope of criminal law

The law is only one means of social control and usually less potent than family, school and workplace. When law is invoked it may often be civil rather than criminal. An effort to achieve redress or compensation through civil procedures may be a more appropriate response to what Louk Hulsman of Erasmus University in Rotterdam calls 'problematic situations' than resorting to the criminal law. The criminal law tends to be a blunt and cumbersome instrument and may be less effective than arbitration, mediation or other means of resolution based upon civil law procedures. Consequently, some reformers would prefer to see much less resort to criminal law. Hulsman has urged that compensatory and educational styles of social control replace those based upon punishment. He goes further than most advocates of de-criminalization, and argues that not only theft but other more serious offences be dealt with as civil matters rather than as crimes. Hulsman uses the word "civilization" to describe the replacement of criminal law by means of the extension and adaptation of compensation procedures through civil law.[1]

Progress in reducing the scope of the criminal law has, at best, been slight. Some criminal statutes have been repealed, mainly with respect to victimless crimes such as prostitution, homosexual relations between consenting adults and attempted suicide. More commonly, decriminalization takes a *de facto* form through decisions made not to make use of criminal law. With respect to many 'problematic situations' it is the victims or other persons involved who decide not to turn to the criminal law. In England, it is estimated that for every one hundred domestic burglaries which are reported to the police, there are a further fifty to one hundred which remain unreported. For many other offences the non-reporting rate is generally estimated to be much higher. With respect to wounding, theft from the person and criminal damage the non-reporting rate may be higher by respectively five, twelve and thirteen times. The victims and witnesses, who are most directly affected by the crime, make the crucial decision as to whether or not to invoke the criminal law. In many cases the persons involved decide to deal with the situation in some other way. Furthermore, when an event is reported to the police, the police may decide to 'no crime' the event, and not record it as a criminal offence.[2]

What little progress has been made to remove the intrusion of the criminal law in certain areas of human behaviour has been greatly surpassed by the proliferation of new criminal statutes. Environmental pollution and misuse of electronic information systems are among recently acquired territories of criminal law. In the United States since the Second World War, there has been a gradual expansion in the scope of offences. Over the period 1948–1978 in only one out of ten states which were examined in a recent study did the number of acts defined as an offence decrease.[3] The American legal scholar, Henry M. Hart wrote: '. . . the criminal law, like all law, is concerned with the pursuit of human purposes through the forms and modes of social organization, and it needs always to be thought about in that context as a method or process of doing something'.[4] It is this 'process of doing something' through the criminal law and the implications this has for the use and nature of prisons that is now beginning to be better understood.

It is important to place stress on the word *process* as there is a frequent and misleading tendency to view criminal justice as a system. Criminal justice as a system suggests an articulation of purposes and a degree of coordination and coherence which bears no resemblance to reality. One consequence of the system's approach is to invite expectations of criminal justice which cannot be achieved. Alternatively, to view criminal justice as a process allows an appreciation of the loose interconnections between the various stages, of different and sometimes competing goals between and within agencies, of the dynamic nature of the forces which determine shape and direction, of the informal nature of much of what takes place, and of the unanticipated consequences which not infrequently ensue.

Criminal justice arrangements may be viewed through two contrasting perspectives. Dominating the period since the Second World War has been the perspective of Great Expectations: the answer to crime lies in the full and vigorous application of the criminal law. More recently, an alternative perspective which might be called Bleak House has begun to emerge. Bleak House regards criminal justice as, at best, tangential in dealing with crime and not infrequently as counter-productive.

Great Expectations

Great Expectations is based upon the presumption that criminal justice arrangements can be applied in a manner which is purposeful, rational and systematic. Given these conditions together with political resolution and considerable resources, reductions in crime are achievable. This perspective, in part, resembles the Crime Control model, developed by Herbert Packer in his pioneering exploration of the criminal justice process.[5]

Great Expectations considers:

- criminal justice to be a system comprised of rationally coordinated bureaucracies;
- criminal justice to be the primary agent of social control. As Packer put it, with reference to his Crime Control model, criminal justice positively guarantees social freedom;[6]
- the primary objective of criminal justice is the control of crime;
- the work of criminal justice personnel is focused upon crime;
- crime is committed by a relatively small and identifiable group of people; with reference to this group there is what Packer calls 'presumption of guilt', which is, 'purely and simply a prediction of outcome';[7]
- the central strategies to be used are those of deterrence, incapacitation and rehabilitation.

Great Expectations promises high returns, given a large investment of resources, and during the 1950s and 1960s ambitious and far-reaching criminal justice programmes were launched in many Western countries. In the United States the airspace over the National Airport in Washington D.C. was thick with criminologists in demand for commissions and task forces, and Congress established the Law Enforcement Assistance Administration to spearhead the fight against crime. Multitudes of new projects were launched along the various stages of the criminal justice process. Resources were made available to evaluate these initiatives, encouraging the establishment of criminal justice institutes and university-based departments of criminal justice studies across the country.

Something of this euphoric mood was also evident in Europe. In England, government white papers referred to the 'war against crime' and urged that increased resources be invested in criminal justice. The 1959 white paper, *Penal Practice in a Changing Society*, although it acknowledged that deep-seated causes of crime are largely beyond government policy, vigorously endorsed expansionist prison policy. Having noted that the number of institutions in the English prison system had been increased from 40 to 73 over the previous thirteen years the white paper described the planned prison-building programme as one of 'formidable dimensions and great urgency'. The purpose of this prison construction was to reduce over-crowding and to replace buildings regarded as obsolete by modern notions of rehabilitation. 'It is no more possible to train prisoners in these obsolete conditions than it would be to provide a twentieth-century system of education in antiquated schools or to carry out modern hospital treatment in the unimproved buildings of the pre-Victorian era.'[8]

Bleak House

By the end of the 1960s it was becoming apparent that the Great Expectations perspective was badly flawed. In particular, the promised breakthrough for criminal justice practice had not occurred. As the quality of research into the effectiveness of criminal justice techniques gained in sophistication, claims for successful outcomes declined. Increasing police resources did not result in improved clear-up rates of serious crimes; similarly the investment of resources into rehabilitative programmes with offenders had no discernable impact upon levels of recidivism. While mostly negative results of carefully conducted studies into the effectiveness of criminal justice activities do not justify total pessimism they have contributed to a more sceptical mood as to what can be delivered through criminal justice. There have been achievements but these are few in number and narrow in scope.

In addition to a new appreciation of the limited effectiveness of criminal justice activities there has been a growing awareness of unintended and sometimes undesirable consequences. Intensive police patrolling methods for example, while making little impact on the level of crime, have been shown to have adverse effects on relations between police and community.[9] Emphasizing rehabilitative purposes for a prison may raise unreal expectations and divert attention from more mundane but basic purposes. Francis Allen, the American legal scholar, commented with some precision on the rehabilitative ideal which for a time imbued the theory, if not always the practice, of juvenile justice in the United States. 'In few localities have we fully achieved the elementary objectives of decency and humanity in dealing with the misbehaving child. The attainment of these objectives, although sometimes obstructed by formidable difficulties is surely not impossible. One difficulty may be that our larger ambitions may sometimes divert us and prevent us from achieving the more modest goals.'[10]

Bleak House sees criminal justice as having only a marginal impact upon the extent of crime. The perspective considers that:

- criminal justice is not a system but a process, which is neither rational nor purposeful;
- criminal justice has a limited role with respect to crime control. The aim is less to maximize benefits than to minimize harm. This position was given some credence by the Home Office in a statement of policy published in 1977, '. . . consideration needs to be given to ways of limiting the input into the system, for example, through slimming the scope of the criminal law, more selective prosecution policy, the development of penalties that do not require the involvement of penal agencies to enforce them, and modifications of the criminal process'.[11] The tone of this viewpoint was summarized succinctly in the foreword to an American report, *Doing Justice*, the report of the Committee for the Study of Incarceration which was published in 1976. 'Permeating this report is a determination to do less rather than more – an insistence on not doing harm . . . we have here a crucial shift in perspective from a commitment to do good to a commitment to do as little mischief as possible.'[12]
- factors responsible for crime are located largely beyond the reach of criminal justice. As expressed by the Home Office review, 'there is ground for re-examining some of the assumptions that underlie current policies and for looking more determinedly for relief beyond the criminal justice system';[13]
- criminal justice should be visible and openly accountable to the community it serves;
- criminal justice should be responsive to the requirements of due process. As Packer noted with respect to his Due Process model, a higher premium should be placed on reliability than on efficiency;[14]
- a great deal of crime is committed by people not generally regarded as criminals, and a sharp distinction cannot be drawn between criminals and law-abiding citizens.

Bleak House underplays utilitarian goals and draws upon the values of justice and humanity. The publication in 1973 of *Struggle for Justice* by the American Friends Service Committee was a landmark event in the United States, rejecting absolutely the liberal goal of rehabilitation and placing a single-minded emphasis on justice.[15] The justice model has since become central to the debate on crime and punishment on both sides of the Atlantic. The other non-utilitarian goal, humanity, extends beyond the notion of justice. As one legal scholar has observed, enjoying the benefits of due process does not rule out ending up in Hell. Alan Roberton, formerly a prison governor in England held that a primary purpose of institutional staff was to humanize the criminal law. Humanization may seem a modest goal, but within the penal context is by no means easily achieved.

Criminal justice consists of a series of loosely connected stages. It is useful to consider the prison system as occupying a mid-point position between decision-making at what might be termed the front and the rear. It is to these decisions that attention is now turned.

Decisions at the front of the process

A crucial and largely unresolved problem shared by national and state governments with respect to prisons is how to influence decision-making at the front of the criminal justice process. Prison systems are generally the administrative responsibility of central government. But the decision-makers who determine the size and composition of the prison population are largely located outside central government. A study of American prisons in the late 1970s found that:

'. . . the rate of prison and jail intake is controlled by a decentralized network of local prosecutors and judges . . . shifts in the rate of intake (as opposed to time served) were primarily responsible for the prison population increase of the seventies. Clearly, how to influence the decentralized 'front end' of the system, as distinct from the centralized 'tail end' of corrections remains a crucial question for the corrections policymaker.'[16]

Arrest and prosecution

The police serve as the principal gatekeepers to the arena of criminal justice, being responsible for crime prevention, the recording, investigation and, exceptionally, as in England, the prosecution of crime. Considerable discretion resides with police authorities as to how resources are deployed and with respect to the handling of individual cases. Of particular importance are questions of priorities in the investigation of crime, recommendations as to bail or remand in custody and decision concerning charging defendants, including the use of cautions. The police provide the first and critical filter, determining who proceeds deeper into the process of justice.

Prosecution has remained the least visible part of the criminal justice process, and in most countries is characterized by the absence of public accountability. Decisions about prosecution, as to whom to prosecute and for what offences have a crucial impact upon prison policy and practice. The general practice is that the office of prosecutor is separate and independent from the police and the courts. However, in England and Wales, but not in Scotland, the police are responsible for prosecution practice except in the case of unusual and politically sensitive cases, which are handled by the Director of Public Prosecutions, or where prosecution is initiated by private citizens or public authorities.

In some countries it has been possible, in part because of the way in which prosecution is organized, to develop some semblance of national prosecution policy. In the Netherlands, prosecution practice, which is directed from The Hague, has since the early 1960s been one of the most important determinants of the declining prison population. The head of the Dutch prison system refers to 'structured consultation' between his department and prosecutors concerning the use of custody. As noted in Chapter 6, prosecutorial dismissals almost equal the number of persons convicted. Similarly in West Germany a substantial proportion of offences which reach the prosecutor do not proceed to court. This is largely achieved through the 'penal order' which accounts for as many cases as do trials. The penal order, which is dispensed by the prosecutor, describes the offence and the evidence gathered and specifies the punishment imposed. The document, which is prepared by the prosecutor, is then routinely signed by a judge. If the offender contests the penal order the case goes to court. It is also permissible for the prosecutor simply to dismiss the case, and since 1976 this power has been extended to include some more serious offences on condition the offender pays a fine or compensation.[17]

In England the police have the powers to caution persons who admit guilt as an alternative to prosecution. However, more than eight out of ten of all persons so cautioned for serious offences are juveniles. With respect to persons aged 17 and over, of all persons cautioned or found guilty, a little under 5 per cent are cautioned compared with about 50 per cent in the case of juveniles.[18] But research findings are casting doubt on the extent to which police cautioning is diverting juveniles from entry into the criminal justice process. A study of police cautioning schemes for juveniles in London concluded that these were followed by a disproportionate increase in the number of juveniles arrested, and resulted in a 'widening of the net' of officially processed juveniles.[19] These concerns about the actual impact of some diversion strategies echo earlier American research in this area. They point to a central problem of reforming criminal justice, namely, how to ensure that changes take effect in the intended direction.

The prosecutorial role is also of crucial importance with respect to decisions and negotiations which shape both the charge and eventual sentence. Plea-bargaining is an important phenomenon in both England and the United States, and compares with the practice in Elizabethan England known as the 'benefit of the clergy'. If defendants could persuade the court that they were literate and therefore clergymen they were spared the death penalty. Clerical credentials could be established by accurate recitation of the first verse of the 51st Psalm (the 'neck verse'), 'Have mercy on me, O God, according to Thy lovingkindness: according unto the multitude of thy tender mercies blot out my transgressions.'

Prior coaching and good memory were particularly recommended.[20]

Plea-bargaining has received its most explicit recognition in the United States, where the practice can be traced to at least the middle of the nineteenth century.[21] Former Federal Judge Marvin Frankel has commented that the process might be more aptly termed 'sentence bargaining'.

Frankel writes: 'The prosecutor indicts exuberantly . . . the defendant is invited to plead guilty to only a part of the charges or to lesser degrees, cutting the the potential sentence, with the understanding that the remainder of the indictment will be dropped.'[21] Plea-bargaining also embraces decisions concerning bail and remand in custody, and defendants are often only able to secure their release from jail by accepting the prosecutor's offer. The alternative may be a long stay in custody awaiting trial, often subject to delays and uncertainty.

In England, although the great majority of defendants plead guilty, plea-bargaining, until recently, has barely been acknowledged to exist and has largely been unexplored by researchers. In a pioneering study, undertaken at Birmingham Crown Court, John Baldwin and Michael McConville found that 70 per cent of their sample of defendants who changed their plea from not guilty to guilty appeared to have taken part in some form of negotiated justice. The research highlighted the sentencing discount practice as a major characteristic of the court's behaviour.[22] The storm of protest which the study produced, with attempts to suppress and discredit the results, exemplified the powerful resistances to disturbing the mythology that sentences are determined within the confines of the courtroom, and that criminal justice is practised as described in the textbooks. The Chairman of the Bar, for example, dismissed the Birmingham study as 'a compilation of unsubstantiated anecdotes . . . and no more than the tittle tattle of the cells'.[23]

Strategies by central government to reduce the prison population only exceptionally address the prosecution stage, although in the Netherlands, Japan and elsewhere it has been demonstrated that later stages of the criminal justice process, including the prison system, can be shielded from increased numbers of offenders coming to the attention of the police. In England, prosecution activities are diffuse and, as the Royal Commission on Criminal Procedure noted, are also varied, haphazard and localized. No attempt has been made to coordinate prosecution practice, and at police regional conferences discussion is largely confined to traffic offenders. There have been only two Home Office circulars on prosecution since 1960, and these were confined to procedural matters. If intake into prison systems is to be regulated, national policy on the screening and charging of defendants is essential. The Royal Commission on Criminal Procedure's recommendation to establish Crown Prosecutors, comprising a locally based service with some national features, represents but a preliminary step towards coherent and rational prosecution policy.[24]

Remand and sentencing decisions

The third filter at the front of the criminal justice process is the amalgam of decisions taken within and around courts, in particular those pertaining to remand, conviction and sentencing. It is to court personnel, especially sentencers, that government exhortations and other efforts to use imprisonment more sparingly are usually directed with little success. In part, the difficulty arises from constitutional arrangements and traditions which provide for a separation of powers between the legislative, executive and judical branches of government. The independence of the courts is regarded as a hallmark of democratic society, and attempts to influence sentencing policy are often resisted on these grounds.

Andrew Ashworth calls this resistance the taboo of encroaching on the independence of the courts, and in its extreme form, 'there is a principle of judicial independence; attempts by the executive arm of government to influence sentencing policy are unconstitutional; attempts by the legislature to interfere with the sentencing discretion of the courts are, even if not strictly unconstitutional, bound to result in both practical confusion and injustice to defendants; the development of sentencing policy should therefore be left to the wisdom of the courts under the guidance of the Court of Appeal and intervention by other bodies can only worsen the situation.'[25] Some judges have attempted to confuse interference by the executive or the legislature in individual cases with Parliament's right to determine the severity of punishments permitted by law.

Attempts were made by government in England in the mid-1970s to reduce the use made by the courts of remands in custody. By means of a circular in 1975, the Home Office set forth criteria to guide decision-making by the courts. In 1976 the Bail Act gave statutory form to exceptions to the granting of bail, and courts were obliged to specify these in writing together with reasons for their application. An assessment of the Bail Act which was carried out six months after the legislation took effect in 1978 concluded that courts did not appear to be greatly affected by the legislation.[26] The proportionate use of custodial remands declined throughout the decade, but it is difficult to gauge the impact of either the circular or the legislation.[27]

A more immediate impact on remand decision-making can be discerned with regard to the events arising from the fifteen-week industrial dispute by prison officers in 1980–81. During this period, remand prisoners accounted for about half of the decline which occurred in prison population size. As a consequence of prison officers refusing to allow prisoners to exceed capacity, the police were unwillingly thrust into the role of jailors. The police cells were ill-equipped to deal with the rapid influx of numbers and the security problems were acute. The police were confronted with the consequences of their own decision-making and recommendations to courts with respect to remand. In order to avert further deterioration in the situation, the number of remands to custody declined.[28]

The sharp increases in the English prison population since the mid 1970s prompted a series of acknowledgements by government officials of the difficulties they faced in shaping sentencing practice. The Home Office, for example, commented in 1977: 'Disposals in individual cases are for the courts, but it is a proper part of the government's responsibility to seek to increase both the courts' and the public's awareness of the purposes and limitations of the various penal sanctions, and of the constraints within which the penal system operates . . . There is an inconsistency between the publically avowed policy of using custody only as a last resort for the really serious offence or dangerous offender, and actual practice.'[29]

The following year, a House of Commons Committee, while firmly endorsing the principle of judicial independence, concluded that, 'more could be done to acquaint the courts at all levels with reliable information about the availability of accommodation in custodial institutions which might help them in making their decisions. We also believe that relevant information about the alternatives to imprisonment should be supplied to the courts'.[30] Efforts to modify sentencing practice also have to overcome local traditions. As an English study of sentencing practice in magistrates courts found, ' . . . the insularity and durability of court traditions as major obstacles to attaining greater consistency between courts. Any attempts to change existing procedures cannot afford to underestimate the strengths and weaknesses of these traditions.'[31]

Efforts have been made by government to avoid imprisonment whenever appropriate and to reduce the length of sentences imposed. Statutory provisions have attempted to ensure that prison be used only as a last resort. New non-custodial sanctions have been created to encourage courts to reduce their use of custodial sentences, but these may supplement rather than replace custodial sentences.

The Criminal Justice Act of 1961 narrowed the powers of courts to sentence young adults, but the resulting howls of protest from the judiciary over the subsequent two decades eventually succeeded in persuading a Conservative government to repeal the offending provision. There had been a recent precedent for repeal. Ten years before, lobbying by the Magistrates' Association led to the repeal of the mandatory suspension of sentences of up to six months imprisonment which had been provided for in 1967. In practice, efforts to structure custodial sentencing amount to very little. Statutory language, dating from the Criminal Justice Act of 1948, has directed sentencers to impose custodial sentences only if no other method is appropriate when dealing with specified categories of offenders.

Later statutes extended the application of this formula, but it appears to have been ignored both by sentencers and the Court of Appeal. David Thomas has commented on the irony that, 'despite the efforts of the Court of Appeal over the last year and a half to encourage a selective reduction in the use of imprisonment, this section (s.20 of the Powers of the Criminal Courts Act, 1973) does not appear to have been mentioned in any decision of the Court during that time, and the Court's efforts to draw attention to the possibilities of reductions of sentence lengths in certain types of cases have not been accompanied by a readiness to explore the use of other means of dealing with offenders.'[32]

The Criminal Justice Act of 1982 resorted once again to this formula, although it does go a step further regarding persons aged under 21 in articulating three criteria. The Act states in its first section that custody should not be imposed unless it is the court's opinion 'that no other method of dealing with him is appropriate because it appears to the court that he is unable or unwilling to respond to non-custodial penalties or because a custodial sentence is necessary for the protection of the public or because the offence was so serious that a non-custodial sentence cannot be justified.' One of the crucial tests in implementation of the legislation is the extent to which these criteria are seriously considered by courts. The danger exists that the criteria will receive a proforma disregard by sentencers and that the legislative language will be little more than hollow rhetoric.

The prospects that reform initiatives may be taken by the judiciary or magistracy should be examined. Until recently there was little indication that the appellate process had served to reduce the use of imprisonment. In 1980 a new Lord Chief Justice, Lord Lane, identified himself with the need for courts to impose shorter custodial sentences, and in a number of property offence cases the Court of Appeal reduced the length of prison sentences imposed. For example, the assistant manager of a supermarket was sentenced to six months' imprisonment at a Crown Court for the theft of items valued at £5. The Court of Appeal did not take issue with the principle of immediate imprisonment, referring to the position of trust held by the defendant and the extent to which pilfering was rife, but it held that the sentence should be one of two months' imprisonment. The Court of Appeal reminded sentencing judges of the very unpleasant nature of imprisonment as a result of overcrowding.[33] The impact of these decisions by the Court of Appeal upon sentencers is uncertain. The preliminary indications are that sentencers took some notice for several months, but reverted to earlier practice the following year.[34]

The initiatives taken by the Court of Appeal, together with the new sentencing powers contained in the Criminal Justice Act of 1982, may provide a new impetus and sense of direction to the training of judges and magistrates on sentencing matters. The training of magistrates is organized at the local level, and is an unwieldy vehicle for assuring sentencing consistency. Judicial training is very much less frequent, and indeed in the opinion of some judges the term itself is a misnomer, as was exemplified by events surrounding the Bridge Committee. The Committee, under Lord Justice Bridge, was originally termed Judicial Training and Information, but this prompted objections to the word 'training'. The Bridge Report on Judicial Studies and Information observed: 'It is said that "training" implies that there are trainers who can train people to be judges, and so long as this concept is capable of influencing the thought of those concerned with the provision of "judicial training", this must, despite all protestations to the contrary, represent a threat to judicial independence.'[35]

Following publication of the Bridge Report in 1978 a board was established to co-ordinate judicial studies. Newly appointed judges now attend a three-day course in addition to periodic sentencing conferences. There appears to be little enthusiasm for a more comprehensive approach to judicial studies either within the judiciary or among barristers. In 1981 it was put to the Chairman of the Bar that the initial training of a judge might usefully be extended to three months. In reply, Mr Richard du Cann, Q.C., replied: 'If he spent 25 years at the Bar, which I think each one of us has, and if he has the width of practice, which I think each one of us has, and if he has a knowledge of humanity, which I trust and believe each one of us has, I would not think that three months was needed.'[36] It does not appear that judicial training, as it is practised in England, is likely to contribute much to rational sentencing practice.

Decisions at the rear of the process

Executive control of the prison population is exercised mainly at the mid-stage and rear of the criminal justice process. These measures, which primarily have to do with remission of sentence length for good behaviour and release by the parole board, determine actual time served in the course of prison sentences. Such activities have no bearing on the 'in-out' decision, whether to imprison or not.

Remission, or 'good-time' allowances, exists in most prison systems. Remission procedures provide prison officials with some degree of control over the prisoner's behaviour. In England, remission amounts to one third of the prison sentence of more than five days, but this can be forfeited as a consequence of prison disciplinary proceedings. Prison officials assert the importance of remission as a control device, and this point is generally conceded even by those in favour of sentences being determined by the courts without the possibility of parole. In addition to remission being earned through good behaviour, there may be other inducements such as, in some American State Prison Systems, contributions by prisoners of their blood.[37] Remission formulae can provide strategic tools for regulating the size of the prison population. In 1975, for example, in response to pressure on space in junior detention centres, the government increased remission from one third to one half. A somewhat similar step was taken the following year with respect to prison sentences in the Northern Ireland prison system. On the other hand, whenever remission is taken away for disciplinary reasons, of course average time served increases.

Parole was not part of the English process until 1967, and has a rather longer history in many other countries. In part, the rationale for the introduction of parole in England was its use as an instrument to regulate the size of the prison population. At that time parole reflected the still prevalent confidence in the rehabilitative ideal. In particular, parole was justified for those long-term prisoners who, in the words of the then Home Secretary, Roy Jenkins, had reached 'a recognizable peak in their training at which time they may respond to generous treatment, but after which, if kept in prison they may go downhill'.[38] Only prisoners serving sentences of eighteen months or more are eligible for parole, and then only after serving one third of their sentence, although the Criminal Justice Act of 1982 gave the Home Secretary power to reduce this threshold. It is some-times argued that if parole did not exist, the number of persons under parole supervision at any one time would be added to the prison popu-lation. This proposition assumes, of course, that the judiciary do not take into account possible release on parole when determining the length of prison sentences. A similar consideration arises with reference to re-mission, although, as with parole, this practice has been discouraged by the Court of Appeal.

In the summer of 1981 the Government published a working party report on parole which suggested extending parole to prisoners serving sentences above six months, and that for sentences of under three years release would be automatic after one third (i.e. the middle third of a sentence would be held in suspense and the prisoner be released under the super-vision of a probation officer for that period). It was estimated at the time by the Home Office that implementation of this scheme might reduce the size of the prison population by up to 7,000 prisoners.[39] The fate of this proposal illustrates the complexities of successfully implementing reform strategies located at the rear of the criminal justice process. At first it appeared that the Home Secretary, William Whitelaw, would back this scheme. However, in the late autumn of 1981 the scheme was abandoned, largely because of pressure from the Lord Chief Justice who had consulted with groups of senior judges as to the merits of the proposal. It appears that the judges had intimated that courts might be inclined to increase sentence length. The headline in the *Sunday Times* was 'Judges dig in heels over Whitelaw's prison reform plan'.[40]

In a public statement, a senior judge declared that the law lords disliked the proposal because it would result in persistent property offenders being let out after six or eight months having been sentenced to periods of eighteen months or two years. 'We appreciated that in these circumstances there would be a risk that some trial judges might pass longer sentences in order to protect the public. I was, however, able to remind those present that when release on parole was introduced in 1967, the then Lord Chief Justice, Lord Parker, had asked the Queen's Bench judges not to take the possibility of the grant of parole into account when fixing the length of sentences. They have not done so.'[41]

A further account of this episode was given by the Lord Chief Justice in a debate on law and order in the House of Lords in March 1982: 'May I try to explode one myth which recently has gained currency in the media: that the judges thwarted Home Office liberal penal proposals by threatening to increase sentences in retaliation against the proposals. They did nothing of the sort. The facts are these: The proposal was that all sentences of, I think, three years and less should be divided into three: a third should be spent in prison, a third should be spent on what is called supervised release and a third should be the subject of remission. So the actual term served in prison would be precisely one-third of that which the judge imposed. There was to be no opportunity for a judge to non-apply the system if he thought the criminal ought to stay inside longer for the protection of the public. The judge consequently would have been in a hopeless dilemma in many cases: should he obey the dictates of Parliament and pass the sentence which was originally in his mind, knowing that only a third world be served, or should he increase the sentence – contrary to the wishes of Parliament? That proposal was mooted first of all at the judicial seminar in September at Roehampton. That seminar was attended by judges of all ranks from all over the country dealing with criminal matters and it was rejected by them unanimously. I took the liberty of seeking the views of the senior Lords Justices presiding in the Criminal Division of the Court of Appeal. They also were unanimously opposed to it and I am very glad to say that the proposal was dropped. But we did not thwart anyone, nor did we threaten anyone.'[42]

Finally the executive branch of goverment may exercise some leverage on the prison population by means of clemency or amnesty. Such measures may provide temporary relief from prison population pressures, but do not constitute an effective long-term strategy. As described in Chapter 6, Winston Churchill, as Home Secretary, made fairly frequent use of executive clemency; his concern to rectify gross sentencing disparities was uninhibited by constitutional niceties.[43] Amnesties, which are hardly ever used in England or the United States, are fairly frequently invoked in some other countries.

The essence of criminal justice is the exercise of discretion under conditions of low visibility. Criminal justice officials tend to regard their discretion as the core of professionalism and are resistant to external review. Furthermore, there is little effective coordination across the various stages of the criminal justice process which may share few common objectives. These endemic qualities make criminal justice activities especially difficult to subject to effective accountability and public control and have three crucial implications for an understanding of the prison system.

First, the diffuse and often hidden decision-making casts a grave shadow of doubt on the fairness of the results. The composite of decisions ultimately selects certain people for the prison system, and this selective filtering poses apparently inexplicable questions as to why some prisoners are accused or convicted of trivial offences while other much more serious offenders are spared the clang of prison gates. Growing concerns about unfairness and disparities are the mainspring of the justice model and efforts to reduce, if not eliminate, discretion. However, discretionary justice, which has something of the dynamics of a waterbed, is not easily eradicated.[44] Attempts to confine or structure discretion at one stage of the process tend to be offset by reappearance of the problem elsewhere. For example, structuring judicial discretion may serve to strengthen the discretionary possibilities open to the prosecutor. While modest gains may be made to minimize injustices along the route to prison, the essential problem remains.

Second, the relative absence of visibility and accountability of much criminal justice activity allow the ideological concerns of criminal justice officials to be a significant factor in decision-making. Walter Miller clearly articulated the concern that '. . . ideology and its consequences exert a powerful influence on the policies and procedures of those who conduct the enterprise of criminal justice, and that the degree and kinds of influence go largely unrecognized. Ideology is the permanent hidden agenda of criminal justice'.[45] The various ideological agendas may range in political terms, from the far Right to extreme Left. Just as authoritarian regimes of both the Right and Left tend to make a heavy investment in criminal justice apparatus, so do individuals with contrasting political orientations endorse a Great Expectations perspective on criminal justice. As Nils Christie points out, the Right and Left often share a belief in strong and centralized state control.[46] Christie has in mind the welfare capitalist societies of Scandinavia, and it might also be noted that prison-system growth has flourished since 1945 under both Conservative and Labour governments in England.[47] As a general rule, however, law and order issues tend to be given most prominence by political parties of the Right and by persons with a conservative orientation. The employees of criminal justice agencies are also likely to be, especially on crime questions, to the ideological Right rather than Left. In England, for example, prison and police officers have, through their unions, repeatedly called for the reintroduction of the death penalty. There are, of course, exceptions, but such persons are often sceptically regarded as mavericks by their colleagues.

Third, the characteristics of criminal justice allow occupational and career commitments of practitioners to shape informally official goals.[48] This is not to suggest that personal agendas of bureaucrats are the most important factors prompting the growth of the criminal justice apparatus. The focus of much of the media on crime, the exploitation by some politicians of law and order issues, and increase in reported crime are perhaps of greater significance. But, for criminal justice bureaucrats, even in times of public expenditure crises, times have been generally good. It is instructive to note developments in England, where a massive investment in resources for the criminal justice process has continued even while other areas of public expenditure were being drastically pruned. Between 1973/1974–1982/83 current expenditure on criminal justice increased by 33 per cent compared with an increase of 26 per cent for all public expenditure. With reference to capital expenditure law and order costs rose by one per cent over the same period, whereas for public expenditure generally there was a 20 per cent decline.[49]

Wherever the mood of Great Expectations is dominant the total capacity of the criminal justice process will expand. There is a dearth of comparative data on criminal justice capacity such as personnel and other resources,[50] and cross-national research is required to assess the relationship of numbers of police officers and court personnel, for example, and the scale of the prison system. It seems probable that the research findings would endorse the theme of this chapter, that efforts to reverse prison-system growth which fail to take close account of the criminal justice process as a whole are unlikely to have a significant and sustained impact.

References

1   Louk Hulsman, 'Penal Reform in the Netherlands: Part II – Criteria for Deciding on Alternatives to Imprisonment', *Howard Journal*, **21**, 1982, p. 38. See also the argument for participatory justice in Nils Christie, *Limits of Pain*, Oxford: Martin Robertson, 1982, pp. 92–116. Christie writes: 'Crime is a concept applicable in certain social situations where it is possible and in the interests of one or several parties to apply it. We can create crime by creating systems that ask for the word. We can extinguish crime by creating the opposite types of systems.' Ibid, p. 74.

2   Results of the General Household Survey, summarized in *Criminal Statistics for England and Wales, 1981*, London: HMSO, Cmnd 8668, 1982, p. 28; also Mike Hough and Pat Mayhew, *The British Crime Survey*, Home Office Research Study No. 76, London: HMSO, 1983, pp. 8–14. Victimization surveys have been extensively conducted in the United States. See e.g. U.S. Department of Justice, *Criminal Victimization in the United States: Summary findings of 1977–78 changes in crime and of trends since 1973*, Washington D.C.: U.S. Department of Justice. For a preliminary English study see R. Sparks, H. G. Genn and D. J. Dodd, *Surveying Victims*, Chichester: Wiley, 1977. The most comprehensive study is the *British Crime Survey*, carried out by the Home Office Research Unit. For a description of the scope of the survey see Pat Mayhew and Mike Hough, 'The British Crime Survey', Home Office Research Planning Unit, *Research Bulletin*, No. 14, 1982, pp. 24–7.

3   Herbert Jacob and Robert L. Lineberry, *Governmental Responses to Crime*, Executive Summary of Final Report to National Institute of Justice. Draft, January, 1982, p. 27.

4   Henry M. Hart, 'The Aims of the Criminal Law', in *Crime, Law and Society*, eds. A. S. Goldstein and J. Goldstein, New York: Free Press, 1971, p. 63.

5   Herbert L. Packer, *The Limits of the Criminal Sanction*, Stanford: Stanford University Press, 1968. See also comments on the rational deterrent model of policing in J. M.

Hough and R. V. G. Clarke's introduction to *The Effectiveness of Policing*, Farnborough: Gower, 1980, pp. 1–16.

6 Herbert L. Packer, op. cit., note 5, p. 158.

7 ibid, p. 161.

8 Home Office, *Penal Practice in a Changing Society* Cmnd. 645, London: HMSO, 1959, p. 21.

9 See e.g. *Report of an Inquiry into the Brixton Disorders, 10–12 April, 1981*, (Scarman Report), Cmnd 8427, London: HMSO, 1981, paras. 4.69–4.80.

10 Francis Allen, 'The Juvenile Court and the Limits of Juvenile Justice' *Wayne Law Review*, **11**, 1965, p. 685.

11 Home Office, *A Review of Criminal Justice Policy 1976*, London: HMSO, 1977, p. 10.

12 Willard Gaylin and David J. Rothman, forward to Andrew von Hirsch, *Doing Justice*, Report of the Committee for the Study of Incarceration, New York: Hill and Wang, 1976, p. xxxiv.

13 *A Review of Criminal Justice Policy*, op. cit., note 11, p. 9.

14 Packer, op. cit., note 5, pp. 163–4.

15 American Friends Service Committee, *Struggle for Justice*, New York: Hill and Wang, 1971.

16 *American Prisons and Jails*, Vol. 1, National Institute of Justice, Washington D.C.: Government Printing Office, 1981, p. 129.

17 Johannes B. Feest, *Imprisonment and the Criminal Justice System in the Federal Republic of Germany*, University of Bremen, 1982, pp. 36–7.

18 *Criminal Statistics, England and Wales 1981*, Cmnd 8668, London: HMSO, 1982, p. 97.

19 David P. Farrington and Trevor Bennett, 'Police Cautioning of Juveniles in London' *British Journal of Criminology*, **21**, 1981, p. 134. A crucial distinction with reference to diversion is whether it results in diversion from or within the criminal justice process. Some American studies refer to diversion from criminal justice as being 'true diversion'. In England there has been rather less concern with the need to focus diversion activities in this direction. The record of formal cautions is made available to the court if the individual is subsequently sentenced. A NACRO working party contrasted its conclusions with much American experience '. . . our own emphasis was rather on the concept of short-term early intervention which in some cases could lead to charges being withdrawn but which in many other cases would have the effect of lessening rather than avoiding criminal penalties'. NACRO, *Diversion From Criminal Justice in an English Context.* Report of a NACRO Working Party, Chichester and London: Barry Rose, 1975, p. 34.

20 See generally Joel Samaha, *Law and Order in Historical Perspective: the case of Elizabethan Essex*, New York: Academic Press 1973.

21 Marvin E. Frankel, *Partisan Justice*, New York: Hill and Wang, 1980, pp. 90–1, for a graphic account of one plea-bargaining episode where the subject was Spiro Agnew, Vice-President of the United States, see Richard M. Cohen and Jules Witcover, *A Heartbeat Away. The Investigation and Resignation of Vice-President Spiro Agnew*, New York: Bantum, 1974, pp. 229–65.

22 John Baldwin and Michael McConville, *Negotiated Justice, Pressures to Plead Guilty*, London: Martin Robertson, 1977. For a study of police bargaining tactics see Barrie Irving, *Police Interrogation. A Case Study of Current Practice*, Royal Commission on Criminal Procedure, Research Study No. 2, London: HMSO, 1980, pp. 138–53.

23 Letter to *The Guardian*, 9 June 1977, quoted by John Baldwin and Michael McConville, 'Plea Bargaining and Plea Negotiation in England', *Law and Society*, **13**, 1979, p. 305.

24 Royal Commission on Criminal Procedure, *Report*, Cmnd 8092, London: HMSO, 1981, pp. 144–70.

25 Andrew Ashworth, 'Judicial Independence and Sentencing Reform', paper presented at the Cambridge Criminology Conference, July 1979, pp. 3–5.

26 Michael Zander, 'Operation of the Bail Act in London Magistrates' Courts', *New Law Journal*, **129**, 1979, pp. 108–11.

27 The percentage of persons remanded in custody of all persons remanded fell between 1978 and 1981 from 18 to 15 per cent. *Criminal Statistics, England and Wales, 1981*, London: HMSO, Cmnd 8668, 1982, p. 188.

28   Home Office Statistical Bulletin, *Changes in the Prison Population during the Industrial Action by the POA*, London: Home Office, issue 12, 1981. Similar tactics were used at Wandsworth prison in London throughout much of 1982.

29   *A Review of Criminal Justice Policy*, op. cit. note 11, p. 7.

30   Fifteenth Report of the Expenditure Committee, *The Reduction of Pressure on the Prison System*, 662–1, London: HMSO, 1978, p. xxxvi.

31   Roger Tarling, *Sentencing Practice in Magistrates' Courts*, Home Office Research Unit Study No. 56. London: HMSO, 1979, p. 45.

32   David Thomas, commentary in *Criminal Law Review*, January 1982, pp. 62–3.

33   R. v. Upton, *Criminal Law Review*, 1980, p. 508.

34   See *Prison Statistics, England and Wales, 1981*, London: HMSO, 1982, p. 66.

35   *Report on Judicial Studies and Information*, Chairman, Lord Justice Bridge, Home Office, Lord Chancellor, London: HMSO, 1978, p. 2.

36   House of Commons, Home Affairs Committee, *Administration of the Prison Service, Minutes of Evidence*, London: HMSO H.C. 412–2, 1981, pp. 155–6.

37   A survey conducted in the late 1970s found that thirteen state prison systems allowed time to be remitted in lieu of blood donations. The variation per pint of blood ranged from five to 30 days. Unpublished paper prepared for the National Institute of Justice Study on American Prisons and Jails. See also, 'A National Survey of Good Time Laws and Administrative Procedures', Texas Department of Corrections, *Research Report No. 17*, 1973.

38   H.C. Debates, vol. 738, col. 70, 12 December 1966. Roy Jenkins was quoting from the White Paper.

39   Home Office, *Review of Parole in England and Wales*, London: Home Office, 1981, p. 15.

40   *Sunday Times*, 22 November 1981.

41   Lord Justice Lawton, Letter to *The Times*, 27 November 1981.

42   H.L. Debates, vol. 428, col. 988, 24 March 1982.

43   See Leon Radzinowicz and Roger Hood, 'Judicial Discretion and Sentencing Standards: Victorian Attempts to Solve a Perennial Problem', *University of Pennsylvania Law Review*, **127**, 1979, pp. 1340–1.

44   See generally Kenneth Culp Davis, *Discretionary Justice: A Preliminary Analysis*, Urbana: University of Illinois Press, 1971; A. Keith Bottomley, *Decisions on the Penal Process*, Oxford: Martin Robertson, 1973; Michael King, *The Framework of Criminal Justice*, London: Croom Helm, 1981.

45   Walter B. Miller, 'Ideology and Criminal Justice Policy: Some Current Issues', *Journal of Criminal Law and Criminology*, **64**, 1973, pp. 141–62. Among the crusading issues of the Right, Miller identifies, 'excessive leniency towards law-breakers' prompting such policy prescriptions as the death penalty for murder and other serious offences; extended prison terms, including life imprisonment, for other dangerous or habitual criminals, with airtight guarantees that these be fully served; and 'the nation's capacity for incarcerating criminals – particularly through maximum security facilities – must be greatly expanded, and prison security strengthened'.

46   Nils Christie, op. cit., note 1, pp. 50–2, and see generally Andrew Fyffe, 'A most peculiar absence of monsters', *Prison Service Journal*, **27**, 1977, pp. 12–14, and J. A. G. Griffith, *The Politics of the Judiciary*, London: Fontana, 1977, pp. 187–216.

47   The respective average daily rates of prison population growth for six periods of office, 1945–83, were as follows:

Labour		*Conservative*	
1945–51	8 per cent (+)	1951–64	2.7 per cent (+)
1964–70	5.3 per cent (+)	1970–74	1.4 per cent (−)
1974–79	2.9 per cent (+)	1979–83*	0.6 per cent (+)

* 1983 = population on 10 June 1983.

48   See e.g. A. S. Blumberg, *Criminal Justice*, Chicago: Quadrangle Books, 1967, p. 34.

49   Report of the Committee of Inquiry into the United Kingdom Prison Service, Chairman, Mr. Justice May, Cmnd 7673, London: HMSO, 1979, p. 149.

50 For example, in 1980 there were 178 police officers per 100,000 inhabitants in the Netherlands compared with 236 in England. For commentary on the relatively low capacity of the Dutch criminal process, see L. H. C. Hulsman, 'The Evolution of Imprisonment in the Netherlands', *Revue de Droit pénal et de criminologie* (Belgium), **57**, 1977, p. 4; and David Downes, 'The origins and consequences of Dutch penal policy since 1945', *British Journal of Criminology*, **22**, 1982, pp. 337–9.

Part Two

Expansion

3   Choosing to Expand

Prison populations are determined, intentionally or otherwise, by policy choices. There are three general policy options: expansion, standstill and reduction. Expansionist policy, which generally reflects a Great Expectations vision of criminal justice, tends to thrive in authoritarian societies, ultra conservative political environments or situations where administrators are able to indulge in empire building. Standstill policy focuses upon holding steady prison population size and balancing the demands made on the prison system with resources of staff and buildings. The reductionist policy option has as its heritage the Bleak House perspective on criminal justice and its possibilities are explored in the final part of the book. This chapter describes the characteristics of expansionist and standstill policy choices, but before doing so it is necessary to address the misleading notion that the number of prisoners is largely beyond the realms of political control, to be regarded in similar fashion to meteorologists tracking an Atlantic storm.

The reactive stance to prison populations tends to seek deterministic explanations, of which the most common is the level of crime. Prisons, after all, are storage receptacles for persons involved in criminal behaviour. It would seem obvious and commonsense that the level of crime and the use made of imprisonment be inextricably related. More crime, it might be expected, will be followed by increased resort to the prison system.

In fact, across a wide spectrum of countries, there is no consistent relationship between crime and imprisonment.[1] Although the direction of rates of crime and imprisonment may sometimes coincide very often they do not. For example, in the United States during the late 1960s prison populations in some states declined against a background of sharply rising recorded crime, and then proceeded to increase rapidly at a time when there was a slowing down in the rate of increase in recorded crime. In the Netherlands over the 25 years up to 1975, recorded crime increased by 300 per cent whereas prison population declined by 50 per cent. In England between 1908 and 1938 recorded crime rates increased by 160 per cent while prison population declined by 50 per cent.

On closer examination, it is less surprising that no direct relationship exists. There are many factors which intervene between the recording of an event as a crime by the police and the prison gates. Two of these may be mentioned briefly. The practice for dealing with juvenile offenders is crucial because juveniles account for a significant proportion of persons involved in serious crime but are generally dealt with outside the prison system. The age up to which the juvenile court has jurisdiction in most countries is 17 or 18, as it is, for example, in England and the Netherlands, respectively. In some American states, the critical age is as low as 15, while in Japan it is 20. Although most jurisdictions have devices to dispatch some juveniles into the prison system, the numbers involved are generally small. Another important consideration is the extent to which the police fail to clear up recorded crime. The clear-up rate for indictable crime in England of around 40 per cent may be compared with rates of 60 and 25 per cent in Japan and the Netherlands, respectively.

A third area intervening between crime and imprisonment encompasses the variety of ways persons are filtered at the various stages of criminal justice. As noted in the previous chapter, prosecutors and sentencers have options open to them in many cases for processing offenders in directions other than the prison system. It has become commonplace to assume that there is an inevitable connection between workload at the front of the criminal justice process and prison population. In England, the phrase 'penal momentum' was coined in 1979 by the May Committee to describe the supposed inevitability of prison system expansion as a response to increased prosecution and sentencing workloads. Superficial consideration of English criminal statistics, as set out in Table 3.1, encourages such a chain-link perspective of criminal justice. For example, a government white paper of 1980, referring to the expanding prison population, stated: 'The main factor in the general year-by-year trend has been the steady increase in the absolute numbers of offenders coming before the courts. Despite some recent levelling-off in the upward trend in recorded crime, a continuing rise is likely in the figures of crime and offenders, and without counteracting policies, further increases in the prison population was to be expected.'[2]

However, *counteracting policies* are available as is demonstrated by means of cross-national comparisons. In Table 3.2, prosecutorial and sentencing practice in England, the Netherlands, Sweden and Japan are compared. It can be seen that with reference to the total number of persons cautioned or proceeded against, significantly more use of custody is made in England and Sweden than in the Netherlands and Japan.

The absence of a consistent relationship between levels of crime and imprisonment is mirrored by other attempts to seek deterministic explanations for movements in prison population. A favourite topic for researchers is the impact of unemployment.[3] While it is conceded generally that

Table 3.1

The processing of indictable offences/offenders in England, 1950–80 (1950 = 100)
(persons refer to persons aged 14 and over)

	Offences recorded by police	Offences cleared up	Percent cleared up	Persons cautioned or proceeded against	Persons cautioned	Percent cautioned	Persons found guilty and sentenced	Persons sentenced to immediate custody	Percent sentenced to immediate custody	Average daily prison population
1950	100	100	(47)	100	Not Known		100	100	(23)	100
1960	151	153	(44)	229	100	(7)	147	133	(21)	132
1970	340	327	(45)	316	290	(8)	332	224	(16)	191
1980	547	457	(40)		580	(12)	433	300	(14)	208

Source: abstracted from the relevant volume of *Criminal Statistics, England and Wales*

Note: changes in the definition of indictable offences and counting rules make comparison by year only approximate.

there is no clear-cut relationship between the levels of unemployment and recorded crime, several studies have sought to locate a direct relationship betwen unemployment and imprisonment. David Greenberg found a positive correlation between prison admission rates and unemployment in both the United States and Canada. With the Canadian data there was also a positive, but weaker, correlation between the unemployment rate and prison population size. He concluded, '. . . changes in commitments to prison can be explained almost entirely by changes in the unemployment rate. Changes in the number of cases entering the justice system and potentially available for imprisonment seem to be unimportant, as does the crime rate, at least as far as we can measure it.'[4]

Table 3.2
Criminal justice processing within selected countries, 1978

	Persons cautioned or proceeded against (= 100)	Persons cautioned	Persons sentenced	Persons sentenced to immediate custody
England	100	4	86	13
Sweden	100	24	76	13
Netherlands	100	51	38	8
Japan	100	33	55	4

Source: cross-national study

Matthew Yeager also reported a positive correlation between the unemployment rate and admissions to the federal prison system in the United States, and asserted: 'The results showed that the unemployment rate alone explains 54 per cent of the variation in the prison population sentenced during the years 1952 through 1978. After considering sentencing practices, a 1 per cent increase in male unemployment results in 1,395 additional prisoners in federal penal institutions.'[5] A rather similar result was reported on the basis of an analysis of English data, with the correlation especially powerful with respect to young males.[6]

However, unemployment is not invariably correlated with the use of prison sentences or with prison population size. In England during the early 1930s unemployment peaked at almost 22 per cent while prison population size remained relatively stable. For example, in 1908 the level of unemployment was 7.8 per cent and the prison population rate per 100,000 inhabitants was 62. In 1932 the unemployment rate was 21.9 per cent and the prison population rate was 32 per cent.[7] It is evident that policy decisions have greater impact on prison populations than does the level of unemployment, as exemplified in the Netherlands and Japan between 1950 and 1975 when prison populations were sharply reduced against a background of rising unemployment.[8]

Prison population size has been explored with reference also to association with psychiatric hospitalization, but again without consistent results. An early study by L. S. Penrose reported an inverse relationship between sentenced prisoner population size and availability of mental hospital beds across fourteen European countries.[9] However, a trade-off pattern between prisons and mental hospitals did not emerge in a recent American study which concluded, '. . . the operations of contemporary American penal systems appear generally uninfluenced by the use of custodial alternatives.'[10] It is also instructive to note, particularly given the discussion of Dutch penal policy in Chapter 6, that the decline in the Netherlands' prison population was not accompanied by an increased number of offenders placed in psychiatric facilities.[11]

Finally, a rather different deterministic approach to explaining prison population size has been pursued by Alfred Blumstein. Using data from the United States, Norway and Canada, Blumstein and colleagues argue that fluctuations in the prison population rate oscillate within a narrow range and that a self-regulating process is at work. Blumstein's work derives its theoretical underpinning from Emile Durkheim's theories of deviance and collective conscience. 'The existence of such a stable imprisonment rate suggests that, as a nation's prison population begins to fluctuate, pressure is generated to restore the prison population to that stable rate . . . Similarly, if the population drops too far below the stable rate, then pressure would develop to sanction (sic) certain kinds of behaviour that previously had been tolerated as more annoying than harmful'.[12] This perspective allows little scope to policy initiatives in shaping the level of imprisonment. Blumstein believes that the focus of the policy debate should shift from absolute levels of imprisonment, which he suggests offer little flexibility, to a consideration of imprisonment policy in terms of the allocation of a fairly fixed resource.[13]

However, Blumstein's stable state model is not consistent with the fluctuating trend towards greatly increased use of imprisonment in the United States.[14] Nor does the model fit sharp shifts in prison population size, as in pre-war Poland, when prison population size more than doubled in a single decade or in England during the first two decades after the Second World War.[15] With respect to the long-term trend data for the United States, Blumstein has acknowledged that fluctuations around one stable rate did shift to a new and higher level in the 1970s, but he suggests that this was the result of unusual changes in American society.[16]

A note on whales and elephants

The alternative to various deterministic explanations is to regard prison populations as primarily the consequence of policy choices and practice. The use made of custody, prison population size and other aspects of the prison system are the result of decisions made throughout the criminal justice process and the wider political sphere. But if prison systems are shaped by policy choices, are there limits on size? The literature on the structure and sociology of organizations suggests that if such limits exist they are unlikely to amount to much. In his general theory of growth, Kenneth Boulding proposed that, '. . . all growth must run into eventually declining rates of growth. As growth proceeds, the growing aspect must eventually run into conditions which are less and less favourable to growth.'[17] Boulding suggests that: 'As any structure grows, the proportions of its parts and of its significant variables cannot remain constant.'[18] For example, as an organization grows, it has to maintain increasingly expanded specialized administrative structures. 'Eventually, the cost of these administrative structures begins to outweigh any of the other possible benefits of large scale . . . and these structural limitations bring the growth of the organization to an end.'[19]

This hypothesis may be valid over the long-term, but as a general rule, the internal pressures for growth will be constant. As noted by one student of the sociology of organizations, Charles Perrow, '(Growth) is a validation of success and thus is a sign of prestige. Perhaps incorrectly, it suggests security for all concerned. It certainly provides status escalators for managers, since it opens up promotions. It makes top management positions higher because, as the pond grows larger, so does the size of the frog. It provides more options for talent, as well as more places to hide whenever more sophisticated younger people come along.'[20]

A further motive for growth for the prison system may be to achieve protection from attacks upon legitimacy. Few organizations, least of all prison systems, can take their existence completely for granted. Perrow suggests: 'In a time of rapid social change and rising social criticism, the legitimacy of organizations in every sector of our society has been questioned, and the questioning has begun to expose the elaborate methods used by some organizations to forestall inquiry, divert attention, and to create legitimacy for questionable activities.'[21] Hugeness may carry the promise of making the organization less vulnerable. As Kenneth Boulding noted: '. . . great size in itself leads to relative invulnerability, and hence very large organizations do not face the same problems of uncertainty and adjustment which face smaller organizations or organisms. The whales and elephants of the universe can afford to have fairly placid dispositions and insensitive exteriors.'[22]

The expansionist option

Expansionist prison systems share most of the following features:

- steady annual increase in prison population size;
- severe levels of overcrowding;

- an ambitious building programme to increase physical capacity;
- strengthening and enlarging the most secure prisons within the system;
- increases in personnel at all levels;
- intensification of the organization's bureaucratic structure.

Much penal practice in the United States, England and elsewhere since 1945 has been consistently expansionist. In the United States the general pattern has been one of rapidly expanding prison systems, especially at the state level of government. The period 1950–81 is displayed in Table 3.3 and shows a national pattern of substantial growth in the 1950s, followed by stabilization and decline in some systems during the 1960s and early 1970s. After 1972, there was a steady increase and by 1978 the total prison population and the imprisonment rate were higher than at any time in the history of the United States,[23] and expansion has continued into the 1980s.[24] The sharp upward rise in state prison populations since the early 1970s took many policy-makers by surprise, coming on the heels of reports by national commissions which had pointed in reductionist directions. In 1967 a presidential commission on crime called for a 'new corrections' that emphasized community-based alternatives to prison.[25]

Table 3.3
Prison population in the United States, 1950–81

	State prison	National total (federal, state and local combined)	National rate per 100,000
1950	166,165*	264,557	174
1960	212,953*	346,015	192
1970	176,403	357,304	177
1972	174,470	357,771	164
1978	268,189	447,742	207
1981	292,245	n.a.	n.a.

Source: data abstracted from *N.I.J.*, vol. 1, p. 7, and *Corrections Magazine*, April 1981, p. 19
* Combined state and federal prison populations

Six years later the National Advisory Commission on Criminal Justice Standards and Goals urged a continuation of the recent trend away from confining people in institutions and towards supervising them in the community. Imprisonment was castigated for its high costs, ineffectiveness in controlling crime and dehumanizing consequences. The Commission urged that states should phase out juvenile institutions and '. . . refrain from building more state institutions for adults over the next ten years except when total system planning shows that the need for them is imperative.'[26]

Ironically, the report of the National Advisory Commission was published just as the sharp rise in federal and state prison populations was getting under way. Furthermore, the upturn in prison population coincided with a considerable slow-down in the rate of increase of recorded serious crime in the United States.[27] The burgeoning prison systems reflected a resurgence of conservative attitudes to the problem of crime. In the late 1970s a spate of new sentencing legislation was enacted, much of it aimed at curbing judicial discretion so as to produce a greater use of custody. By early 1980, more than half the states had enacted mandatory minimum sentencing laws, mostly during the preceding year.[28] One analysis of recent sentencing legislation concludes that, although early initiatives were, in some cases, taken by liberal legislators guided by a justice model of criminal justice, 'politicians have responded to pressure from voters who are more concerned with their safety than with doing justice, and from the law enforcement lobby seeking stiffer penalties for reasons relating to occupational ideology and interests.'[29] In 1981 the Reagan administration proposed federal legislative action to restrict opportunities for bail and to increase the severity of penal sanctions.[30]

The most spectacular expansion in the United States has taken place within a number of state prison systems in the South. The prison population rate for every 100,000 inhabitants for state and local levels of government combined in the South in 1970 was 211, and by 1978 the rate had increased to 273. In 1970, 30 per cent of the nation's state and local prisoners were housed in the South, with 31 per cent of Americans residing in the South. By 1978 the South accounted for 45 per cent of all prisoners and 32 per cent of the nation's inhabitants. The prototype Southern expansionist prison system is the Texas Department of Corrections (TDC) which, since 1979, has become the nation's largest prison system. Between 1955 and 1981, the prison population of the Texas state prison system increased from 9,000 to 30,000, an average annual growth of 9 per cent.[31]

The Texas state prison system, together with most other prison systems in the South, continued to expand throughout the 1960s and early 1970s when prison populations elsewhere were falling. In a single decade, 1971–1981, the number of prisoners held by TDC doubled, as did the prison populations of several other states, including some outside the South. In Texas, as in most states, jails are administered at the local level of government, and in 1978 the jail population of 11,000 contributed to a total prison population rate per 100,000 Texas inhabitants of 282 compared with 207 for the nation as a whole.

The Texas prison system is comprised of eighteen maximum security prisons which vary in size from 400 to over 4,000 prisoners. Construction plans for the 1980s include huge maximum security prisons which, similar to existing institutions, are to be geographically isolated from metropolitan centres. The new prisons which include a 4,000 bed facility are not expected to eliminate overcrowding. In 1980, United States District Judge Wayne Justice concluded: 'It appears that, under TDC's own plans, the elimination of triple-celling will not be achieved in the near future and overcrowding will only get worse'. The court found that the contention by prison system administrators 'that future building plans will eventually alleviate the aggravated conditions that now exist is extremely suspect'.[32] TDC has not been expansionist in terms of personnel, as staff numbers have not kept pace with the escalating prison population. The prison officer to prisoner ratio in 1979 was 1:12 compared to the national average of 1:5.[33] The very low level of staffing, extensive overcrowding and the agricultural produce from huge penal plantations contributes to TDC having the lowest operating cost per prisoner for all state prison systems in the United States.[34]

The appalling conditions within America's most expansionist prison system were brought to light during long drawn-out litigation in a federal court. Judge Wayne Justice concluded his opinion by summarizing his view of the Texas prison system:

'. . . It is impossible for a written opinion to convey the pernicious conditions and the pain and degradation which ordinary inmates suffer within TDC prison walls; the gruesome experiences of youthful first offenders forcibly raped, the cruel and justifiable fears of inmates, wondering when they will be called upon to defend the next violent assault; the sheer misery, the discomfort, the wholesale loss of privacy for prisoners housed with one, two, or three others in a forty-five square foot cell or suffocatingly packed together in a crowded dormitory; the physical suffering and wretched psychological stress which must be endured by those sick or injured who cannot obtain adequate medical care; the sense of abject helplessness felt by inmates arbitrarily sent to solitary confinement or administrative segregation without proper opportunity to defend themselves or to argue their causes; the bitter frustration of inmates prevented from petitioning the courts and other governmental authorities for relief from perceived injustices. For those who are incarcerated within the parameters of TDC, these conditions and experiences form the content and essence of daily existence. It is to these conditions that each inmate must wake every morning; it is with the painful knowledge of their existence that each inmate must try to sleep at night'.[35]

If Texas has the political environment for an aggressively expansionist prison system so does the Republic of South Africa, where between 1950–80 the size of the prison population more than trebled.[36] South Africa's prison population rate per 100,000 inhabitants in 1978 was 456, one of the highest rates of any prison system in the world. There is also a vast turnover of persons through South Africa's prison system. Of the 274,000 sentenced persons received into the South African prison system, one third were sentenced for infringements of 'influx control measures', mostly for being longer than 72 hours in a prescribed area.[37] That a high reliance on criminal justice, including the prison system, exists in racialist South Africa is not surprising. As Albie Sachs suggests, racial theory leads to the view that 'the only realistic approach to crime in South Africa is to have strong laws, a strong police force and escape-proof jails.'[38]

Aggressive prison system expansionism was also dramatically evident in Italy and Germany during the inter-war years. In 1934 the prison population rates for 100,000 inhabitants in Italy and Germany were 126 and 157 respectively, much higher than in most other European countries.[39] These figures, which excluded persons in concentration camps, reflected a vigorous application of criminal law. Georg Rusche and Otto Kirchheimer point out that in National Socialist Germany, 'the elements of a biological race and predestination doctrine are mixed with the retaliatory principles of classical German penal theory.'[40] A distinct feature of the Italian and German prison systems at this time was an engineered decline in living conditions, including severe levels of overcrowding.[41] The underlying principles were set out in 1935 by the Secretary of State in the German Ministry of Justice to delegates attending the Congress of the International Penal and Penitentiary Commission which was held in Berlin. 'For the National Socialist State, criminal law becomes an instrument of the national community which serves the purposes of the nation's need for cleansing and protection. The need for cleansing is a moral need for atonement, which is explained at bottom by the fact that the nation considers that it is itself defiled by the objectionable conduct of its members.'[42]

England: Stop (but mostly) Go Policy

The pattern of prison system growth in England since the Second World War, as in much of the United States, has been steadily expansionist, although efforts were made after the mid-1970s to effect a standstill policy.

Between 1945 and 1970, the size of the prison population increased from 15,000 to 39,000, an average annual rate of growth of 5 per cent. The prison population rate per 100,000 inhabitants over this period rose from 33 to 80. The rapid expansion of the English prison population contrasts sharply with the thirty year period preceding 1938 when, as described in Chapter 6, there was a sharp fall to a low level maintained until the early 1940s. But the Second World War was not accompanied, as had been the War of 1914–18, with reductions in prison population. In 1940 the population fell to 9,377, the lowest figure in the history of the English prison system, largely due to early release of prisoners into the military services. However, in the following year prisoner numbers began to climb and by 1945 the average daily prison population total was at its highest level for thirty years.[43] Seven years later, the total surpassed the peak of 1908 which preceded the great reduction which began at that time. The expansion of the English prison system after 1945 was based on the reactive policy assumption that growth is inevitably driven by factors, such as the crime rate, largely beyond the control and influence of government.

On taking office in 1945 the Labour Government heralded a period of social reconstruction with a legislative programme of welfare reform of unprecedented scale in Britain. The Criminal Justice Act of 1948, while preserving many features of the Bill which was scrapped on the outbreak of War, nevertheless, reflected a more conservative orientation. The proposals for community-based hostels for young offenders, to be known as Howard Houses, were dropped in favour of the starkly different concept of the detention centre, presented as a tough alternative to corporal punishment and to prison. The regime was to be deliberately deterrent in nature so as to provide sentencers with the option of imposing a 'short sharp shock'. Support for the detention centre reflected parliamentary anxiety regarding increases in recorded crime involving young people and, since 1952 when the first centre was opened, the sanction has proved to be highly durable.[44] Over the next 30 years detention centres were to contribute substantially to the increased throughput of persons handled by the English prison system. The Criminal Justice Act of 1982, as noted in Chapter 8, promises to further extend the role of the detention centre in this respect.

During the first forty years of the century, placing more than one prisoner in a cell designed for one person was virtually unknown. In 1950 some 2,500 prisoners, 12 per cent of the prison population, were sharing cells and by 1980 the number of prisoners sharing cells exceeded 17,000, 40 per cent of the prison population. The increase in overcrowding and the general decline in living conditions in many prisons coincided with a large-scale prison building programme. The capacity of the English prison system, as measured by certified normal accommodation (CNA) increased by 170 per cent between 1945–81, not much less than the 195 per cent rise in prisoners over the same period. The increase in numbers of staff in the English prison system was more spectacular. In 1923 there were 2,150 personnel of prison officer grade, representing a ratio to prisoners of 1:5. In 1947 the number of prison officers was very similar, although the ratio of prison officers to prisoners had become 1:7. However, in the early 1950s with prison staff increasing at a much faster rate than prisoners, the ratio returned to its pre-war level.

As shown in Table 3.4, between 1950 and 1980, the number of prison officers increased at more than twice the rate of increase in prison population. The escalation in prison systems personnel was not confined to prison officers. Total prison system staff, excluding headquarters, in 1960 amounted to 8,250, a total which by 1970 had increased to 15,950 and by 1981 to 24,000.[45] Account also needs to be taken of the 1,700 staff at headquarters and regional offices,[46] the 460 probation officers seconded to prisons and the 1,100 educational staff working within the prison system.[47]

The grand total of personnel in the English prison system in 1981 was around 27,200, representing a ratio of all staff to prisoners of 1:1.6.

Table 3.4

Growth of the English prison system 1950–80 (1950 = 100)

	Prison officers	Capacity	Prison population
1950	100	100	100
1960	175	120	132
1970	321	156	191
1980	430	183	208

Source: derived from annual reports of the Prison Department

The huge increase in personnel was accompanied by the development of a complex bureaucratic structure. The Prison Commission, which administered the English prison system between 1878 and 1963, had a relatively modest headquarters office. The number of commissioners varied between two and four and there was a small support staff. After 1945, the Prison Commission created several new posts and by the early 1960s there was criticism by prison governors and others about poor communication within the prison system.[48] At this time moves were under way to dissolve the Prison Commission and to incorporate its functions within the Home Office.[49] One reason put forward for the change was to create greater career mobility for Home Office civil servants, especially in the adminstrative grades. An important dynamic in the administration of the English prison system is the relatively more powerful position within the bureaucratic structure of administrative grade civil servants in comparison with persons who have been or still are members of the governor grade.[50] In 1970 four regional offices were added and, following a further reorganization in 1980 subsequent to the May Report, the prison system's headquarters was enlarged to encompass nine divisions.[51]

Trying to stand still

Since the mid-1970s efforts have been made in England, several other Western European countries and some jurisdictions in the United States to curb prison system growth. The principal features of standstill policy are:

- exhortations to sentencers to make less use of custody, by using non-custodial sanctions and by reducing the length of prison sentences;
- the development of non-custodial sanctions intended to replace some use of the prison system;
- a prison construction programme intended to replace outdated buildings rather than to increase the total capacity of the prison system;

- attempts to widen discretion exercised by the executive branch of government regarding length of time spent in prison;
- attempts to place a ceiling on prison population size, but the total number of persons passing through the prison system may increase;
- the avoidance of fundamental questions regarding the purposes of prison, with the energies of standstill policy consumed in pragmatic efforts to maintain operations.

Standstill policy, born of expediency, is commonly couched within a pragmatic rather than philosophical rationale. In part the impetus for standstill policy arises from the overall economic situation. Widening restraints and cuts in public expenditure have not entirely spared prison systems, especially with regard to capital expenditure. However, financial factors have sometimes been given undue emphasis. Andrew Scull, in his book *Decarceration*, writes with reference to Britain and the United States: '. . . the pace of expansion of state expenditures on 'social services' in both countries increased markedly during the 1960s and 1970s. As it does, the incentives to accelerate the movement towards deinstitutionalization likewise intensify. And it is precisely in this period that the momentum of the drive to shut down institutions and minimize incarceration gathered its greatest force.'[52]

Scull's thesis is not supported by the recent experience of many prison systems. Since the early 1970s when the economic recession began to take hold, the new gaol fever has been at its most rampant. Public spending crises may at least impose restraints. The Home Office argued against a severer penal policy in 1977 on the grounds that, '. . . an increase in the number or length of custodial sentences would require a substantial rise in capital and current expenditure on the prison service. This could be obtained only from the budget of the non-custodial agencies (the police and courts being protected as agencies of the severer policy) or from outside the Home Office budget. Both of these alternatives, in the current climate of opinion and present financial circumstances seem to be non-starters.'[53]

Standstill policy in England began to take shape in the late 1960s with the focus on prison population size. In 1965 the English prison system had an average daily population of 30,421 and a capacity shortfall of 354. By 1970 the average daily population had increased to 39,028 and the capacity shortfall to 6,036. The Home Office in 1976 articulated, as one of its particular preoccupations for the preceding decade, the reduction of both the size of the prison population and the proportionate use of imprisonment as a court disposal. However, despite standstill policy, prison population had continued to increase, largely because of sentencing practice. The Home Office noted: 'There is an inconsistency between the publicly avowed policy of using custody only as a last resort for the really serious offence or dangerous offender, and actual practice.'[54] Standstill policy was given its most precise articulation by Roy Jenkins as Home Secretary who said in 1975: 'The prison population now stands at over 40,500. It has never been higher. If it should rise to, say 42,000, conditions in the system would approach the intolerable, and drastic action to relieve the position would be inescapable. We are perilously close to that position now. We must not just sit back and wait for it to happen. If we can prevent it, we must do so.'[55]

The average daily prison population hovered around 41,500 over the next three years.[56] Standstill policy amounted to an effort to hold the line on prison population size but did not include a concerted strategy to effect substantial reductions. In fact, the various strategies most often canvassed in the late 1970s did not offer the likelihood of other than marginal reductions.[57] By the end of the 1970s, standstill policy was near to collapse. The Conservative government which took office in May 1979 was committed to increasing significantly criminal justice resources, especially police manpower, and to strengthening the sentencing powers of the courts. It was the government's purpose to protect criminal justice, to the extent possible, from public expenditure cuts. In this endeavour government policy has been successful. An analysis of changes in central government staff numbers between 1979 and 1982 showed that while total personnel declined by 9 per cent, Home Office numbers, mainly prison staff, increased by over 3 per cent.[58] In 1979 the average daily population of the English prison system for the first time exceeded 42,000, the crisis level identified four years earlier.

By the early 1980s, English prison system administrators defined standstill policy in terms of achieving an 'alignment between the resources of the prison system and the demands made upon it'.[59] In the early part of 1981, it seemed for a while that the government might seek to offset the demands made upon the prison system through legislative action. In February 1981, William Whitelaw, the Home Secretary, declared: 'It is I think common ground that a continued increase in the prison population could not be sustained. So, on present trends, I should be obliged to consider what legislative measures could be taken.'[60] It was soon clear that what the Home Secretary had in mind was a form of automatic parole for short-term prisoners. This scheme was set out in a Home Office report published in July which, under the most optimistic scenario, promised to cut the size of prison population by about 15 per cent. But by the late autumn it was evident that Whitelaw was backing away from this strategy and in November, in the wake of the summer's inner city rioting, judicial opposition and the defeat of his law and order motion at the Conservative Party Conference in October, he scrapped his plans to extend parole release. The Home Secretary told the House of Commons: 'We are determined to ensure that there will be room in the prison system for every person whom the judges and magistrates decide should go there, and we will continue to do whatever is necessary for that purpose.'[61]

This announcement, during a debate on law and order following increased reported crime figures for 1981, signalled the abandonment of standstill policy on prison population in England. In effect, the decision was made to re-embark on an expansionist course and to allow prison population to rise to the level forecasted by the Home Office of 47,800 by 1984–85.[62] Early in 1982, the prison system, through the Home Office, successfully pressed the Treasury for additional cash so as to increase further the recruitment of prison officers. The English prison system is preparing itself for a prison population in excess of 50,000 by the end of the 1980s together with a much accelerated throughput of prisoners.

Standstill policy is unlikely to curb expansionist pressures from within or outside the prison system. The invariable result is that efforts to replace existing arrangements supplement and enlarge the prison system. If new non-custodial sanctions supplement rather than replace custodial sentences, these serve to increase pressure in the prison system as a consequence of action taken when persons reappear in court. Similarly, new prisons are likely to operate alongside the outdated and crumbling prisons they were intended to replace. Old and decrepit prisons are useful in making the case for prison building programmes, but such places rarely are closed.

Any success in imposing a ceiling on the average daily prison population may well be offset by increases in the total numbers of persons passing through the prison system. Under these circumstances, the rationale for using custody is likely to shift from the convenience of dumping society's misfits to providing a taste of custody for a wide range of petty offenders. This approach contrasts with the once prevalent view that very short sentences did not allow enough time for treatment and training efforts to bear fruit. In the 1950s and early 1960s, courts were advised by prison system personnel, on grounds of rehabilitation, not to send people to prison for short periods of time. With the demise of rehabilitative goals, this view has given way to the notion that penal institutions provide a salutary but short shock to relatively unsophisticated offenders. This idea is given its most explicit and powerful endorsement with reference to young offenders.

Magistrates visiting detention centres often return with the message from staff that the regime would be more effective if youths were sentenced earlier in their penal career. The question is, more effective than what? Certainly the success rate would be higher if detention centres dealt exclusively with first offenders. The success rate would no doubt be higher still if the youths passing through detention centres had no criminal record whatever! This special pleading is reminiscent of the remark by Lester Maddox, a former governor of Georgia, on his state prison system: 'We are doing the best we can, but before we can do much better we are going to have to get a better grade of inmate.'

It has not been demonstrated, however, that 'tastes of custody' are more effective in cutting short a criminal career than non-custodial sentencing alternatives. On the principle, therefore, of using the least restrictive punishment, shock custody has to be rejected. It does, however, provide an example of prison system personnel departing from the passive role of recipient by seeking to encourage the use of custody.

It is not suggested that these views lack genuine intent and are cynically aimed at assuring brisk business, although examples of blatant cynicism are not hard to find. Officers who remark to youths as they leave the institutions: 'you are my pension' or 'come back and bring a friend with you',[63] provide an echo of the following feature of eighteenth century penology, described by Seán McConville: 'So necessary was a good and constant flow of prisoners that some gaolers felt it improvident to trust in the normal workings of the law. Instead, they had themselves placed as commissions of the peace and indicted quite innocent parties who between committal and release paid numerous fees and charges.'[64]

The consequence of expansionist and standstill policies is that prison systems are engaged with both serious and trivial offenders. This state of affairs resembles the dualism revealed by Georg Rusche and Otto Kirchheimer in their classic study of pre-Second World War Europe, *Punishment and Social Structure*. Fascist penal policy differentiated between serious offenders who were treated with severity and the great mass of minor offenders who were dealt with leniently and often pardoned by amnesty. 'It is noteworthy, however, that many minor offences (whole categories or merely individual cases) are singled out as injurious to the welfare of the nation and classed with the more serious crimes.'[65] The dualistic role of contemporary expanding prison systems is to incapacitate very serious offenders for long periods but also to provide brief and salutary prison sentences for minor offenders. With regards to both groups, there is considerable elasticity, and under conditions of expansion the incapacitation net is stretched to include persons other than those convicted of serious offences. Habitual property offenders and institutional trouble-makers become likely candidates for inclusion. At the same time, the custodial threshold is lowered to include persons who earlier would have been fined or dealt with by some other non-custodial means.

In this chapter, two choices open to policy-makers, expansionism and standstill, have been described. It has been argued that standstill policy is unlikely to be an effective counter to expansionist pressures. One regular source of prison system expansion are crises of a scale that would threaten the survival of other organizations. It is with this penal paradox that the next chapter deals.

References

1 The measure of crime generally embraces all but trivial offences, and is covered by such terms as indictable (England), penal code offences (most European countries and Japan) and index offences (USA). The measures of imprisonment are the number of prison sentences and prison population size.

2 Home Office. *The Reduction of Pressure on the Prison System, Observations on the Fifteenth Report from the Expenditure Committee*, Cmnd 7948, London: HMSO, 1980, p. 2.

3 For reviews of the literature on unemployment and crime, see Roger Tarling, 'Unemployment and crime', *Home Office Research Unit Bulletin*, No. 14, 1982, pp. 28–33. Also, Roy Carr-Hill and Nicholas Stern, 'Crime, unemployment and the Police', SSRC Programme on Taxation, Incentives and the Distribution of Income, *Research Note No. 2*, January 1983.

4 David F. Greenberg, 'The dynamics of oscillatory punishment processes', *Journal of Criminal Law and Criminology*, **68**, 1977, pp. 645–50.

5 M. G. Yeager, 'Unemployment and Imprisonment', *Journal of Criminal Law and Criminology*, **70**, 1979, pp. 586–8.

6 Steven Box and Chris Hale, 'Economic Crisis and the Rising Prisoner Population in England', *Crime and Social Justice*, **21**, 1982, p. 28. Box and Hale suggest, '. . . after controlling for other related factors, that for every 1,000 increase in youth unemployment, 23 additional young males get sent to prison'. They go on to argue that, '. . . among the superordinate class, prisons are *believed* to play an important part in disciplining and containing problem populations, and irrespective of the truth-value of this belief, it has real consequences, particularly during periods of economic depression when the size of the surplus labour force rapidly expands.' ibid., p. 31.

7 Hermann Mannheim, while holding there was a relationship between unemployment and crime rates, acknowledged that no such relationship existed with prison statistics. See Hermann Mannheim, *Social Aspects of Crime in England Between the Wars*, London: George Allen and Unwin, 1940, pp. 123–52.

8 David Greenberg concluded from an analysis of Polish data, that changes in prison population rates appeared to vary in response to policy decisions, e.g. amnesties, made for reasons unrelated to either unemployment or conventional forms of crime. See, David F. Greenberg, 'Penal Sanctions in Poland: A Test of Alternative Models'. *Social Problems*, **28**, 1980, pp. 194–204.

9 L. S. Penrose, 'Mental Disease and Crime: Outline of a Comparative Study of European Statistics'. *British Journal of Medical Psychology*, **18**, 1939, pp. 1–15. See also, David Biles and Glenn Mulligan, 'Mad or Bad? The Enduring Dilemma', *British Journal of Criminology*, **13**, pp. 275–9, for a similar finding based on Australian data.

10 P. N. Grabosky, 'Rates of Imprisonment and Psychiatric Hospitalization in the United States', *Social Indicators Research*, **7**, 1980, pp. 63–70.

11 See, David Downes, 'The origins and consequences of Dutch penal policy since 1945', *British Journal of Criminology*, **22**, 1982, pp. 332–3.

12 Alfred Blumstein and Soumyo Moitra, 'An analysis of the time series of the imprisonment rate in the states of the United States: A further test of the stability of punishment hypothesis'. *Journal of Criminal Law and Criminology*, **70**, 1979, pp. 376–7. See also, Alfred Blumstein and Jacqueline Cohen, 'A Theory of the Stability of Punishment', *Journal of Criminal Law and Criminology*, **64**, 1973, pp. 198–207.

13 Alfred Blumstein and Daniel Nagin, 'Imprisonment as an Allocation Process', in *Prisons: Present and Possible*, ed. M. E. Wolfgang, Lexington, Mass: Lexington Books, 1979, pp. 169–200.

14 See, e.g., Margaret Cahalan, 'Trends in Incarceration in the United States since 1880', *Crime and Delinquency*, January 1980, pp. 9–41.

15 See generally, Irvin Waller and Janet Chan, 'Prison Use: A Canadian and International Comparison'. *Criminal Law Quarterly*, **17**, 1978, pp. 47–71.

16 Alfred Blumstein and Soumyo Moitra, comment on Cahalan's article, *Crime and Delinquency*, January 1980, pp. 91–2.

17   K. E. Boulding, 'Towards a General Theory of Growth', *Canadian Journal of Economics and Political Science*, **19**, 1953, p. 327.

18   ibid., p. 355.

19   ibid., p. 336; see also, Peter N. Blau and W. Richard Scott, *Formal Organisations: A Comparative Approach*, London: Routledge and Kegan Paul, 1963, pp. 214–17.

20   Charles Perrow, *Organisations Analysis: A Sociological View*, London: Tavistock, 1970, pp. 152–3. Perrow's analysis was anticipated by Peter Ryland MP, during the debate in the House of Commons on the Prisons Bill of 1877, who suggested that civil servants 'were always awake to their own interests; and whenever public opinion slept they took advantage of the opportunity of increasing the flow of promotion by the creation of new offices, and by advances in the rates of pay. They constituted, in fact, a great trade union, and every year were increasing in number and in influence', cited by Seán McConville, op. cit., p. 476.

21   Perrow, op. cit., note 20, p. 122.

22   Boulding, op. cit., note 17, p. 336.

23   The following data for the United States are available from 1850 (combining all persons in prisons for adults):

	Total prisoners	Rate per 100,000 inhabitants
1850	6,737	29
1880	57,760	115
1910*	111,498	121
1933*	189,433	151

* Data available only for sentenced prisoners.
Source: M. Cahalan, op. cit., note 14, pp. 12–13.

24   Data on local prisoner populations are not available since 1978. It is interesting, however, to note that the total local prisoner population remained at much the same level, around 150,000, for years 1970, 1972, and 1978, when counts were conducted.

25   President's Commission on Law Enforcement and Administration of Justice, Task Force Report, *Corrections*, Washington D.C.: U.S. Government Printing Office, 1967, pp. 13–16.

26   National Advisory Commission on Criminal Justice Standards and Goals, *A National Strategy to Reduce Crime*, Washington D.C.: Government Printing Office, 1973, p. 121.

27   See, Alfred Blumstein, Jacqueline Cohen and William Goulding, 'The Influence of Capacity on Prison Population: A Critical Review of Some Recent Evidence', unpublished paper, 1982, p. 2. The annual growth in index crime from 1965–74 was 9.2 per cent compared with 3.5 per cent from 1975–80.

28   Kevin Krajick, 'The Boom Resumes', *Corrections Magazine*, vii, April 1981, pp. 16–20.

29   David F. Greenberg and Drew Humphries, 'The Cooption of Fixed Sentencing Reform', *Crime and Delinquency*, **26**, 1980, p. 223.

30   *Attorney-General's Task Force on Violent Crime, Final Report*, Chairman, Griffin Bell, U.S. Department of Justice, Washington D.C., 1981, xiii; see also Congressional Quarterly, 10 July 1982, p. 1669.

31   The Texas state prison population increased as follows between 1955–81:

1955	8,622	1975	18,937
1960	10,081	1980	26,522
1965	12,054	1981	29,886
1970	14,331		

Other state prison systems which doubled their prison population between 1970–81 included Florida, Georgia, Tennessee and New York.

32   *Ruiz v. Estelle*, 503, F.Supp. 1265, 1280–1, (E.D. Tex., 1980).

33   ibid., p. 1290.

34   National Institute of Justice, *American Prisons and Jails*, Vol. III, (Conditions and Costs of Confinement), 1981, p. 118. The operating cost per prisoner in the Texas state prison for fiscal year 1977 was $2,241 compared with a national average of $5,662. ibid., pp. 115–17.

35   *Ruiz v. Estelle*, op. cit., note 32, pp. 1390–91.

36 South Africa's prison population and rate per 100,000 inhabitants 1952–79:

	Total	Rate per 100,000 inhabitants
1952	31,903	236
1962	62,769	355
1972/73	95,014	446
1978/79	98,292	452

Source: Albie Sachs, Justice in South Africa, Berkeley and Los Angeles: University of California 1973, 189 (for 1952–62); and Report of the Commissioner of Prisons for 1978/79, 1980, p. 24 (for 1972/73 and 78/79).

South Africa also makes extensive use of the death penalty, with the number of executions increasing steadily since 1945. In the twelve months ending June 1978, 105 persons were executed.

37 Report of the Commissioner of Prisons, op. cit., note 36, p. 12 and p. 28. Over 80 per cent of sentenced receptions into the prison system are sentenced to periods of six months or less. Because of the high turnover, persons serving sentences within this category constitute about 15 per cent of the average daily population, whereas 65 per cent are serving sentences of two years or longer, ibid., p. 12.

38 Albie Sachs, op. cit., 185; Sachs provides a comprehensive overview of the South African criminal justice process.

39 Howard League for Penal Reform. The Prisoner Population of the World, London, 1936.

40 Georg Rusche and Otto Kurchheimer, Punishment and Social Structure, New York: Russell and Russell, 1939, p. 182.

41 ibid., p. 188.

42 Actes du Congrès Pénal et Pénitentiare International de Berlin août 1935, Berne: Bureau de la Commission Internationale Pénale et Pénitentiare, 1936, Volume 1a, pp. 434–456; for an English perspective on the Berlin Congress see G. H. C. Bing, 'The International Penal and Penitentiary Congress, Berlin, 1935', Howard Journal, IV, 1935, pp. 195–8. Bing comments on the unusual way the host government organized the proceedings. The second largest national delegation was the United States with thirty-six delegates. Germany had 443 delegates. Bing comments, 'It appeared, for example, that the German view of sterilization was carried by an overwhelming majority. Actually those few hands which were raised against it in the Plenary Assembly represented the opinion of at least half the civilized world.' ibid., p. 198.

43 It is interesting to note that women prisoners increased numerically and as a proportion of the total prison population during the Second World War. This is shown below:

	Women prisoners	Women as percentage of total prison population
1938	698	6.3
1939	664	6.4
1940	934	9.9
1941	967	9.1
1942 } 1943	not available	
1944	1,477	11.4
1945	1,538	10.4
1946	1,233	7.8
1950	1,107	5.4

44 See especially, Hilary Land, 'Detention Centres: the Experiment Which Could Not Fail', in Change, Choice and Conflict in Social Policy, ed. Phoebe Hall et al., London: Heinemann, 1975, pp. 311–70.

45 Sources for these data are Prisons and Borstals, England and Wales, London: HMSO, 1960 (for 1960); Home Office evidence to May Committee, vol. II, 1979, p. 81 (for 1970), and Report of Prison Department for 1981, 1982 (for 1981).

There are indications that procedures for selecting prison officers became less rigorous in 1969 with the result of encouraging staff recruitment. When selection was an integral part of the training process at the Officers' Training School, between 25–35 per cent of recruits failed the course. A departmental working party, set up in 1968, aware of 'the present need to recruit more officers', noted the separation of selection from training to be put into operation from early 1969. While these changes were welcomed by the working party, it was concerned that these should be accompanied by a greater understanding between headquarters and governors about appropriate action in the case of unsuitable officers on probation. (Report of the Working Party on the Initial Training of Prison Officers, unpublished paper, February 1969, pp. 9–10). However, one senior official involved in staff training in the early 1970s has estimated that under the new procedures the failure rate of officers on probation did not exceed about 1 per cent.

46 *Memorandum Submitted by the Prison Department of the Home Office* to the Home Affairs Committee, House of Commons, Session 1979–80, Administration of the Prison Service, Minutes of Evidence, London: HMSO, 3 November 1980, p. 6.

47 Probation officers and educational staff are not appointed by the Prison Department, although their cost is met by the system's budget. The respective sources for the data cited are Probation and After-care Statistics 1981, London: Home Office, 1982; data on educational staff supplied by the Prison Department, which in detail for 1980/81 were:

education officers	121
teachers (full-time)	287
sessional day teachers (full-time equivalent)	600
sessional evening teachers (full-time equivalent)	400

48 See, Prison Department, *Report of the Working Party on Communications*, 1964. The report concluded: 'We have come to the general conclusion that the increase in size and complexity of the penal system has not been matched by adequate development of the system of communications. There is a great deal of evidence for this; it is implicit in most of the criticisms that have been made to us. Members of the Service with long experience can recall the days when the organisation was smaller and simpler, when there were fewer both of individual specialists in establishments and specialised sections at Head Office, when there was a simple chain of command and everyone knew exactly where he, and other people with whom he came into contact, stood in the organisation. There were fewer different types of establishment and less variety of treatment. The risk of confusion and misunderstanding was correspondingly less'. ibid., p. 8.

49 Legislative moves to dissolve the Prison Commission were first made with the Criminal Justice Bill of 1938. The Bill was withdrawn in 1939, and a similar clause in the Criminal Justice Act of 1961 allowed for the abolition of the Prison Commission which, after some controversy, took place in 1963.

50 The tension between these two groups has contributed to several major structural reorganizations since 1963. The key positions, however, in the early 1980s have remained with administrative grade civil servants. This is illustrated by the diagram of Prison Department headquarters, as of 1980, from which it is obvious that the four key positions on the Prisons Board are all held by administrative grade civil servants. See Minutes of Evidence taken before the Home Affairs Committee, *Memorandum Submitted by the Prison Department of the Home Office*, 3 November 1980: 5. For an excellent discussion of the power plays of Home Office mandarins, see Peter Evans, *Prison Crisis*, London: George Allen and Unwin, 1980, pp. 110–38.

51 Memorandum submitted by the Prison Department to the Home Affairs Committee, op. cit., p. 2. The Director of Personnel and Finance told the Committee with respect to the 130 persons in the Personnel Division that: 'it strikes me that the ratio, in military jargon, of tail staff to teeth is extraordinarily small . . .', ibid., p. 10.

52 Andrew Scull, *Decarceration: Community Treatment and the Deviant: a Radical View*, Englewood Cliffs: Prentice-Hall, 1977, p. 140.

53 *A Review of Criminal Policy 1976*, London: HMSO, 1977, p. 9.

54 ibid., p. 7. For a description of Home Office policy-making at this time, see, M. J. Moriarty, 'The Policy-Making Process: How it is seen from the Home Office', in *Penal Policy-Making in England*, ed. Nigel Walker, Cambridge: Institute of Criminology, 1977, pp. 131–2.

55 Roy Jenkins, Unpublished speech to NACRO, 21 July 1975, draft, p. 13.

56 A new prison population peak of 42,400 was reached in October 1976.
57 See, e.g., Ken Pease, 'The Size of the Prison Population', *British Journal of Criminology*, 21, 1981, pp. 70–74.
58 David Walker, *The Times*, 17 June 1982.
59 Director-General's Review in *Prison Department Annual Report for 1981*, Cmnd 8543, London: HMSO, 1982, p. 3.
60 William Whitelaw, unpublished speech to Leicestershire magistrates, 13 February, 1981.
61 H.C. Deb. Sixth Series, vol. 21, col. 1122, 25 March 1982. Mr Whitelaw repeated this phrase, with considerable emphasis, at the Conservative Party Conference in 1982.
62 *The Government's Expenditure Plans, 1982–83 to 1984–85*, Cmnd 8494–11, London: HMSO, March 1982, p. 36.
63 These perhaps apocryphal comments were repeated by young men in at least one borstal in the early 1970s.
64 Seán McConville, *A History of English Prison Administration*, vol. I, 1750–1877, London: Routledge and Kegan Paul, p. 11.
65 Rusche and Kirchheimer, op. cit., note 40, p. 206. The notion of dualism has some similarities with the bifurcation process, as described by Tony Bottoms, and makes a split between the dangerous and the rest with, for example, the use of long prison sentences increasing alongside a general decrease in sentence severity. See, A. E. Bottoms, 'Reflections on the Renaissance of Dangerousness', *Howard Journal of Penology and Crime Prevention*, 16, 1977, pp. 88–9.

4　Growth through Crisis

The complexity of the functions of the prison system ensures that it is especially prone to crises. The paramount functions are security and control. The security function is to prevent, or at least to minimize, possibilities of escape. The control function is to ensure good order and discipline within the prison. The third function, providing prisoners with adequate conditions, invariably is afforded a lower priority than security and control. Crises may erupt when the prison system fails with respect to any one of these three functions. Prison crises can only be understood in terms of the political environment within which the prison system is located. The political environment is comprised of groups with special interests in prisons of whom the most important are legislators, the media, staff associations, the judiciary, reform groups and prisoners. The relative powers and interests pursued by these groups shape the character and course of prison system crises. [1]

Prison systems, compared with many other organizations, are remarkably resilient to the eruption of crises. Two features of this resilience require emphasis. First, crises occasioned by a much publicized escape or a large-scale disturbance are likely to result in an immediate shift of resources from the provisions of adequate conditions to the functions of security and control. For this and for other reasons, discussed in the next chapter, efforts to provide decent conditions are inherently vulnerable. Second, a long-term consequence of security or control crises is likely to be the injection of additional resources into the prison system. Much of the internal impetus for expanding prison systems gathers momentum in the wake of control and security crises.

The first section of this chapter reviews general problems which arise with respect to the prison's tasks of security and control. Much of the material refers to prison systems in the United States, mostly over the period since the mid-1970s, where events are often taken to a further extreme and the issues more finely drawn than in Europe. There are, of course, features of the American prison scene which are less commonly found in Europe. The concentration of non-whites, the level of violence and the generally larger scale of operations are among the factors which suggest caution in generalizing from American experience. However, it is contended that the basic functions of the prison systems are similar across industrialized democratic societies and that the problems faced in the United States, where expansionist prison policy has become the rule rather than the exception are, although posed rather starkly, relevant elsewhere. As a comparison to the American situation, some issues arising in Scandinavian prison systems are explored.

The second section addresses the English prison system during the period 1965–80 and examines three critical events, each of which fuelled expansionist tendencies. In the mid-1960s, attention focused on major breaches of prison security. In the early and mid-1970s the theme was collective disorder by prisoners threatening traditional assumptions as to the distribution of power within the prison system. By the late 1970s and early 1980s, attention had shifted from prisoners to prison officers, with administrators and managers facing a severe test as to where the real power lay. The three developments overlapped and interlocked, and each significantly contributed to the scope and paraphernalia of the prison. When, in the mid 1970s, efforts were made by government to fashion standstill policy with respect to prison system size, these were doomed to failure. Pressures prompting expansion within and outside the prison system were already out of control.

The security function

Fundamental to any prison is the assurance that prisoners do not absent themselves without authority. The security task is paramount with regard to prisoners who have committed serious offences or who are notorious for other reasons. Lionel Fox, a former head of the English prison system, put the point squarely: 'The essence of commitment to prison for any purpose being that the prisoner is deprived of his liberty, the basic charge on the keepers of the prison is, today as yesterday, safe custody . . . The prison officer of today is a good deal more than a turnkey, but turning keys, checking them and accounting for them remain a prominent and permanent feature of his daily life.'[2] Even ultimate fortress prisons such as Alcatraz have not been immune from security crises. As noted in a new study of 'The Rock', 'with such an experienced and sophisticated group of men looking for the slightest opportunity for escape, it is not surprising that several of the most ingenious escape attempts in American penal history occurred at Alcatraz.'[3]

Prison security relies upon architecture, categorization of prisoners, physical paraphernalia, routine procedures and staff. The key architectural dilemma is whether to rely upon cellular or perimeter security. Early prisons, including most of those constructed in the nineteenth century, were designed around the notion of the prisoner spending most, if not all, of his or her time locked in a cell. Movement within the prison, if it occurred, was tightly restricted, thereby achieving the tasks of both security and control. More recently, and typically in many prison systems in the United States, security has been placed at the periphery. The prison is surrounded by high walls, fences or other barriers with armed guards posted in watchtowers. This approach permits movement inside the prison, for example within the yard, with security concentrated at the boundaries of the prison and the world beyond. In most prisons there is reliance on both cellular and perimeter security, especially at night. In 1952, Lionel Fox, in rather ironic terms given the crises a decade later, wrote: 'Having broken out of the cell, it is necessary to get over the wall, and this seems to present surprisingly little difficulty to the enterprising.'[4]

Prison systems generally categorize institutions, units within institutions and prisoners in terms of gradation of security. Prisoners and prisons are categorized as to maximum, medium and minimum security. The difference between maximum and medium security is often marginal, reflecting defences around the perimeter, numbers of security cells and investment in security technology. In most prison systems, as shown in Table 4.1, the great majority of prisoners are held in conditions of maximum or medium security. Exceptionally, as in Sweden, the proportion of prisoners held in minimum security approaches one quarter.

Table 4.1
Distribution (by percentage) of prisoners, by level of security which housed them on a given day in 1978

	Maximum	Medium	Minimum
England	28	53	9
Sweden	51	25	24
Netherlands	NIL	85	15
Japan	69	27	3
USA (federal and state systems)	51	38	11

Source: cross-national study, and American Prisons and Jails, vol. 1, p. 57

The security catergorization of prisoners is in large part determined by the architectural structure of existing institutions. In many state systems in the United States the majority of prisoners are held in fortress prisons of maximum security design, constructed prior to 1925, and generally holding at least 2,000 prisoners. In some systems security categorization of any sort hardly exists. For example, in Texas the state system categorizes ninety-five per cent of its prisoners as maximum security, despite the fact that the head of the system has testified to the legislature that forty per cent of the male population do not need to be imprisoned.[5] The tendency to over-utilize maximum security facilities, the deepest end of the prison system, and to under-utilize minimum security facilities is a hallmark of the expanding prison system.

Security paraphernalia take many forms. It can be applied directly to the prisoner in its most crude form by shackling or chaining the prisoner to the cell floor. In many prison systems the use of mechanical restraints is no longer permitted, except in the case of medical or other narrowly defined and exceptional circumstances. Special prison garb to identify prisoners is general practice, and in England and some other systems prisoners on the 'escape list' wear coloured patches on their clothing. Most security technology, however, is applied to the prison buildings and grounds, and may include such items as geophones (electronic alarms buried in the ground or located on the walls), closed circuit television, razor-ribbon fencing, a large variety of lethal weaponry, searchlights, dogs and so forth. In some prisons security arrangements are largely computerized. The official description of a Minnesota prison, opened in 1982, states: 'A computerized building status system monitors security. Routine events, such as the opening and closing of doors, are programmed into the computer. Any deviation must be cleared with security officers to avoid triggering alarms.' Once in place, security paraphernalia tend to proliferate rapidly. Prior to 1967 there were no guard dogs in the English prison system. By 1982 dog sections were maintained at 23 prisons at an annual cost of £5 million. A wide range of prison security gadgetry is advertised in the pages of American prison journals and is lavishly displayed at conventions attended by system personnel.

Associated with security hardware is a variety of procedures designed to avert escapes. These include searches of cells and prisoners, movement of prisoners around the prison or between prisons, and scrutiny of prisoners' contacts with the outside world. The security technology and procedures, despite their sophistication, depend upon an intelligent and vigilant staff. Prison staff are routinely reminded that they are responsible for security. As a report on English prisons observed: '. . . the first and most important element in the security of any prison is an adequate, alert and well-trained staff.'[6] However, even in the most secure prisons, staff sometimes make extraordinary oversights. One prisoner, who escaped from Brixton prison while awaiting terrorist offence charges, has decribed how while being searched he asked an officer to hold the box containing tools he was using to carve a hole in the wall of his cell.[7]

The emergence of security specialists may ironically result in other staff giving less attention to security than they otherwise would. In England, security staff have developed close links with the police in order to maintain checks on both prisoners and staff. Prison staff, of course, may become especially vunerable when prisoners have financial resources at their disposal, as described later with reference to the escape of one of the Great Train Robbery gang.

Finally, the prison system's security function is closely associated with the regime within the prison. The reasons why prisoners contemplate escape are often related to intimidation and fear of violence, and these are but two facets of the function of control.

The control function

Prison routine is as much focused on control as upon security. The day-to-day concerns of administration and management are less focused on the likelihood of escape than on disruptive incidents ranging from collective disorder, which may be peaceful or violent, to events involving small groups or individuals. A principal and highly complex responsibility for prison management is to prevent prisoners from exploiting and mistreating each other and to discourage staff from exceeding their lawful powers. The available tools include classification procedures, disciplinary practices, segregation facilities, the deployment of staff and staff training. Of paramount importance to effective control of the prison by management is the tenor of prison life, and this reflects the quality of relationships, especially between prisoners and custodial staff. The governor of an English maximum security prison has written: 'Control in a prison can be achieved in many different ways but the only successful control is when there is a true understanding between staff and prisoners and where, to some extent, there is a ready level of give-and-take, when the boundaries are clearly understood and where there can develop – dare I say – a certain amount of mutual respect.'[8]

Prisoners and staff share the same environment and have a common interest in good order, and it is to be expected that informal understandings are established between these two groups. While these arrangements are often useful in terms of maintaining an apparently orderly regime, they pose certain dangers. Effective order may be replaced by a surface placidity, agreed to by prisoner leadership and staff, but at the expense of other prisoners.[9] Selective rule-enforcement and privileges for informal leaders are exchanged for cooperation. Sociological studies of the prison, especially in the United States, emphasize the importance of these informal arrangements as sources of social control within the prison. Richard Cloward found that elite prisoners '. . . stand between the inmate system and the formal system, bridging them and binding them together. They mediate and modify the diverse pressures emanating from each system. They bring order to an otherwise strife full situation.'[10]

In some prison systems, prison management formally delegate responsibility for control, and sometimes even for security, to particular prisoners. An extreme example is described by Tom Murton, former director of the Arkansas state prison system: 'Incredible as it may seem, the inmates were in complete control of Tucker (the main prison). The gates, towers, cell blocks, kitchen, hospital, dog kennel, chicken house, barns and everything else were all supervised by the inmates who, in turn, were watched over by other inmate guards and the troopers. Inmates carried weapons, and they would not allow the state troopers to have weapons. A first step in gaining control of the institutions and weakening the power of the trusties, therefore, was to get the state police armed.'[11] Murton gained control of the prison system for a short period, but his reforms, together with the highly publicized discovery of the remains of prisoners murdered some years earlier and buried in the prison grounds, led eventually to his removal. The use of armed 'trusties' in the Arkansas prison system was later condemned in the following terms by a federal court: 'The reasons for penological disapproval of the use of trusty guards are that it creates an unhealthy prison climate and atmosphere: it breeds fear and hatred between the guards on the one hand, and those guarded on the other hand; it tends to be brutal and to endanger the lives of inmates who live and work "under the guns" of other convicts; and it leads to other abuses.'[12]

The ultimate in contemporary prison order, it is sometimes claimed, is to be found in the institutions of the Texas state prison system which gained a national reputation for its tight and rigid grip on 30,000 prisoners. This model of orderly and efficient control was severely tarnished by the findings emerging during the course of a lawsuit, *Ruiz* v. *Estelle*, which was filed originally in 1973. In a decision made in 1980, Federal District Judge Wayne Justice found that as the result of severe overcrowding and low numbers of staff, '. . . inmates are routinely subjected to brutality, extortion and rape at the hands of their cellmates'. The court also found that certain prisoners, known as 'building tenders', were permitted to carry weapons, despite the fact that Texas state law expressly prohibits the use of prisoners in a supervisory capacity over other prisoners. The court found that the Texas prison system had disregarded this statutory provision and made up for its manpower shortages by using prisoners to perform security duties. In 1974 there were 800 formally approved building tenders, constituting about five per cent of the prison population, and by 1979 this number had increased to 2,260, nine per cent of the prison population.

The court observed that the Texas prison system was not absolved by the legislature's failure to appropriate funds to significantly increase custodial staff. Furthermore, it appeared that although prison system administrators had earlier requested a custodial staff–prisoner ratio of one to six, the 1978 budget request only maintained a ratio of one to ten.[13] The court concluded: 'This implies that TDC (Texas Department of Corrections) officials have chosen to accept and bear with the building tender system.'

The court found that building tender positions were routinely filled with, 'violent, corrupt and brutal inmates – some particularly notorious'. One former building tender testified to the court that he was promised certain favours if he would cooperate with officers. The court noted: 'One of his commissioned tasks involved the intimidation of a writ writer (prisoner skilled at preparing civil suits) by the officials.' Although the writ writer had his throat slit, not fatally as had been intended, the building tender who carried out that assault was not charged, as the injury was characterized by the authorities as self-mutilation.[14] The court found that in some parts of the Texas prison system, '. . . building tenders have and exercise more authority than low-level correctional officers. Several former TDC officers stated that they were taught their duties by building tenders and learned quickly never to challenge them, particularly if the officer the building tenders 'worked' for was of high rank.'[15]

Several instances of crude brutality are cited in the court's judgment, some of which appear to have been condoned by prison management. Building tenders involved in serious incidents retained their positions after receiving either minimal disciplinary action or none at all. In summary, the court found that the prison system administration, '. . . had not adequately controlled the unlawfully maintained building tender system, and they have directly and indirectly permitted its abuses on the inmates of Texas prison'.[16]

There are two ready measures of the degree of confidence held by staff in their control over prisoners. The first type of measure, which lends itself to empirical test, is the extent to which prisoners are locked in their cells as opposed to being free to associate with others during certain periods of the day. The second measure is more qualititative and has to do with the freedom enjoyed by staff to move around all parts of the prison.

In the United States, the fragile control exercised in many prison systems by management and staff is symbolized by 'lock-up', which entails the entire population of a prison being confined within their cells throughout the day for weeks or even months at a time. James Jacobs, in his study of Stateville prison in Illinois, traces the use of lock-up since the prison was opened in 1925. Following a riot in 1931 the entire prison was placed on lock-up for seven months, a practice which became tradition at Stateville in times of crisis. During the next quarter of a century the prison was managed rigidly by the same warden, assuming the character of a paramilitary organization, and resort to lock-up was rarely necessary. Jacobs writes: 'Every person and every aspect had its place. From the award-winning gardens to the clock-like regularity of the movement of prisoners in precise formations from assignment to assignment, the prison reflected its warden's zeal for order and harmony.'[17] By the 1960s control problems resurfaced, and lock-up again became routine. Control crises throughout the Illinois prison system between 1970 and 1980 resulted in five changes of heads of the system and frequent shake-ups of prison management. In 1979 a new warden at Stateville commenced a six week lock-up. An arsenal of weapons was removed from prisoners, gang leaders were transferred and new personnel employed. The warden described the situation prior to the lock-up as follows: 'The only thing that inmates were not permitted to do was escape. We just controlled the perimeter. The rest was free territory.'[18]

The use made of administrative segregation is also an index of control problems within the prison system. Cellular confinement of prisoners, when not used as a disciplinary sanction, has the dual purpose of providing protective custody for victims and for isolating prisoners viewed as potential aggressors or predators, to use the new American prison term. Rulings by courts in the United States have, however, placed restrictions on the use of administrative segregation of prisoners suspected of violence. One prison manager concluded: 'It's easier to let the predator run around and to lock up the guy who needs protecting'.[19] Upward trends in the use of protective custody in many prison systems in the United States have been dramatic. In California the number of prisoners in protective custody increased from two per cent of the state prison population in 1977 to twelve per cent in 1980. In Illinois some seventeen per cent of the state prison population were in protective custody in 1980.[20]

There are several reasons for the escalating use of protective custody in the United States. Racial factors are important and in some prisons, for example, Stateville, the protective custody unit is the only part of the prison that is predominantly white. An associated factor is the growth of prisoners gangs, and these are especially active in the prison systems of California and Illinois. A particularly difficult group to protect are police-paid informers, many of whom are involved in narcotics cases. A recent development in the federal prison system is the setting up of special units to hold high-risk witnesses in cases involving drugs. The huge profits in the narcotics business place these witnesses at dire risk even when the most extraordinary measures are taken for their protection.

The extent to which staff are able to move freely around the prison provides a general indication of the degree of staff control. In many prison systems in the United States attacks on staff, some of them fatal, have become more frequent. For example, in the mid-1970s certain parts of Stateville prison were declared by prisoners to be off-limits to guards with threats to kill those who trespassed. In 1976 a senior guard was fatally attacked and thrown forty feet off a cell tier.[21] Staff may also be fearful of being taken hostage.

The emergence of 'no-go' areas for staff is, of course, a threat to prison security. In one of the more notable recent escapes in the English prison system, involving three high-security prisoners from Brixton prison in 1980, the official inquiry concluded: 'Although there is conflicting evidence on this point, I am reasonably satisfied that the association area was, in practice, a "no-go" area for the staff and that, therefore, the prisoners involved in the escape could, over a period of time, work on the dividing walls of the cells under cover of the noise of personal radios during the day without the risk of observation by the wing's staff.'[22]

The good order of prisons can be challenged by prisoners through either peaceful or violent means. The peaceful demonstration by prisoners poses particular difficulties. For management there are concerns that the legiti-macy of the prisoners' position may be enhanced if force is used to reassert control. For custodial staff, the peaceful demonstration undermines their authority without providing a ready pretext for that authority to be demon-strably restored. In the late 1960s and early seventies the prisoners' rights movement, as part of the broader Movement, flowered for a while in the United States and some European countries. John Irwin, in his com-prehensive account of the development of the rights movement within American prisons in the late 1960s, points out: '. . . Although racial hostility simmered below their new radical perspective, in the late 1960s many of the heads of black prisoner organizations and other respected black leaders were ready to cooperate with whites to achieve shared political goals.'[23]

Irwin, who was close to the prisoners' movement in California, describes how it originated with an underground newsletter, *The Outlaw*, in San Quentin prison in 1967. The following year there were demonstrations and strikes on behalf of prisoners' rights, some of which received support from radical groups outside the prison system. Irwin comments that the San Quentin strikes marked a turning point in the developments inside American prisons. 'After these events, more and more prisoners through-out the country began redefining their legal and social status, adopting political ideologies, and becoming involved in various forms of political activities.'[24] A series of violent episodes in California and in prison systems elsewhere fuelled the movement for a while. On occasion the semblance of a national prisoners' network was evident, largely through underground newsletters. However, strikes by prisoners had minimal impact, and attempts at collective organization by prisoners made little headway. By the mid-1970s the prisoners' rights movement in the United States had largely dissipated. The prisoners' movement had become dependent upon groups outside the prison system for direction and impetus. Once these groups lost interest in prisons, the movement was doomed. However, matters did not revert to where they had been when the prisoners' move-ment began. As Irwin comments, '(the old guard) returned to full power with renewed strength and considerable vengeance'.[25]

Even in Scandinavia, where the prisoners' rights movement in the early 1970s made most progress, the position of prisoners remained weak. In Sweden the Association for the Humanizing of the Penal System (KRUM) was founded in the autumn of 1966 with a gathering, dubbed 'the Thieves' Parliament', which brought together ex-prisoners and assorted profes-sionals to discuss policy and to improve prison conditions. Two of KRUM's early demands were quickly granted. In 1968 prisoners were allowed to vote in a general election, and the first prisoners' council was set up. Thomas Mathiesen, in his analysis of KRUM and related developments in Norway and Denmark, has described the shift of emphasis from humani-tarian and treatment concerns to a radical questioning of the total penal process. In Norway a prison reform organisation, KROM, was founded in 1967 and, according to Mathiesen, was adversely reacted to by the authorities and the media because it disturbed significant social functions of imprisonment, such as the scapegoating and expurgating of convicted persons.[26]

In Sweden various attempts were made in the early 1970s to improve the lot of prisoners through attempts at establishing collective bargaining procedures. Organization among Swedish prisoners first took place in 1968 at Håll prison resulting in demonstrations together with work and hunger strikes. The developments at Håll were given press coverage, and the idea of organization spread to other prisons. In October 1970 a hunger strike at Österåker prison, just outside Stockholm, gained support through a sympathy strike which involved about half the country's five thousand prisoners. On the fourth day of the hunger strike talks commenced at Österåker prison and continued for three days. They were attended by representatives of the prison officers' union, other staff representatives, the head of the prison system and some of L.T. staff. Gunnar Marnell was present as regional director and provided a frank description of the event:

'In the beginning the atmosphere was very tense. In spite of great informality – all were on first-name terms – the prisoners were very firm and logical in their arguments. And they were, of course, sceptical towards the prison authorities! The local questions – demands for improved visiting conditions, a new education department as an alternative to one of the workshops, enlarged exercise yards, etc. – were apparently only an excuse for their most important demands, negotiations between inmates representing all eight regions and the central administration itself.

This demand succeeded. Nearly all the demands were met. On the local level: enlarged exercise yards, the creating of an education centre, improved and much more liberal conditions for the prisoners' council to work within the institution including the use of the prison radio for sending regular radio programmes produced by the prisoners' council. But the most important and far-reaching decision was the final one – central talks a month later.'[27]

The central talks were held during the winter of 1970–71; and agreement was reached to end censorship of letters, to increase visits and furlough arrangements and on other matters. Further talks at the national level took place in November 1971 but these broke down on the first day. Agreement could not be reached that decisions be made on every point raised if there were no legal obstacles.

The formal dialogue between prisoners, staff representatives and prison system administrators was a consultative rather than a bargaining process. KRUM was critical of the 'pseudo-democracy' which the new arrangements suggested, and the events underscored the relative powerlessness of prisoners.[28] By the mid-1970s KRUM's membership had dropped sharply and as noted by one commentator, the failure of prison democracy in Sweden provides '. . . evidence of the difficulty inmates have in bringing about fundamental changes in even the most enlightened system'.[29] Mathiesen's assessment points to the fundamental weakness of the prisoners' situation: 'The prisoners have no built-in possibility of threatening the prison system. They do not contribute to the system, and therefore have nothing permanent which they may threaten to withdraw.'[30]

When the prisoners' representatives walked out of subsequent talks in November 1971, Mathiesen, who was present as an adviser, saw this as an attempt to break out of a system in which their position was weak, towards a situation where strategic relationships might be developed with outside organizations. There was some negative reaction by staff in the Swedish prison system. Mathiesen comments that with 'the feeling of being overlooked, and of the prisoners' demands being unreasonable . . .', staff felt they had reached boiling point.[31] However, staff reaction was mild compared with what occurred in England and the United States. The mildness of the Swedish staff union may have been due to their involvement in the national negotiations and to the close ties of the union with the Social Democratic Party which was in office. In the end, the negotiations came to nothing, in part because the administration was under pressure from staff unions not to give in to far-reaching demands by prisoners.[32]

The margin between peaceful and violent protest within the prison is often narrow. Collective protests and strikes may erupt into violent episodes. This pattern was exemplified by the events surrounding the life and death of George Jackson, a black prisoner who became a celebrated Movement figure. Jackson's eloquent testimony, *Soledad Brother*, caught the mood of the times.[33] A series of violent incidents inside and outside the prison system culminated in his death, along with two other prisoners and four guards in San Quentin prison in 1971.

Collective violence may have nothing or little to do with prisoner protests. Traditionally, the violent disturbance, including the prison riot, reflects a breakdown in the informal arrangements between prisoner leadership and custodial staff. The collapse of such arrangements may well be prompted by the zealous reforms of the new management. Riots may also result from power struggles between various prisoner factions or, more rarely, may be linked with a mass escape attempt. While the traditional pattern of prison riots in the United States suggests contagion, more recently riots have tended to be spontaneous and unpredictable.

On occasion, there is considerable loss of life as was the case at the state prison at Attica in 1971 when 43 staff and prisoners died, most of whom were killed during the retaking of the prison by the state police and prison staff.[34] Appalling as the events at Attica were, the riot at the state prison in Santa Fé, New Mexico in 1980 is surely prison management's ultimate nightmare of total loss of control to prisoners. The events started with several members of staff being taken hostage in the early hours of the morning of 2 February 1980. Within an hour or so, prisoners had taken over the control centre, and the ninety prisoners inside the segregation unit had been released. Negotiations by means of two-way radio between prisoners and prison officials commenced almost immediately, but while these were proceeding up to fifty prisoners were engaged in a series of killings. Thirty-three prisoners were killed and a further two hundred were seriously injured. Many of the deaths were of prisoners held in the protective custody unit after rampaging prisoners burned their way in using acetylene torches.

Scenes of horrific dimensions followed, including prisoners being soaked in petrol and set on fire. Other prisoners met a variety of ghastly deaths and, although the victims included known informers, there was no obvious pattern to their selection. No guards were killed but three were injured, and more staff casualties would have occurred had the hostages not been protected by prisoners. The negotiations continued in a protracted form and eventually involved journalists who were allowed to enter the prison. The riot ended, with the release of the last two hostages, thirty-six hours after it began. In the five years prior to the riot the prison had had five wardens, and the state prison system headquarters had undergone similar upheavals. The riot was followed by further firings and new appointments, but it also resulted in very considerably increased expenditure on the state prison system.[35]

Management's control task extends beyond prisoners to staff. In this sense, the prison and the system of which it is a part are similar to other organizations where controlling the activities of personnel is a paramount management concern. During the 1970s, the English prison system was confronted by two control crises. As outlined later in this chapter, the challenge by prisoners was short-lived but had far-reaching repercussions and, in particular, fuelled a militancy among prison officers which carried over into the 1980s. The extent of this challenge by prison officers to English prison system administrators and managers far surpasses what has occurred elsewhere. In the United States, for example, there are some states, mostly in the South, where unionization by prison staff is still not permitted. Where the unionization of guards has occurred, it has made much impact on the entire prison system in only a few states.[36]

The growth of unionism among guards at Stateville prison has been described by James Jacobs. Prior to 1970 the union, a local of the American Federation of State, County and Municipal Employees (AFSCME), was concerned mostly with salary, overtime and pensions. After 1970 the union widened the scope of its activities to encompass the security of the prison and made demands which displayed a lack of confidence in the prison

administration. Gradually senior uniformed staff joined the union including eventually the chief guard. Soon afterwards, collective bargaining
arrangements were established on a statewide basis, although this had not
been provided for by the legislature.[37] In New York State at Attica prison,
the guards' union negotiated a contract seventeen months prior to the riot
which enabled experienced and senior guards to position themselves in the
watchtowers. This arrangement reversed previous practice and resulted in
the least experienced staff being in most direct contact with prisoners.[38]
Later in New York State, the guards' union were active in blocking the
appointment of a liberal law professor as head of the agency with oversight
responsibilities for the prison system.

In other states too, guards' unions have turned their attention to prison
system policy. In Massachusetts, for example, in 1973 a progressive and
black head of the state prison system, John Boone, was fired partly as
the consequence of pressures exercised by the guards' union. Boone was
regarded by the guards' union as being sympathetic to the emerging
prisoners' rights movement, and his departure encouraged resistance by
the guards' union to significant reform of the state prison system.

From the preceding review of problems arising regarding the prison
system's functions of security and control, it is not difficult to appreciate
why administrators have a tendency towards the defensive. Many prison
systems lurch from one crisis to another, and in some instances managing
these recurring crises has become routine. For the administrator, the
challenge is professional survival and this largely depends upon considerations in the political environment. For the prison system as a whole, the
crisis may provide the springboard for seeking additional resources. While
heads roll the prison system is consolidated, often to be further expanded.

Escapes and Eruptions in England

Three major crises buffeted the English prison system between 1964 and
1980. In part, crises of security and control represent bids for attention by
the two largest prison system interest groups, prisoners and prison officers.
The dynamics of the relationship between these two groups has been a
mainspring of the reactive and expansionist prison policy pursued over this
period. The prison system was more successful in securing financial
resources than most other areas of public expenditure. Ironically, despite
this massive investment of resources, living conditions for prisoners have
deteriorated and in some respects there has been a decline in staff working
conditions.

The security crisis
The English prison security crisis of the mid-1960s was unusual in the
ferocity with which it rocked the entire prison system. The tidal waves

of alarm exhibited by Home Office politicians and administrators and set loose by these events went far beyond the particular prisons involved and enveloped the prison system as a whole. The crisis began to brew as a sequel to the Great Train Robbery, one of the most notorious crimes of the century. In the early hours of 8 August 1963, the Glasgow-to-London mail train was brought to a halt near Cheddington, Buckinghamshire and robbed of 120 mailbags containing cash amounting to two and half million pounds. The money, in used notes, was on route to be shredded. The gang which consisted of about fifteen men displayed a nerve and style which produced in a startled public emotions ranging from outrage to admiration. Some but not all of the persons involved in the robbery were arrested and brought to trial. On conviction in April 1964, six members of the gang received prison sentences of thirty years imprisonment which, with full remission, meant twenty years in custody. Only the spy, George Blake, had ever been given a fixed prison sentence of greater length.

Not all the stolen money had been recovered and, in part, the rationale for the long sentences was to postpone enjoyment of the proceeds. However, two of them were not to be delayed. Before day-break on 12 August 1964, Charles Wilson was removed from Birmingham prison by accomplices who had scaled the wall. While one night patrol officer was in the prison kitchen putting on the porridge for breakfast, his colleague was knocked down, bound and gagged. Aided by keys not carried by night patrols and therefore provided through internal cooperation, Wilson's accomplices made their way to his cell. Wilson had served four months of his thirty year sentence. Almost eleven months later on 8 July 1965, Ronald Biggs, also serving a thirty year sentence, escaped from Wandsworth Prison. Since Wilson's escape three prison officers had stood guard outside Biggs' cell at night, but despite special daytime precautions, security had failed to take account of all contingencies. Accomplices parked a furniture removal van near to the prison wall which bordered the main exercise yard and, standing on its roof, threw ladders into the exercise yard. Biggs and three other prisoners were over the wall and away within one or two minutes.

Public interest in prison system security was rekindled on 25 May 1966, when nine prisoners escaped from a coach after appearing as witnesses at Winchester Crown Court. By now, media attention was focused on every security incident, including absconding from open institutions. The prison system was subjected to considerable ridicule and the escapes provided regular copy for cartoonists. One television news programme displayed a scorecard of escapes each evening. The climax came at 7 p.m. on 22 October 1966, when it was discovered that George Blake had vanished from Wormwood Scrubs prison. Blake had been sentenced in May 1961 to a total of 42 years imprisonment on five counts under Section 1 of the Official Secrets Act. On sentencing Blake, the Lord Chief Justice said:

'Your case is one of the worst that can be envisaged in times of peace.' In refusing Blake's application to appeal against his sentence, the Court of Appeal stated: 'It is of the highest importance, perhaps particularly at the present time, that such conduct should not only stand condemned, should not only be held in utter abhorrence by all the ordinary men and women, but should receive, when brought to justice, the severest possible punishment. This sentence had a threefold purpose. It was intended to be punitive, it was designed and calculated to deter others, and it was meant to be a safeguard to this country.'[39]

Blake was placed in Wormwood Scrubs prison in London and five months later special precautions against escape were relaxed. Despite recurrent suggestions that he might be planning to escape, stringent security steps were not taken regarding Blake, even after the escape of six prisoners from Wormwood Scrubs on 6 June 1966. The prison governor, however, did request Blake's transfer on security grounds in 1965, but to no avail.[40] During the early evening of 22 October 1966, Blake was able to kick out a window frame and get quickly into the prison yard only sixty feet from the wall where later a rope ladder was found on one side of the wall and on the other side, still in florist's paper, a pot of pink chrysanthemums.[41]

The political impact of Blake's escape was recorded by Harold Wilson, then Prime Minister, who recalls an interrupted discussion on defence proposals in the House of Commons, '. . . there was a sudden and serious disturbance to our talks. We had only just begun when the news came through that the spy, George Blake, serving a sentence of 42 years at Wormwood Scrubs, had escaped. This really was a shock and it was clear there would be a rowdy parliamentary reaction. The Home Secretary (Roy Jenkins) went off to the telephone to deal with the situation.'[42] Later that evening, Richard Crossman was with Harold Wilson when Roy Jenkins telephoned the Prime Minister. After putting down the phone, Wilson said to Crossman, 'that will do our Home Secretary a great deal of good. He was getting too complacent and needs taking down a peg.'[43]

The Blake escape produced in Home Office ministers and administrators a reaction little short of sheer panic. The Home Office moved with unusual speed to bring forward the retirement of the governor of Wormwood Scrubs. Roy Jenkins headed off the political storm by appointing Lord Mountbatten of Burma to conduct an enquiry into prison security, including the escape by Blake. The Conservative opposition, sceptical of a wide-ranging investigation by a distinguished public figure, unsuccessfully pressed for a judicial enquiry into the circumstances of Blake's escape. Mountbatten began work at once, extending his enquiry to take account of yet one further escape, the disappearance on 12 December 1966 from a farm working party at Dartmoor Prison of Frank Mitchell, dubbed the 'mad axeman' by the popular press.

Published in December 1966, the Mountbatten Report made over fifty recommendations on the security of the prison system and legitimized huge increases in expenditure on prison security hardware which had got underway even prior to Blake's escape. These included floodlighting and the installation of closed circuit television and electronic devices in several prisons.[44] The new security provisions also had significant expenditure implications arising from additions to total manpower and revised manning levels. The Home Office later estimated that 40 per cent of the increase in prison system manpower between 1965 and 1978 was due to implementation of the Mountbatten Report.[45]

The central feature of the Report was the proposed categorizing and allocating of prisoners according to security criteria. Mountbatten recommended that prisoners be placed in one of four security categories. Category A to encompass those prisoners, 'who must in no circumstances be allowed to get out . . .' Category B are those 'in respect of whom the very high expenditure on the most modern escape barriers may not be justified, but who ought to be kept in very secure conditions'. Category C are those who, 'although they lack the resources and will to make escape attempts, have not the stability to be kept in conditions where there is no barrier to their escape'. Category D are those for whom open conditions are appropriate.[46] Mountbatten also recommended that Category A prisoners be placed in a specially constructed top security prison. He suggested that this facility be known as Vectis, be located on the Isle of Wight and hold about 120 prisoners. He foresaw that a second similar prison might eventually be required.

Security categorization was accepted by the government, but the Vectis notion was eventually to be rejected. In February 1967 the Home Secretary asked his Advisory Council on the Penal System to consider the type of regime appropriate for Category A prisoners. A sub-committee was set up under the chairmanship of the Cambridge criminologist, Professor Leon Radzinowicz and, having widened its terms of reference, it eventually recommended against the concentration of high-risk prisoners, preferring their dispersal in three or four prisons where security would be strengthened. The Radzinowicz report commented that: 'the immediate capital expenditure needed would seem to be limited to the construction of the towers, and the building of a small segregation unit in the prisons.'[47]

One member of the sub-committee, Leo Abse, MP, has provided a curious account of his own participation in the recommendation for dispersal prisons: '. . . I came to the conclusion that public anxiety about security would have to be allayed by some tangible and emphatic innovation, if we were to succeed in our aims of dispersing these Category A prisoners into liberal prisons rather than concentrating them into an oppressive fortress that would cast a shadow over our whole prison system. I cynically decided, therefore, to embark upon a diversionary tactic: to shift attention from the real issue of dispersal or concentration to another issue which would arouse the hostility of all the liberals, and place me on the side of the devils.[48] The issue selected by Abse was the arming of officers to be located in watchtowers on the perimeter of dispersal prisons. The government, as Abse expected, rejected firearms but accepted the notion of dispersal prisons.

Abse's liberal instincts on this occasion may have been misplaced. Once the principle of dispersal was accepted it was not long before prison system administrators concluded that three or four dispersal prisons were insufficient. By 1970 there were five dispersal prisons, and by 1980 there were seven. In 1973, after a policy review following riots at two dispersal prisons and disturbances in others, it was decided that Category A prisoners required dispersal across a wider selection of prisons. A further prison was therefore converted for dispersal use that year and a new dispersal prison planned for the early 1980s. After the riot at Hull Prison in 1976 the Chief Inspector in his report recommended that existing dispersal prisons, allowing for the new prison when completed, were still insufficient.[49] The Home Office, however, rejected the argument that the system of dispersal has experienced remarkable growth, a view which was pressed upon the May Committee in 1978 by one of its witnesses.[50] Indeed, the Home Office has justified the policy on grounds of cost and appears sanguine as to the prospects of further expansion. 'Current experience suggests that seven dispersal prisons are barely enough for present needs and that the number of Category B prisoners needing dispersal conditions is likely to grow . . . there is no reason to think that the intended addition of two purpose-built dispersal prisons as envisaged in 1973 will be over-provision.'[51]

The Home Office rationale for dispersal policy has shifted beyond Category A prisoners. Attention is drawn to those Category B prisoners who require the security provided by dispersal prisons, although the Home Office acknowledges that there is a lack of reliable information on which to base a judgment.[52] The financial costs per prisoner held in dispersal prisons are almost twice those of other closed training prisons. The total costs of the seven dispersal prisons in 1979–80 represented ten per cent of total current expenditure by the English prison system although these prisons contained less than five per cent of the average daily population. These cost differences largely reflect the much higher levels of staffing in dispersal prisons where the ratio of prison officers to prisoners is 1:1 compared with 1:3 in other closed training prisons.[53] The high staffing ratios in dispersal prisons are a consequence of manning levels agreed with the Prison Officers' Association and, as noted later, they present a severe obstacle to any attempt to reduce the level of costs.

The policy of dispersing high security prisoners has become an integral aspect of the expanding English prison system. By increasing resources at the deepest end of the prison system, impetus for growth of the total system

is encouraged. More than fifteen years after the security crisis, its repercussions remain powerful and, together with crises concerning control, it
has fuelled the pressures towards relentless expansion of the prison
system.

The Control Crisis: Prisoners

For England, the year of the prisoners' rights movement was 1972. PROP
(Preservation of the Rights of Prisoners) was established in April of that
year by a group of academics and former prisoners. A week later a sit-down
demonstration took place at Brixton prison, the main remand prison for
London. The Home Office announced an immediate inquiry into conditions
at Brixton and certain reforms were announced. PROP, claiming an early
success, announced a national prisoners' strike for July unless further
demands were met. These included the right to vote, to join a trade union
and to receive conjugal visits. Immediate reactions included the Home
Secretary's analysis that the main problem was overcrowding in old prisons.
The chairman of the POA decried support given to PROP by academics
and others and commented that: 'the dividing line between a passive
demonstration and a riot is very thin.' Over the next five months, 130
demonstrations took place in over forty institutions. In August, PROP
called for a national prisoners strike, and about 4,000 prisoners in 26
prisons took part in sit-down protests.

Reactions by the Prison Officers' Association were swift, threatening
a work-to-rule unless the Home Office responded firmly to prisoner
demonstrations. One POA official remarked: 'there is a very real danger
that the clock will be turned back in prisons. The thing which in the past
made it possible to have a humane prison system was goodwill between
both sides. The latest series of demonstrations is clearly aimed at the
cooperation that existed. The likelihood now is that to work at all, the
system may have to be more repressive.'[54] During the next few weeks,
the scene changed with threats of militant action by staff, including a
national work-to-rule or walkout unless the Home Office responded firmly
to prisoner demonstrations. In a directive to local branches, the POA
called for:

- rigid application of prison rules and reporting of acts of indiscipline.
- officers not to prepare food outside normal meal times, or do any
  work normally done by a prisoner.
- a ban on overtime which normally would allow prisoners to see
  special television events, etc. When prisoner demonstrations made
  extra demands on staff time, other activities such as classes and
  letters to and from prisoners would be stopped.

PROP offered to meet with the POA and, although this was immediately
rejected, PROP was not discouraged from announcing that in September

it would hold a one-day strike in sympathy with the demands by prison officers for better working conditions.

Prison governors began to take a harder line in dealing with prisoners reported for disciplinary offences arising from the demonstrations. The Home Secretary, Robert Carr, declared: 'There is a strong distinction between those who wish to promote penal reform and those who seek to ferment discontent and indiscipline in prisons.' The demonstrators would be dealt with firmly and severely, and governors were asked to see that all prisoners be so warned. He said he had no intention of recognizing PROP. In the aftermath of the disturbances nearly one thousand prisoners were disciplined. PROP forwarded a list of rather mild demands to the Home Office in exchange for ending the protests, but it was clear by this time that PROP was in serious trouble. In part because of internal conflicts, the initiative had shifted from prisoners to prison officers. As Mike Fitzgerald comments in his account of PROP: 'No longer were the prisoners to call the tune and lead the dance. On the contrary, they were to be on the receiving end of the full-scale, bitter and personalized recrimination of the POA.'[55]

Although short-lived, the prisoners' rights movement in Britain played a crucial part in generating a more militant mood among prison officers. As a response to prisoner demonstrations, custodial staff in some prisons by working to rule were able to restrict certain privileges enjoyed by prisoners. Although prisoners involved in the protests were firmly dealt with in disciplinary hearings, staff militancy did not subside. By the late seventies and early eighties, it was not prisoners but unionized custodial staff who posed the greatest challenge to Home Office control of the prison system. The peaceful protests orchestrated by PROP in 1972 were to be over-shadowed later that year by violence in two of the new dispersal prisons, Albany and Gartree. The violence at Gartree, which was especially serious, was triggered by an escape attempt. Four years later, in the late summer of 1976, an even more destructive riot took place at Hull dispersal prison. About two hundred prisoners, two-thirds of Hull's prisoner population, took part and most of the prison was taken over by prisoners during the four day incident. The damage to the physical fabric of the prison was estimated at £¾ million.[56]

The reassertion of control by prison staff in the absence of careful precautions is likely to be accompanied by excessive force. Both the riot and the peaceful demonstration represent a stark challenge to the basic function of custodial staff. The insult to professional standing cannot be over-estimated. Despite precedents it is remarkable how rarely prison management takes sensible steps to avoid or minimize excesses by staff during and after the retaking of the prison. The Hull riot was no exception, and considerable damage and injury occurred in the immediate aftermath of the riot. These events were not within the terms of reference of the prison system's enquiry but were described in the unofficial investigation carried out under the auspices of PROP and in a report prepared by the local Member of Parliament.

The events of the aftermath also featured subsequently in the prosecution of some prison staff for conspiring together and with others to assault prisoners. A member of the prison system's inspectorate, P. L. James, a senior prison governor, said during the committal proceedings: 'Prisoners are inclined very quickly to smash up government property and that issued to them by the prison authority. They do not, in my experience, destroy transistor radios, record players; they do not destroy gramophone records. They certainly do not tear up their photographs of relatives and loved ones, let alone write obscenities on them. And I have never known them to destroy caged birds. I came away from B Wing with the feeling, that I still hold, that 95 per cent of all that damage was certainly done by uniformed staff (let me say that I am aware that not all may have been Hull officers) in what I can only describe as an orgy of destruction.'[57]

By contrast, the presence of members of the board of visitors, as observers in the prison after the second riot at Gartree prison in October 1978, contributed to the absence both of staff violence and protected staff from false allegations.[58] The experience at Gartree prison, however, had pervasive and long-term consequences. Over the next three years, the prison operated at half capacity with two of the four wings, each badly damaged in the roof, remaining closed. In 1981 the Chief Inspector of Prisons commented: 'The scale of that unnecessary expenditure can be judged from the present cost of £6–£7 million per annum to run Gartree as a two-wing prison . . . Continued anxiety about the prospect of further disturbances has manifested itself in a determination to exercise strict control over the prisoners. This has placed significant restrictions on the regime, for example, prisoners are locked up earlier in the evenings than previously, so that the time spent locked in the cells has increased to 14 or 15 hours a day.'[59] This level of control was maintained despite the fact that prison officers outnumbered prisoners by more than two to one. Gartree, in effect, had become a sick institution. The governor of another dispersal prison has written: '. . . staff confidence in the ability to remain in control and handle any prisoner, or situation, is absolutely critical. Once their confidence has been lost, it is exceptionally difficult and costly to restore.'[60]

The aftermath of disturbances occasionally highlights the relative power of custodial staff with respect to both management and specialist staff. This was illustrated by the events following a sit-down demonstration in August 1979 by prisoners at the dispersal wing of Wormwood Scrubs prison. Reassertion of control was achieved by a specially trained squad of officers.[61] However, the official inquiry into circumstances surrounding the disturbance found: 'The indications are that members of the POA committee played a more intrusive role in the operational decision-making process than is appropriate, whereas some members of the management team, notably the Deputy Governor, the duty Medical Officer and the Assistant Governor in charge of D Wing, were either not involved at all or were inadequately consulted and briefed.'[62] The inquiry had this to say about the failure by prison management to determine how many prisoners had been injured: 'The initial report that no prisoners had been injured was later amended to the effect that 5 prisoners had been admitted to the prison hospital on 31 August. It was not until 25 September, when the Governor submitted a written report to Headquarters, that any mention was made of the other prisoners, at that time said to number 53, who had sustained injuries as a result of staff intervention.'[63]

Of particular significance was the role played by the POA in the aftermath of the disturbance. The official inquiry found: 'During this period the local branch of the POA, particularly, though not exclusively, those of its members who were not D Wing staff, sought to prevent a return to anything like the former regime in D Wing, and there are strong indications that the Governor came under pressure from the POA so severe that some of the policy decisions affecting the Wing that he made at that time were against his own better judgment and the advice of his own most senior advisers . . .'[64] Policy for the prison over the next few months was determined in effect by the local branch of the POA. Prisoners were transferred, exercise and bathing curtailed, visits were stopped and association was suspended for over four months. Furthermore, specialist staff, including probation officers, chaplains and teachers, were excluded from the wing for varying periods of time after the disturbance. POA anger was especially directed at psychologists following questions raised by a psychologist at a senior management meeting twelve days after the disturbance as to the number of prisoners who had been injured. On the following day, the psychology department was informed by the POA that psychologists were not among the specialists to be permitted entry into the wing. The POA local branch also adopted a policy of '. . . total non-cooperation with psychologists throughout the establishment with the result that psychologists had such limited contact with prisoners that they were unable to perform their normal established duties.'[65]

At first the POA had suspected a psychologist of leaking information about injured prisoners to the media, but their position was unchanged even after this suspicion was laid to rest. As the report of the inquiry puts it: 'They defended their action on the grounds that they did not know what the psychologists did, they did not like them and finally, that the figure of injured prisoners quoted at the heads of departments meeting was inaccurate.'[66] It was not until four months after the disturbance that the POA permitted psychologists to fully resume their duties within the prison.

Early research on prison organizations, which was carried out largely in the United States, centred on tensions between custodial and specialist staff. This conflict usually was explored in terms of the dichotomy of the custodial and rehabilitative purposes of the prison. The source and shape of the conflict in the contemporary prison system is rather different. With the decline of fortunes experienced by the rehabilitative ideal, the position of many specialist staff has become problematic and has been further undermined by the relative gain in power by prison officers. The form of some industrial disputes has given symbolic significance to these develop-ments. As in the case of Wormwood Scrubs, specialist staff have found themselves not only excluded from certain parts of the prison but on occasion from the institution as a whole. The events following the distur-bance at Wormwood Scrubs prison illustrate the second control crisis to confront the English prison system during the 1970s, namely the extra-ordinary growth of the power of the Prison Officers' Association.

The Control Crisis: Staff
By the late 1970s concern about control held by English prison system administrators focused less on prisoners than on staff. Although the Prison Officers' Association was active in putting down the prisoners' rights movement in 1972, it was not until the second half of the decade that custodial staff militancy fully emerged. Most of the industrial disputes were locally based, initiated at branch rather than at national level. Between 1976 and 1980 there was an annual average of 74 industrial disputes compared with an annual average of seven over the preceding three years.[67] In 1978 a record of 119 disputes took place in 63 of the prison system's institutions. The Home Office categorized industrial action by prison officers as actions which interfere with the administration of justice such as refusals to escort prisoners to court; actions which affect prison administration such as refusals to allow vehicles in and out of the prison; and actions which directly affect prisoners such as denials to prisoners of bathing, exercise and association.[68]

At both the local and national level the POA has challenged the authority of administration and management of the prison system. Exchanges be-tween members of the House of Commons Home Affairs Committee and national leaders of the POA were often illuminating. After hedging on the issue of the implementation of policy on the introduction of telephones, the secretary of the POA had this to say on the censorship of prisoners' mail: 'The whole issue as far as we are concerned is that if in fact they want censorship of inmates' mail to cease then of course we have a right to be consulted over the matter. If the Home Secretary decides administratively to introduce that then he will do so without the assistance of the Prison Officers' Association. Our arguments for not removing censorship are not on the grounds of dogma, that we want to read prisoners' mail *per se*. There are excellent reasons why we maintain that the mail of prisoners has to be read. It is not a paternal argument.'[69]

The POA instructed its members not to co-operate in internal investigations which may be held following allegations by prisoners against staff,[70] and in many respects pursued a policy which made management's position untenable. Prison system administrators have remained reticent in public on the growing power of prison officers. Similarly, prison governors have avoided public criticism of actions taken by the POA, although in private they have voiced sharp criticism of the apparent disregard shown by prison officers of the consequences of industrial action for prisoners and other staff. The Chairman of the Prison and Borstal Governors' Branch of the Society of Civil and Public Servants commented to the Home Affairs Committee: '. . . in pursuance of an industrial dispute, prison officers decide to do certain things. That means that they, for practical purposes, disobey management instructions so management's control is diminished. However, I think it is a by-product of their trying to achieve something else. What is absolutely true is that in this situation the people who in some ways have been most seriously affected have been the senior uniformed staff, in their authority, and to some extent the more junior governor grades, because the question has arisen as to where the boundaries lie, they have become very uncertain.'[71] In more direct terms another prison governor has written: 'The control of prisons had by the mid-seventies to a very large extent passed into the hands of the Prison Officers' Association.'[72]

Areas of concern such as manning levels and overtime opportunities are of course not unique to the prison system, but by 1976 there was strong criticism of the English prison system by the Treasury for the overall level of overtime by prison officers. This resulted in an effort to save £2 million a year. However, from July 1977 the POA adopted a policy of non-cooperation in the deployment of manpower and instructed members not to supply the Department with data on staffing. The May Committee commented two years later: '. . . sometimes it almost appears as if there were some sort of collusion between local management and staff, at least to the extent that each group did not in the past look too closely into the motives of the other for cooperating with high overtime demands.'[73] With regard to manning levels the May Report concluded: 'Over the entire area there appears to rest a pall of uncertainty, if not incomprehension,'[74] to which the wry comment on prison officers' industrial action was later added: 'Branches have been careful, for example, except in the most extreme cases, to avoid action which would adversely affect the level of overtime and thus take-home pay.'[75]

In the preceding chapter it was seen that the strategic position of the prison system within the criminal justice process makes it especially vulnerable to expansionist pressures whenever there are Great Expectations for the administration of criminal law. Pressures favouring an expansionist prison policy are compounded by events arising within the prison system in pursuance of the functions of security and control. In the case of the

English prison system, the security crisis of the mid-1960s and the control crises which pervaded the system since the early 1970s added to the momentum towards expansion. One consequence of this accelerated growth has been the diversion of resources away from ensuring that minimum living standards are achieved. Establishing and maintaining standards cannot be resolved within a prison system where resources are consumed primarily in the course of relentless expansion. It is with this problem that the next chapter deals.

References

1 The American criminologist, Lloyd Ohlin, has described prison interest groups as follows: 'Interest groups constitute the basic organizational structure which gives form and content to correctional activities. The power and influence of interest groups are not static, however, but change with their fortunes over time'. Lloyd Ohlin, 'Conflicting Interests in Correctional Objectives' in *Theoretical Studies in Social Organisation of the Prison*, eds. Richard A. Cloward *et al.*, New York: Social Science Research Council, 1960, p. 126.

2 Lionel W. Fox, *The English Prison and Borstal Systems*, London: Routledge and Kegan Paul, 1961, pp. 161–2.

3 David A. Ward and Annesley K. Schmidt, 'Last-Resort Prisons for Habitual and Dangerous Offenders: Some Second Thoughts about Alcatraz', in *Confinement in Maximum Custody*, eds. David A. Ward and Kenneth F. Schoen, Lexington, Massachusetts: Lexington, 1981, p. 63.

4 Lionel W. Fox, op. cit., note 2, p. 163.

5 *Ruiz* v. *Estelle*, 503 F.Supp. 1282, 1284 (E.D. Tex, 1980).

6 Advisory Council on the Penal System, *The Regime for Long-Term Prisoners in Conditions of Maximum Security*, chairman of sub-committee, Professor Leon Radzinowicz, London: HMSO, 1968, p. 20.

7 *Sunday Times*, 4 October 1981.

8 Ian Dunbar, unpublished paper, 1981, p. 3. The author is grateful to Mr Dunbar for permission to quote from this paper.

9 For a discussion of the goal of surface placidity, see Andrew Rutherford, 'Formal Bargaining in the Prison: In Search of a New Organisational Model', *Yale Review of Law and Social Action*, **2**, 1971, pp. 5–12.

10 Richard A. Cloward, 'Social Control in the Prison', in *Theoretical Studies in Social Organisation of the Prison*, op. cit., note 1, p. 48.

11 Tom Murton and Joe Hyams, *Accomplices to the Crime, The Arkansas Prison Scandal*, London: Michael Joseph, 1970, pp. 26–7.

12 *Holt* v. *Sarver*, 300 F.Supp. 825, 831 (E.D. Ark. 1969).

13 *Ruiz* v. *Estelle*, op. cit., note 5, pp. 1298–9.

14 ibid., pp. 1295–6.

15 ibid., p. 1296.

16 ibid., p. 1298.

17 James B. Jacobs, *Stateville, The Penitentiary in a Mass Society*, Chicago: University of Chicago Press, 1977, p. 31.

18 Kevin Krajick, 'At Stateville, The Calm is Tense', *Corrections Magazine*, June 1980, pp. 8–10.

19 Quoted by David C. Anderson, 'The Price of Safety: I Can't Go Back Out There'. *Corrections Magazine*, August 1980, p. 10.

20 By comparison, in England (1980) three per cent of prisoners (excluding women's prisons, borstals and detention centres) were held on Rule 43 for their own protection. H.C. vol. 986 (Written Answers), 12 June 1980, cols. 277–8.

21 Kevin Krajick, op. cit., note 18, p. 10.

22 *Report of an Inquiry by the Deputy Director-General of the Prison Service into the escape of three prisoners from H.M. Prison Brixton on 16th December 1980*, H.C. 450, 1981, para. 52.

23 John Irwin, *Prisons in Turmoil*, Boston: Little, Brown & Co., 1980, p. 77.

24 ibid., p. 87.

25 ibid., p. 123.

26 Thomas Mathiesen, *The Politics of Abolition*, Oxford: Martin Robertson, 1974, pp. 76–9.

27 Gunnar Marnell, 'Penal Reform: A Swedish Viewpoint', Howard Journal, **14**, 1974, p. 14.

28 Mathiesen, op. cit., note 26; David A. Ward, 'Sweden: The Middle Way to Prison Reform?', in *Prisons: Present and Possible*, ed. Marvin E. Wolfgang, Lexington, Massachusetts: Lexington, 1979, pp. 116–27.

29 Ward, ibid., p. 126.

30 Mathiesen, op. cit., note 26, p. 135.

31 ibid., p. 172.

32 Ward, op. cit., note 28, p. 123. See also Gunnar Marnell, op. cit., note 27, pp. 12–13.

33 See George Jackson, *Soledad Brother*, New York: Bantam Books, 1970.

34 The most comprehensive account is *Attica, The Official Report of the New York State Special Commission on Attica*, New York: Bantam Books, 1972. For a vivid description by one of the observers, see Tom Wicker, *A Time To Die*, New York: Balantine Books, 1976. The events at Attica contrast with the peaceful resolution in January 1983 at another New York prison, Sing Sing, when 600 prisoners held 19 guards for two days. See, *The Times*, 12 January 1983.

35 This summary is based on M. Serrill and P. Katel, *Corrections Magazine*, April 1980, pp. 7–16 and 20–24; see also, Office of the Attorney-General, *Report of the Attorney-General on February 2 and 3 Riot at the Penitentiary of New Mexico*, Santa Fé, New Mexico, 1980.

36 Between 1973 and 1977 only fifteen episodes of industrial disputes in prison systems across the United States were reported in the *New York Times*, see James B. Jacobs and Norma Meacham Crotty, *Guard Unions and the Future of Prisons*, Cornell University: Institute of Public Employment, New York State School of Industrial and Labour Relations, 1978, pp. viii–ix.

37 James B. Jacobs, op. cit., note 17, pp. 191–2.

38 *Official Report of the New York State Special Commission on Attica*, op. cit., note 34, pp. 126–7.

39 *R. v. Blake* (1962), 2 Q.B. 383.

40 *H.C. Debates*, vol. 741, col. 842, 16 February 1967.

41 These had been used by Blake's accomplice, Seán Bourke to conceal the two-way radio used in planning and executing the escape. See Seán Bourke, *The Springing of George Blake*, London: Mayflower, 1971, pp. 91–2.

42 Harold Wilson, *The Labour Government 1964–1970. A Personal Record*, London: Weidenfeld and Nicolson, 1971, p. 297.

43 Richard Crossman, *The Diaries of A Cabinet Minister*, vol. 2, London: Hamish Hamilton and Jonathan Cape, 1976, p. 81.

44 *Report of the Prison Department for 1966*, Cmnd 3408, London: HMSO, 1967, p. 2.

45 Unpublished study by the Home Office, referred to in the paper by the Treasury, see Central Departments, evidence to Inquiry into the UK Prison Services, vol. III, 1979. London: Home Office, p. 15. The components percentage of the manpower increase for the period 1965–78 were estimated by the Home Office as:

– improvements in security following Mountbatten   39
– growth in prison population, new capacity, etc.   30
– improvements in staff conditions of service   12
– improvements in regime, etc.   12
– introduction of new attendance scheme for staff   7

The details as to how these estimates were reached were not published.

46 Lord Mountbatten, *Report of the Inquiry into Prison Escapes and Security*, Cmnd 3175, London: HMSO, 1966, pp. 56–8.

47 Advisory Council on the Penal System, op. cit., note 6, p. 25.

48   Leo Abse, *Private Member*, London: McDonald, 1973, pp. 132–3.
49   *Report of an Inquiry by the Chief Inspector of the Prison Service into the Causes and Circumstances of the Events at H.M. Prison Hull, During the Period 31st August to 3rd September, 1976*, London: HMSO, 1977, para. 52.
50   See paper on dispersal policy submitted to the May Committee by Roy King, and the Home Office response to King's paper, in Evidence by Home Office to May Committee, vol.II, 1979, London: Home Office, pp. 183–202.
51   Home Office Evidence to May Committee, ibid., p. 196. Although the May Committee endorsed dispersal policy, it should be noted that in 1982 it was decided that Frankland prison which had been designed as a dispersal prison should be used for non-dispersal purposes. This decision was taken on grounds of the staffing costs involved.
52   ibid., pp. 188–9, see also Prison Department, *Working Party on Categorisation Report* (unpublished), August 1981, Appendix 3, which shows considerable regional variation in proportions of prisoners by security category.
53   data abstracted from unpublished paper on Prison Department costs, 1981.
54   *The Guardian*, 24 August 1972.
55   Mike Fitzgerald, *Prisoners in Revolt*, Harmondsworth: Penguin, 1977, p. 161.
56   Fowler Report, op. cit., note 49, para. 44; riots in the English prison system have been less frequent and generally much less serious than in the United States. Until the riot at Hull prison in 1976, the most serious incident on record had occurred in Dartmoor prison in 1932. As at Hull, the Dartmoor riot was preceded by a rumour that a prisoner had been assaulted by staff. The incident lasted for twelve hours, there was one serious injury, a prisoner who was shot, and no escapes. Prison officers entered the prison with rifles, but there was little shooting. See, *Report on the Circumstances Connected with the Recent Disorder at Dartmoor Convict Prison*, Chairman Herbert du Parcq KC. Cmnd 4010, London: HMSO, 1932.
57   Cited in J. E. Thomas and R. Pooley, *The Exploding Prison*, London: Junction Books, 1980, pp. 117–18.
58   See J. P. Martin, 'Jellicoe and After: Boards of Visitors into the Eighties', *Howard Journal of Penology and Crime Prevention*, **19**, 1980, pp. 91–3.
59   Report by H.M. Chief Inspector of Prisons, *Gartree*, London: Home Office, 1981, p. 5.
60   Ian Dunbar, unpublished paper, 1981, p. 3.
61   Specially trained squads, known as MUFTI (minimum use of force and tactical intervention) were established in 1978 largely as a result of the riot at Hull prison two years earlier.
62   *Home Office, statement on the background, circumstances and action taken subsequently relative to the disturbance in 'D' wing at H.M. Prison, Wormwood Scrubs on 31 August 1979; together with the Report of an Inquiry by the Regional Director of the South East Region of the Prison Department*. H.C. 199, London: HMSO, 1982.
63   ibid., p. 44.
64   ibid., p. 59.
65   ibid., p. 60.
66   ibid., p. 61.
67   Data abstracted from annual reports of the Prison Department for 1978 and for 1980. Information was not given for 1979.
68   For fifty examples of industrial action taken by the POA, see Home Office Evidence to May Committee, vol. II, op. cit., note 50, pp. 124–5.
69   House of Commons Home Affairs Committee, *Administration of the Prison Service*, Minutes of Evidence from the Prison Officers Association, 8 December 1980, para. 292.
70   ibid., 19 January 1981: paras. 401–2.
71   ibid., Minutes of Evidence from the Prison and Borstal Governors Branch of the Society, 1 December 1980: para. 193.
72   Arthur de Frisching, 'Are Prisons Out of Control', forthcoming article in *Journal of Criminal Law and Criminology*.
73   *Report of the Committee of Inquiry into the United Kingdom Prison Services*, Chairman, Mr Justice May, Cmnd 7673, London: HMSO, 1979, p. 119.
74   ibid., p. 120.
75   ibid., p. 236.

5 High-cost Squalor

As the twentieth century draws to a close, two frequently cited propositions on imprisonment evoke a note of hollow rhetoric. These are that the pains of imprisonment should not exceed what is required for the deprivation of freedom and that persons are sentenced to prison as a punishment and not for punishment. Both propositions are refuted by the daily experience of imprisonment provided within most prison systems.

A prominent feature of many expansionist prison systems is the juxta-position of declining conditions and escalating costs. Deteriorating living conditions, often due to gross overcrowding, persist despite huge increases in prison system budgets. There are, of course, expanding prison systems such as in Texas where appalling conditions within prisons are accom-panied by low budgetary-provision, but it is all too evident that the injection of additional resources into prison systems makes little impact on the conditions of imprisonment. Successful strategies to humanize or, even more ambitiously, to normalize the prison remain as elusive as ever.

In many countries, spending on prison systems is rapidly increasing. For example, in England during the period 1956–78, the cost of the prison system increased at a rate two and a half times as great as for public expenditure generally.[1] The English prison system, in terms of increased current expenditure, has fared very much better than hospital services and education. Over the five-year period up to 1978–9, current spending on the English prison system rose by 36 per cent compared with 15 per cent on hospital services and 9 per cent on education.[2]

Operating costs per prisoner need to be viewed with some caution as these are reduced as a consequence of overcrowding. The greater the degree of overcrowding the lower the costs per prisoner. In the United States, prison systems with the lowest costs per prisoner also had the highest prison population rates. On the other hand, state prison systems with high costs per prisoner, such as Minnesota and Massachusetts, also had higher staff–prisoner ratios, tended to be less crowded and had lower prison population rates.[3] In expansionist prison systems, increased current expenditure is likely to be greater than any increase in costs per prisoner.

For state prison systems in the United States, the annual rate of increase in direct current expenditure (not adjusted for inflation) over the period 1972–7 was 16 per cent compared with an increase in costs per prisoner of 9 per cent.[4]

Progress in upgrading prison conditions remains marginal even where the concept of normalizing the prison has been taken most seriously by administrators, as in the prison systems of Sweden and Denmark. The two components of the prison normalization strategy as pursued in these Scandinavian countries have been to reduce barriers between the prison and the general community and to preserve individual autonomy across certain areas of decision-making. While these reform efforts have been shaped in part by theoretical perspectives on the prison as a social organization, the principal impetus has come from considerations as to what constitutes the least damaging penal environments. Efforts have been made in Scandinavian countries to challenge those features of the prison which characterize, to use Erving Goffman's term, the total organization. These features include geographical isolation, the organization's hierarchical structure and the caste-like distance between staff and prisoners. The pragmatic accent on prison reform efforts in Sweden and Norway is exemplified by prison administrators' attempts to respond to human needs, in particular contact with prisoners' families and home communities. In addition, attention has been given to physical comforts, to work satisfaction and to psychological well-being.

In Sweden the Treatment in Correctional Institutions Act was enacted in 1974 to further localize prisons so as to encourage frequent contacts by prisoners with their home districts. The Act declares: 'Correctional treatment in an institution shall be so designed as to promote the adjustment of the inmate in society and to counteract the detrimental effects of deprivation of liberty.'[5] Local institutions are limited to about fifty prisoners, serving sentences of up to a year or who are in the final months of a longer sentence. Prisoners serving long sentences or who pose escape risks are allocated to national institutions. The Swedish legislation has taken a stage further the main theme characterizing prison administration in Sweden and Denmark since the 1950s.

In Denmark, the state prison of Renbaek on Jutland provides a good example of humanizing zeal. In the early 1970s, an American criminologist commented: 'The principal pains of imprisonment at Renbaek appear to be the stigma that goes with a criminal conviction and some limits on a man's ability to come and go as he would in the free world.'[6] As is the case for the other open prison in Denmark, but not the closed prisons, visiting arrangements at Renbaek are remarkably liberal. Prisoners are allowed an eight hour visit away from the prison every other week, and unsupervised visits of up to three hours within the prison are permitted.

Research conducted within the Scandinavian prison systems provides a warning to those tempted to conclude that some form of penal utopia has been created. Ulla Bondesson, in a large-scale study of the effectiveness of prison organizations, concluded: 'It thus seems that not only do the benign Swedish correctional institutions produce as few positive effects and almost as many negative effects as the more repressive American institutions, but that the treatment-orientated institutions . . . create as much of a criminal subculture as the more custodially orientated prisons.'[7] Indeed, given the custodial function of imprisonment, notions of humanizing or normalizing the prison may only make sense at the margins. By its very nature, the prison can hardly be other than inhuman and abnormal. A Swedish Minister of Justice, Lennart Geijer, who was closely identified with prison reform efforts, put the point well: 'I do not mean that it is wrong to 'humanize' the stay in prison – but a cage is still a cage, even if gold-plated.'[8]

Progress towards humanizing prisons in Sweden and Denmark, however modest, has been achieved in the context of prison systems which have remained relatively small and, indeed, which have been inclined towards reductionist policies. Elsewhere despite efforts by reformers and the massive injection of resources, most prison systems are characterized by conditions which remain abysmal. Where improvements have occurred, these have often been so fragile as to require constant vigilance. As the pioneering commentator, John Howard, shrewdly observed: 'A person may now look into many a prison without gaining an idea of the condition it was in a few years ago. I wish the reformation to be not for the present only, but lasting. If the motive for amendment has anywhere been merely temporary, there is no doubt that the effect will cease with the cause: those who from such inducement have obeyed, will in future follow the examples of others who have disregarded the law; and prisons that have been amended will relapse into their former state.'[9]

Four conditions are considered which have a direct bearing on the dismal quality of life which typifies contemporary and, in particular, expanding prison systems. These are the principle of less eligibility which has remained a pervasive force in penal practice; the trade-off between manpower and conditions; the impact of overcrowding; and the low public visibility of the prison system.

The Principle of Less Eligibility

In the early eighteenth century one of the rather less enlightened schools of thought on capital punishment held that hanging was not punishment enough.[10] The practical consequence of this view was the development of techniques to prolong and intensify the pain and degradation of the death penalty. From the earliest use of imprisonment, the view has persisted that depriving the prisoner of his freedom is not punishment enough. Jeremy Bentham articulated the principle of less eligibility in 1843. 'Saving the regard due to life, health and bodily ease the ordinary conditions of a convict doomed to a punishment, which few or none but individuals of the poorest class are apt to occur, ought not to be made more eligible than that of the poorest class of citizens in a state of innocence and liberty.'[11] Explicit espousal of the less eligibility principle has become unusual. Sir Edmund du Cane, the first head of the English prison system, enthused as to the merits of 'hard bed, hard fare' but this approach was repudiated as early as 1895 by the Gladstone Committee on the prison system.

Specific strategies to make the life of a prisoner especially unpleasant, such as the imposition of hard labour and the treadmill, have been removed from most prisons. British enthusiasm for the deliberately rigorous regime of the detention centre is exceptional with respect to modern penal systems. Even with the detention centre, there are difficulties in sustaining the required level of discomfort. After visiting a senior detention centre for young adults, setting for the revitalized notion of the 'short, sharp shock', the Home Secretary, William Whitelaw declared: 'It could be that it works with younger boys, but not with older ones. They seem to be enjoying it . . . that was obviously not the idea,'[12] Nor was there widespread support at the meeting held in Berlin in 1935 of the International Penal and Penitentiary Congress for the effort launched by the German government to articulate precisely the steps required to eliminate all comforts from the prison regime.[13]

Less eligibility, of course, is a relative concept and prison conditions inevitably are shaped by the quality of life in the society within which the prison system is located. The American criminologist, David Ward, has commented that in many parts of the United States there is '. . . too much work to be done to meet the basic needs of their law-abiding citizens before they are likely to turn to efforts to bring about any significant improvements for their citizens who are in jail and prison.'[14] Ward argued that efforts at prison reform must be considered in the context of social policy generally, and that what has been achieved in Swedish prisons does not stand out as any more innovative or progressive than other areas of social policy in that country.[15] A related point was made during a House of Commons debate in 1981 by a Conservative member: 'There are no votes in improving conditions for prisoners . . . Politics is about priorities in spending money. It is extremely difficult for our government to spend large quantities of money on improving the conditions of prisoners. There are so many areas in society, and so many people who are at the bottom of the economic strata such as the disabled, who have a difficult time, for whom no money is available. How can we possibly trust arguments to spend increasing resources of which we are so short on improving the conditions for prisoners?'[16]

General socio-economic conditions are reflected also in the living and working conditions of prison staff. Indeed, prison officers are society's carriers into the prison system of the less eligibility principle. Custodial staff are inclined to resist reforms which they consider improve the relative position of the prisoners. In England, for example, the Prison Officers' Association has thwarted attempts to liberalize mail censorship and blocked the introduction of pay telephones. At Wormwood Scrubs prison, one consequence of demands by the Prison Officers Association for a substantial increase in manning levels was the decision in 1979 to terminate educational classes for prisoners. In the official enquiry into a subsequent disturbance at the prison, it was found: 'There is no doubt that the decision to economize on staff deployed to supervise the extensive education programme was popular with the POA who regarded such provision for prisoners as an unnecessary extravagance. The closure of the education centre was re-garded by prisoners as a major deprivation and it was the most frequently expressed and keenly felt of the grievances which contributed to the break-down of relationships between staff and prisoners . . .'[17]

These considerations suggest that a principal obstacle to upgrading the quality of prison regimes may be prison staff carrying the banner of less eligibility. However intellectually and morally bankrupt the notion of less elibigibty may be, it is not without a vibrant emotional quality. An interesting observation has been made by the sociologist, John Irwin, as to the emotional basis for guards regarding prisoners as being less eligible: '. . . guards must co-mingle constantly with other humans, some of whom they know and like, who live in obviously reduced circumstances and are unhappy in them. This poses a moral dilemma for the guards. They must have an explanation and justification for the disparity between the prisoners' circumstances and their own, and a rationale for refusing to respond to the prisoners' frequent supplications for special favours or contraband. Their solution has been to embrace the readily available theory that prisoners deserve their fate.'[18] Essentially, less eligibility is closely tried to the caste-like relationship between staff and prisoners in most prison systems. The function of caste as a control device within specific social systems is widely reported.[19] Humility and lack of direct demands characterize the behaviour patterns of the low caste in these social systems. The caste system also tightly controls members of the high caste in not allowing members of the low caste to forget their place.

A related characteristic of the prison is the reciprocal practice of staff and prisoners to stereotype the other as inferior and childish. Donald Cressey has suggested that this serves to minimize staff decision-making about inmate conduct for, 'if guards are inferior inmates will not readily approach them with requests that require decision-making, and if offenders are inferior, they do not deserve the privilege which special decision-making would involve'.[20] He goes on to suggest that staff have few personal skills, for 'their duty in the organization is primarily one of being present, and by their presence symbolizing a show of force'.[21] In a situation in which their own autonomy is low, it is expected that staff will insist that minimal choices be available to prisoners. In addition they may consider that they have sacrificed much in the way of personal autonomy in exchange for security by becoming prison officers and that inmates have forfeited any claim to autonomy by becoming involved in crime.[22]

Manpower Versus Conditions

Within expanding prison systems, much of the increased finance has been absorbed by escalating manpower costs. Where a trade-off is made between manpower and conditions, it has been manpower which has gained. In England this conclusion was set forth by the Treasury in evidence to the May Committee enquiry into prisons in 1979: 'There can be no question that the increase in manpower costs have been at the expense of other purposes, including conditions of confinement.'[23]

In England staff costs account for a little over seventy per cent of the total current expenditure by the prison system. The 26 per cent increase in current expenditure during the 1970s was largely accounted for by escalating manpower costs. These additional manpower costs arose because of sharp increases in the number of staff, especially prison officers, and as a result of the large amount of paid overtime. As noted in Chapter 3, the rate of increase in the number of prison officers in England between 1950 and 1980 was about twice that of the prison population.

Responses by management and prison officers to the security and control crises of the 1960s and 1970s played a critical role in providing a rationale for additional resources. The new security and control procedures and paraphernalia were accompanied by restrictive practices which are as complex to understand and regulate as they are difficult to dismantle. Manning levels were agreed, leading to a much higher authorized manpower strength. The extra staffing requirement was met partly by large scale recruitment and partly by huge increases in overtime worked. In 1975 the Prison Department reported on Gartree dispersal prison that, 'despite a relatively low population and a high staff:inmate ratio, overtime for Gartree is excessive, and there tend to be too many staff chasing too few jobs'. Six years later, the newly created Chief Inspector of Prisons wrote of Gartree: 'In 1981, with staff substantially as large, but with an even lower inmate population the position is considerably worse.'[24] In fact, in 1981, with only half the prison operational following the riot of 1978, there were nearly two and a half staff persons for each prisoner. The increasing prison officer to prisoner ratio between 1947 and 1981 is shown in Table 5.1.

As the Treasury commented in 1979 '. . . productivity within the prison service, as measured (crudely) by the ratio of staff to inmates, has been declining for some time'.[25]

Table 5.1

Prison officer: prisoner ratios,
English prison system 1947–81

1947	1:7	1965	1:4.2
1950	1:6.3	1970	1:3.4
1955	1:4.7	1975	1:2.4
1960	1:4.8	1981	1:2.6

Source: data abstracted from annual reports of English prison system

Despite the growth in numbers of prison system personnel, extraordinarily high levels of overtime worked by prison officers have become the norm. In the late 1970s there was mounting discontent by English prison officers concerning the impact on their earnings by government pay restraint policy. In 1976 when the prison system administration achieved a slight saving in overtime costs, the result was extensive industrial action by prison officers. However, the average number of hours per week incurred in overtime rose from eight in 1967 to thirteen in 1981. In 1978, when the issue was examined by the May Committee, overtime accounted for 37 per cent of average gross earnings of basic and senior officers in Great Britain compared with 15 per cent for all manual occupations. The May Report was not over-stating the situation in commenting that the situation was 'not one to generate confidence that management at all levels was firmly in control'.[26] The Report went on to state: '. . . the construction of the daily detail takes on the air of a mystery understood only by the detailing officer and in circumstances which have made us wonder whether he is subject to effective supervision. Not only does it seem that governors have withdrawn from trying to manage the use of the most important and expensive resource at their disposal, but chief officers too.'[27]

The task of determining the optimal staff–prisoner ratio, despite its complexities, is one of high priority and has crucial implications for the prison regime. The experience of several prison systems in the United States indicates that gross under-staffing contributes to appalling levels of violence which place both staff and prisoners in considerable fear and risk of assault. In the Texas state prison system the custodial officer–prisoner ratio of 1:12 is the highest of state prison systems in the United States, with about half the states having ratios of between 1:3 and 1:6. During daytime hours in Texas prisons it is not uncommon for one guard to be responsible for supervising two to four cell blocks, each consisting of three tiers with twenty or thirty cells on each tier. A large percentage of prisoners are not at work, in part, due to staff shortages. Officers are never stationed inside dormitories at night; a guard is assigned to supervise several hundred inmates, virtually all in doubly or triply occupied cells or cramped dormitories. In *Ruiz* v. *Estelle* the court found: 'This lack of supervision means that aggressive and predatory inmates are free to do as they wish in the living areas, and their victims can be threatened, extorted, beaten or raped, in the absence of protection from civilian personnel.'[28] Although frequent shakedowns reduced the number of weapons among prisoners, contributing to the relatively low homicide rate in Texas prisons, the court concluded that the '. . . institutions are unsafe and charged with a climate of fear'.[29]

At the other extreme there are dangers arising when prisons have too many staff. In English dispersal prisons the custodial staff prisoner ratio averages 1:1, and the governor of a dispersal prison has noted that from the standpoint of control there is an optimal point of staffing which should not be exceeded, because, 'it can change drastically the crucial nature of the relationship between officer and prisoner'. He elaborated on this point in an interesting way: 'The reason is not difficult to identify. If the ratio of staff to prisoners is at certain levels, the only way to maintain control is by the officer using his personality to influence the prisoner, which as a by-product, maintains a reasonable atmosphere within the prison. Raise staffing levels, and contact between staff and prisoner can reduce quickly as contact between officer and officer increase. If this happens not only can 'no go' areas develop but staff virtually become guards who have minimal contact with individual prisoners, both sides become more insecure, stereotypes build up, the subtleties of relationships between the two vanish and contempt grows as each side develops superficial but strong anti-stereotypes of the other; any meaningful concept of community breaks down and the atmosphere becomes tense, prisoners sullen, staff defensive and threatened.'[30]

Not surprisingly, decarceration has not been championed by employees' unions. Institution staff opposition to the decarceration movement in the United States was evidenced in the publication by the largest public employees' organization of a pamphlet entitled, *Deinstitutionalization: Out of Their Beds and Into the Streets*.[31] Preferring to work in a growth rather than declining industry is understandable, and there is no reason why criminal justice personnel should not share this preference. Growth industries offer not only security and perks, such as generous overtime, but also increasing prospects for advancement. The English prison system increased from 77 to 120 institutions between 1960 and 1982, and the number of governor grade positions more than doubled over the same period.[32] Growth of this magnitude carried the promise of greatly enhanced career prospects. Although reductionist policy may not involve redundancies or even a hiring freeze, it is unlikely to be readily attractive to employees, be they custodial staff, managers or administrators.

The Consequences of Prison Crowding

A principal tactic of the expansionist prison system is to squeeze an increasing number of prisoners into existing space. It can take up to ten years to bring a new prison into commission, and there are serious constraints, primarily those of staffing, with respect to using emergency accommodation such as military camps. A short-term strategy used especially by prison systems in Britain and the United States has been to insist that two or even more persons share cells originally designed for individual use.

In England although certified normal accommodation [CNA] starts from considering the number of persons for which the prison space was designed, it fails to amount to a clearly definable formula. The CNA of most prisons fluctuates, sometimes considerably from year to year. For example, cells may be converted into offices or, on the other hand, accommodation provided for recreation or work purposes may be converted into living accommodation. The Home Office has observed: 'There are no objective criteria for deciding the extent to which a cell can be overcrowded. The governor decides this on a common-sense basis, consulting the medical officer if necessary.'[33] The arbitrariness of CNA determination, especially with respect to dormitory accommodation, has received some adverse comment.[34] Similarly, a study in the United States found the terms 'rated' and 'design' capacity to be almost meaningless. An effort was made therefore to obtain a measure of capacity based upon actual square footage of all living units. Using 1978 data, it was found that cell space accounted for 63 per cent of measured living space capacity in state systems and 54 per cent in the federal system, the balance being dormitory space. Two or more prisoners occupied 19 per cent of state system cells, 15 per cent of cells in local jails and 11 per cent of federal cells. Over 70 per cent of all celled state and federal prisoners were accorded less than 60 square feet each of floor space.[35] Two out of every three prisoners in the United States have less than the minimum standard of 60 square feet of floor space.[36]

The extent of prison crowding in England has increased greatly over the last thirty years and is very much more severe than the situation in most systems elsewhere. Two out of every five prisoners are accommodated with others in cells designed for single usage.[37] A Swedish principal prison officer wrote in 1982 after a study tour of the English prison system: 'Worst of all is, however, the state of overcrowding which, especially in the big prisons with 1,500–2,000 inmates, creates enormous problems. When you see those old and outdated prisons and hear the old-fashioned and conservative views of the staff you get the impression that time must have come to a standstill in England.'[38]

Without question, living conditions in the English prison system are considerably inferior to what existed a century ago. Nineteenth-century legislative attempts to ensure single cellular confinement need to be viewed against a belief in rehabilitation through penance together with an overriding concern with criminal and moral contamination. Cellular isolation by day and night was the hallmark of the separate system. While the silent system allowed some carefully supervised activity outside the cell by day, no compromise was allowed with respect to separation at night. Legislative intent as to minimum standards often falls far short of practice and is especially the case when operations are decentralized. The Gaols Act of 1823 and the Prison Act of 1865 attempted to set minimum standards which were perhaps not attainable by local government. The Act of 1823 did not endorse solitary confinement, allowing local prisons to abandon it whenever overcrowding made it necessary to do so.

Michael Ignatieff has written: 'A generation later, the idea of solitude was to be revived again, but in 1823 it was in retreat, tarnished by the excesses of its enthusiasts.'[39] Commenting on the Act of 1865, Sidney and Beatrice Webb observed: '. . . the provision of separate cells for all prisoners involved an enormous building programme, which neither County Justices nor Municipal Corporations were willing to undertake at the ratepayers' expense.'[40] The Prison Act of 1865 provided: 'In every prison separate cells shall be provided equal in number to the average of the greatest number of prisoners, not being convicts under sentence of penal servitude, who have been confined in such prisons at the same time during each preceding five years.'[41] Prison Regulations were appended to the Act, and Regulation 26 stated: 'Every male prisoner shall sleep in a cell by himself, or under special circumstances in a separate bed placed in a cell containing not fewer than two other male prisoners . . .' The Act of 1865 attempted to define capacity more precisely by replacing the term 'maximum available accommodation' with 'number of separate sleeping cells'.

This change in terminology reduced the capacity of prisons in 1867 by 12 per cent. In other words, for the same year, in local prisons the occupation factor (prisoners as a percentage of capacity) increased from 89 to 102.[42] Similarly, a recent study of prison systems in the United States found dramatic differences between capacity as reported by the prison systems and definitions based upon physical measurement. For example, the result of replacing reported capacity by measured capacity, defined as a minimum of 60 square feet per prisoner, was to reduce total capacity in the United States by 49 per cent.[43]

Prison overcrowding, however, was not unknown in nineteenth century England, as is evident from reports of Inspectors of Prisons for various parts of the country. McConville comments that even when prisons were enlarged, committals often overtook new capacity. For example, Liverpool prison after some easing of pressure at the end of the 1860s was by 1873 reported to be again grossly overcrowded.[44] With the formation of a national prison system following the 1877 Prison Act, in the words of Sidney and Beatrice Webb, a 'fetish of uniformity' was applied. The Webbs concluded that although overcrowding ceased, '. . . the system of cellular isolation for everyone was maintained with inflexible vigour, and the Prison Commissioners remained to the end, absolutely complacent about it.'[45] However, instances of overcrowding continued to be reported and some of these were the direct consequences of the allocation practices of the new Prison Commission. It was the public complaints of overcrowding at Wandsworth prison by the Revd W. D. Morrison, a former prison chaplain which, in part, led to the setting up of the Gladstone Committee in 1894. In his evidence to the Committee, Morrison showed that at Wandsworth, in the five years prior to the Prison Act of 1877, the occupation factor was 88 compared with 104 for the years 1889–93.[46]

With the fall in prison population size after the First World War, over-crowding in the English prison system ceased to be a problem. During the inter-war years, the average daily population hovered between ten and thirteen thousand, comfortably below available capacity. However, after the Second World War prison overcrowding steadily escalated. In 1948 up to 2,000 prisoners were sharing a cell with two other persons. In 1952 the statutory language on cellular usage was considerably weakened, merely requiring the Home Secretary to, 'satisfy himself from time to time that in every prison sufficient accommodation is available for all prisoners'.[47] By 1958, the number of prisoners sharing a cell with two other persons had reached 6,000. A revision of the Prison Rules in 1964 weakened the statutory requirement yet further to a prohibition on exceeding the maxi-mum number certified for each cell or dormitory without authority of the Home Secretary.[48] Also in 1964, the Home Office allowed the practice of placing two men in a cell instead of a minimum of three persons when cell-sharing occurred. In what the Prison Department called 'an interesting experiment at Chelmsford', 148 men were in that year so sharing cells.[49]

The Wolfenden Report in 1957 had recommended the decriminaliza-tion of homosexual behaviour between consenting adult males,[50] and this encouraged the Prison Department to be less worried about possible homosexual behaviour arising from two prisoners sharing a cell. It was not long before 'doubling up' became the standard form of overcrowding, and the end of 1973 saw 9,000 men two to a cell and 3,000 three to a cell. It is important to note that 12,000 persons were required to share cells in 1973, despite the near equivalence of total capacity of the prison system and average daily population.

The policy decision had been made by administrators that overcrowding would be largely confined to local prisons and that 'training prisons' would be maintained at or under-capacity. By 1980, when the total number of prisoners sharing cellular accommodation had risen to almost 18,000, Roy King and Rodney Morgan persuasively made the link between crowding pressures and the rhetoric 'training and treatment'. Under-occupation of many training prisons means that perhaps a quarter of total cell sharing 'is created as a matter of deliberate policy and constitutes a fraudulent claim for additional cells.'[51] King and Morgan have argued that elimination of the distinction between local and some training prisons would lead to a fairer distribution of resources and significantly reduce the overall level of crowding.

Concern in England about the level of prison crowding and its consequences reached a peak in the early 1980s. The phrase 'affront to a civilized society' was used by both the head of the prison system and by the Home Secretary to describe conditions in local prisons. Prison governors publicly complained about the condition of the institutions for which they were responsible. In a much publicized letter to *The Times*, the governor of Wormwood Scrubs stated that he could no longer tolerate the inhumanity of the system within which he worked.[52] The reports of Her Majesty's Chief Inspector of Prisons, which began to appear in 1982, substantiated the scale of the problem. In Gloucester Prison, inspected in March 1981, 253 men were found in 112 cells designed for individual use. The Chief Inspector observed: 'The consequence of this policy of overcrowding is that conditions are so cramped in the multiple occupancy cells that, even when some items of furniture are removed, the remaining floor space does not allow two men to pass each other without difficulty . . . They must eat in their cells and there is no means of sanitation other than a chamber pot . . . We consider these conditions to be deplorable and degrading both for the inmates and for the staff who work on the wings.'[53] At Leeds prison, 1,200 prisoners were jammed into 520 cells designed for one person and 18 larger cells suitable for multi-occupancy. The bath-house, situated in a dirty and primitive basement area, had 16 baths and three showers. 'If that were not bad enough, the water supply is so unreliable that only four baths can be used at any one time, and the showers cannot be used at all because they interrupt the flow of water to the baths.'[54] The practice of 'slopping-out' entails 60 or 70 prisoners sharing one slop sink. The report on Leeds prison commented on the 'daily miracle in juggling numbers and processing people . . . The prison is a humane, efficient conveyor belt, but we consider it highly undesirable that a prison should have to function like a production line.'[55]

The Chief Inspector identified overcrowding as a direct cause of many of the 'suffocating difficulties' besetting the English prison system. The crowded cells are described as 'spartan, gloomy and stagnant', and in the majority of local prisons there is no integral sanitation. 'Therefore, an inmate wishing to urinate or defecate at a time when the cell is locked must use a chamberpot within six or eight feet of his companions, and either retain the contents until 'slopping out' is possible, which may be many hours later, or, as an alternative sometimes resorted to, throw them out of the window.'[56] On occasion it is argued that cell sharing, even when enforced, is preferable to solitary confinement, the implication being that overcrowding and solitary confinement are the only options. Rod Caird, a former prisoner, has provided a vivid description of what it means to share a cell with two others. Caird notes that: 'No compulsive habit escapes attention. No dirtiness can be hidden. No frustration can fail to be seen.'[57]

In several leading cases in which American prison systems have been sued in federal courts, overcrowding has been the central issue. In *Pugh* v. *Locke* overcrowding was found by the court to be 'primarily responsible for . . . all the other ills of Alabama's prison system'.[58] It was the totality of these ills that led the court to conclude that the living conditions in Alabama prisons amounted to cruel and unusual punishment and therefore breached the Constitution. In another case, the court found that overcrowding in the Texas prison system '. . . exercises a malignant effect on all aspects of inmate life . . . Crowded two or three to a cell or in closely packed dormitories, inmates sleep with the knowledge that they may be molested or assaulted by their fellows at any time. Their incremental exposure to disease and infection from other inmates in such narrow confinement cannot be avoided. They must urinate and defecate, unscreened, in the presence of others. Inmates in cells must live and sleep inches away from toilets; many in dormitories face the same situation.'[59] Cells of 45 square feet invariably house at least two prisoners, sometimes even five. 'When four inmates are present, two of them must sleep on the floor, across the width of the cell with their feet under the lower bunk. Since the cells are only five feet wide, those two cannot stretch out fully during the night. With five inmates, three must sleep on the floor, squeezed between the bars in front and the toilet in the rear of the cell . . . At one unit, inmates being quarantined for possible exposure to gonorrhoea were housed, four to a cell, in an administrative segregation wing for several consecutive weeks.'[60]

The court judge's ruling went on to describe conditions in dormitories which housed between 10 and 136 persons. In one dormitory, two rows of double-decker bunks, directly adjacent to each other, run down the middle of the dormitory. The scene was described as resembling one giant bed. The court found: 'Except for his bed, an inmate has no assigned space. Even while asleep, an inmate so confined is within easy and immediate reach of three other inmates (those sleeping at his side, at his head and at his feet), and he is directly above or below a fourth inmate.'[61] The results of these levels of overcrowding are obvious: 'Since the dormitories are unsupervised, violent inmates have free access to their fellows. The record indicates that these risks frequently turn into the repulsive actualities of sex malpractices, barbarous cruelties, and extortions, all of which have been shown to be commonplace in the dormitories.'[62]

Gross overcrowding serves to focus political attention on the prison system, and its resolution may become closely tied to the reductionist policy set out in the final section of this book. In the United States, when courts have ordered reductions in the number of prisoners by setting population ceilings, such orders have at least three types of consequences.

First, prison system administrators may be encouraged to move in a reductionist direction by making more use of minimum security institutions, expedite parole hearings or to consider early release schemes. Officials may also be encouraged to establish new community-based sanctions. For example, in Mississippi the state set up restitution centres as one means of meeting a court imposed ceiling on the size of the state prison population.[63] There is, of course, the danger that new non-custodial sanctions will be used by sentencing courts to replace not imprisonment but measures such as fines or probation orders. Early release schemes are regarded very much as a last resort both by courts making orders on prison conditions and by prison administrators and, with the exception of Michigan, have not been used to any substantial degree.[64] In Michigan, a prison overcrowding statute was enacted in 1980 and was used three times during the next twelve months to effect the early release of prisoners.[65]

Second, litigation may result in shifting the problem of crowded conditions elsewhere. In 1978 four of the six states, all in the South, with increasing jail populations, had their state prison systems under court orders to reduce overcrowding. In Alabama the federal court, having found that substandard conditions throughout the state prison system constituted cruel and unusual punishment in violation of the Eighth Amendment, set a ceiling on prisoner numbers. The consequence was that 3,000 state prisoners were soon backed up in local jails, and the crowding problem was simply transferred from one jurisdiction to another; and litigation was commenced at the local level. Similarly, in Louisiana overcrowding at the Orleans Parish prison, as a result of a court order on the state prison system, led the master appointed in a separate case to recommend that the local sheriff be directed to refuse to accept 500 state prisoners.[66]

Third, prison population ceilings may become both a consequence of and contributor to expansionist policy. They are a consequence when prison population outstretches physical resources; they are a contributor which provides a lever to extract yet further resources for the prison system. In Texas, the response by prison system administrators to overcrowding has been to secure additional funds from the legislature for prison construction. However, the federal court found that these capital expenditure plans promised little significant relief from overcrowding in the foreseeable future and that Texas officials had failed to explore other measures. Facilities providing work release opportunities consisted of only fifty beds, a third of which were empty.[67] The court also found that Texas prison administrators had not sought reductions in prison population size by using their powers regarding remission or by increasing the number of prisoners eligible for parole consideration.

Low Visibility – Protection from the Ravages of Outsiders

Once central government established prison systems, prisons became increasingly secret places. The clamp of secrecy on the operation of English prisons was firmly imposed at the take-over of local prisons by central government in 1878. The dismissal of the Revd W. D. Morrison in the early 1880s by Sir Edmund du Cane made the point that public information about prisons would be limited to what was contained in annual reports to Parliament. The dictate to prison system staff was reinforced by provisions of the Official Secrets Act of 1911 and its subsequent amendments. The cloak of secrecy covered not only events within the prison system but also formal regulations.

As a refinement to statutory rules, which are approved by Parliament, the practice developed of issuing confidential standing orders and circular instructions. As early as 1895, the Gladstone Committee recommended that these be published but this was not acted upon. When in 1919 the unofficial Prison System Enquiry Committee requested a copy of standing orders from the Home Office, it was informed that, in the view of the head of the prison system, it would not be desirable for this to be provided. Although subsequent efforts by the Committee's chairman, a retired colonial governor, were rebuffed by Home Office officials, it was from other sources that the committee 'had the good fortune to obtain a copy of the official volume containing the Rules and Standing Orders for Local Prisons (1911 edition)'.[68]

The Webbs wrote in the early 1920s of a '. . . silent world, shrouded so far as the public is concerned in almost complete darkness'.[69] The tradition of secrecy remains strong despite more frequent public glimpses behind prison walls and the barriers of bureaucracy. In 1952, the head of the English prison system wrote that criticism that prisons were characterized by undue secrecy was made '. . . without reference to the facts.' As evidence that this criticism was unfair, he gave the example of an official film on the prison system prepared by the Central Office of Information for private showing to audiences of magistrates and others concerned with the criminal justice process.[70]

Thirty year later, another head of the system declared that a recent reorganization of the prison system sought to meet wider demands for public accountability. He commented: 'The Prison Department has a reputation for secrecy. That reputation is, in my view, unjustified.'[71] To support this proposition, he mentioned a BBC television series on Strangeways prison and departmental encouragement to prison governors to be more forthcoming with the media. These steps, however, remain highly tentative and, despite rhetoric to the contrary, the prison system remains largely hidden from public view. The new spirit of openness received something of a setback when, following the letters to newspapers from prison governors on the consequences of overcrowding, governors were warned that any repetition would find official disfavour.[72]

Prison administrators generally strongly discourage access to prisons by the media unless it can be closely regulated. In England, journalists allowed to visit prisons are obliged to submit their copy to the Home Office press officer for clearance. Staff are prohibited by departmental regulations from communicating with the press without authorization. Although English newspaper investigations were important in reporting allegations of violence by prison staff during incidents at Parkhurst, Hull and Wormwood Scrubs prisons in 1969, 1976 and 1979 respectively, the American media, with its strong traditions of investigative journalism, has more regularly drawn attention to widescale abuses within prison systems. American journalists have also on occasion played an important role during hostage-taking incidents. Tom Wicker of the *New York Times* was called to Attica at the time of the 1971 uprising due to the urging by prisoners that he be one of the observers.[73] In New Mexico during the Santa Fé prison riot in 1980, negotiations between prisoners and the administration involved the exchange of guard hostages for newsmen. Prisoners have learned the value of the media in the negotiating process in ensuring the honouring of agreements made and in protecting them from recriminations by staff.

Perhaps inevitably, the attention of the press will be attracted to news-making incidents rather than to policy issues. However, in recent years the higher quality media on both sides of the Atlantic have followed the crisis enveloping prison systems with the result that it has become more difficult for policy-makers to keep the issues hidden from public scrutiny.[74] The better informed approach by the media to prison policy problems owes much to the working relationship established between journalists and representatives of prison reform and other key interest groups.

Independent inspection

An inspectorate for English prisons was first established by the Prison Act of 1835, empowering the Home Secretary to appoint persons to inspect local prisons on his behalf and to report to him. Reports by prison inspectors were published, and many of these demonstrated a strident independence. Centralization of the English prison system in 1878 effectively destroyed independent inspection. With the setting up of the Prison Commission the Home Office inspectorate was replaced by an inspectorate reporting to the Commission, and more than a century passed before an element of independence was restored. In 1895 the Gladstone Committee concluded that the intention of the 1877 Act was that the inspectorate should be independent of the Prison Commission and recommended that inspectors should report directly to the Home Secretary and that annual reports be laid before Parliament.[75] This recommendation was resisted by the prison system, and it was not until the May Committee reconsidered the issue eighty-five years later that action was taken.[76] In 1981 offices of H.M. Chief Inspector of Prisons for England and Wales and for Scotland were created. The inspectorate is located outside the prison system, but within the Home Office.[77]

Research

Prison systems have remained largely immune from academic research and other external enquiries. Since John Howard's monumental and pioneering study, *The State of English Prisons*, published in 1777, developments have been largely downhill. Howard's enquiries began with his concern for prisoners being held at Bedford jail and, as High Sheriff of Bedfordshire, he decided to review the experience of neighbouring counties before instigating reform measures. In the event, Howard's travels and visits to prisons took him some fifty thousand miles, mostly on horseback. On only three occasions was he barred from gaining access to prisons, and once inside he had a free range of the prison. As Leon Radzinowicz has commented: 'Being the first in the field gives a certain advantage to any researcher, and there is no doubt that Howard exploited it to the full.'[78] Howard revisited many prisons, noting any changes, and he soon appreciated the immensely complex task of effecting real change.

Because of difficulties of access, prison research is usually effectively regulated by prison system administrators. In most instances, the administration is able to determine access, scope and sometimes the published findings. Moreover, a considerable body of research remains unpublished, including several studies carried out by members of the Home Office Research Unit and by psychologists working in the English prison system. Occasionally, research is undertaken without the authority or knowledge of prison system administrators; for example, the carefully documented and sharply critical report by the Prison System Enquiry in 1922, and fifty years later, Stan Cohen and Laurie Taylor's study of the security wing at Durham prison which was carried out while the authors were involved as part-time teachers within the prison.[79]

Prison research takes four broad forms. First, there is research carried out within prisons on prisoners or, less frequently, on prison staff. In these studies, the prison setting is incidental. Cesare Lombrozo's attempts to establish a criminal anthropology were based upon his physiological observations of Italian prisoners towards the end of the nineteenth century. The more rigorous work carried out by Charles Goring in Wandsworth Prison just prior to the First World War essentially refuted Lombrozo's notions of 'criminal types'.[80] Secondly, there are studies of the prison as a community and organization. Clemmer's pioneering research in the late 1930s of Menard prison in Illinois remains the most comprehensive study of this kind.[81] Clemmer, a criminologist employed by the Illinois prison system, gave particular attention to the informal culture developed by prisoners which took the form of solidarity against the formal purposes of the prison.

The third type of research concerns effectiveness of prison using measures such as the criminality of prisoners after release.[82] These studies approach the prison as the context for treatment activities which range from specific interventions by treatment staff to viewing the total institution as a treatment tool. Some of these studies include detailed descriptions of institutional activities, formal and informal, but the focal point is usually outcome rather than process. Fourth, there are studies interested in exploring the prison within its political environment. The pioneering study of this type is Richard McCleery's account of Oahu prison in Hawaii during the decade following the Second World War.[83] A neglected area has been the prison system as a totality with particular attention to headquarters and regional structure, comprising the immediate political environment of the contemporary prison, and it is curious that this area has received so little research attention.[84]

Incursions by the Courts

Civil litigation in the courts has begun to play an important part in making some prison systems both more visible and accountable. Although in the United States, West Germany and elsewhere a body of case law on the administration of prison system is emerging, in England the courts have continued to show considerable reluctance to intervene. Lord Denning summarized the prevailing situation in England: 'If the courts were to entertain actions by disgruntled prisoners, the governor's life would be made intolerable. The discipline of the prison would be undermined. The prison rules are regulatory directions only. Even if they are not observed they do not give rise to a course of action.'[85] This opinion reflects a 'hands-off' policy by the courts, similar to that which existed in the United States up to the late 1960s.[86]

With the impact in the United States of the Civil Rights Movement, litigation increased at a rapid pace, largely within the federal courts, reflecting a shift away from earlier practice which had viewed the prisoners as a 'slave of the state' without enforceable rights.[87] Traditionally, American courts provided several rationales for non-intervention, including separation of powers, federalism, judicial inexpertise and subversion of prison discipline. The 'hands-off' doctrine was seriously eroded in 1964 when the Supreme Court recognized an individual's right to bring an action against state officials under the Civil Rights Act of 1871.[88] By 1978 there were over 8,000 pending cases filed by prisoners. Where court orders have been made these have varied from redressing individual grievances to dealing with virtually every aspect of the prison system. Prison overcrowding has become a frequently litigated issue and prompted judicial supervision in 1980 of state prisons in 19 states in order to remedy overcrowded conditions in one or more facilities.[89] One of the most comprehensive of these orders arose from the Alabama case, *Pugh* v. *Locke*, where the federal court's remedial order addressed virtually every aspect of prison life, including severe crowding and its consequences.[90] The Supreme Court declined to review this case on its merits, leaving the lower court's order intact. In an Arkansas case[91] the Supreme Court upheld a lower court ruling that conditions in isolation cells violated the Eighth Amendment on cruel and unusual punishment. Other aspects of the lower court's order, which was applied to the entire prison system and which included overcrowding, were not challenged on appeal.

Judicial intervention in the United States with respect to prison conditions is most frequently based upon the Eighth Amendment's ban on cruel and unusual punishment. In practice, judges, in considering whether confinement violates the Eighth Amendment, inquire whether the conditions are such as to 'shock the conscience' of the court.[92] In approaching prison overcrowding, courts have drawn attention to its various effects, including reductions in the quality of medical care, violence and psychological damage. Although housing two or more persons in a cell designed for one person has been addressed in several cases resulting in a finding that such conditions are unconstitutional, clearly articulated criteria have not emerged for determining constitutionally acceptable standards. Double-celling, for example, has been prohibited by the courts with reference to cells ranging in size from 35 to 88 square feet.[93]

A relatively new approach to finding that the Eighth Amendment's ban on cruel and unusual punishment has been breached is to refer to the totality of conditions. There are three leading cases, each resulting in comprehensive orders against state prison systems. The first of these, *Holt* v. *Sarver*, involved the Arkansas prison system and revealed conditions of extraordinary depravity and squalor.[94] Six years later in *Pugh* v. *Locke*, U.S. District Court Judge Frank Johnson established a detailed set of minimum standards to govern the operation of the entire state prison system in Alabama.[95] The third and most recent example, also dealing with a southern state prison system, is the Texas case, *Ruiz* v. *Estelle*, where the judge concluded: 'Based on a review of the exhaustive evidence and the applicable law, separate constitutional violations have been found in the areas of overcrowding, security and supervision, health care delivery, discipline, and access to the courts at TDC (the Texas State prison system). Basically, these violations exist independently of each other, although the harms caused by each have been exacerbated by the others. However, even if the conditions in any one of these areas were considered not sufficiently egregious to constitute an independent violation, their aggregate effects upon TDC inmates undeniably contravene the Constitution. The grave consequences of rampant overcrowding, inadequate security, substandard health care, inappropriate disciplinary practices, and substantially impeded access to the courts manifestly dictate this result.'[96]

One commentary suggested three important features of the approach based upon totality of conditions. First, the approach is consistent with the expansive inquiry necessary to examine the cruelty and unusualness of punishment in American prisons; second, a multifaceted complaint is more likely to succeed than a single issue; and third, the court will be faced with the task of fashioning and enforcing minimum standards throughout a large prison system.[97] In reaching decisions, courts have used exhaustive discovery procedures resulting in considerable information becoming available about the prison system. This information has served to increase public awareness of prison problems and to shape the remedial action required.

Prison systems have differed in their response to litigation. In some instances, officials have welcomed the court's order because it strengthens their own case for additional political support and resources. Alternatively, litigation may be vigorously opposed at every stage of the suit. For example, the issues raised in *Ruiz* v. *Estelle* were contested relentlessly by the Texas state prison system. The far-reaching order by U.S. Judge Wayne Justice went to appeal with little sign that the authorities were prepared to acknowledge either the merits of the case or the need for change. Eventually the sheer financial costs to the state forced the reaching of consent decrees.[98]

Despite the volume of litigation and the wide scope of some of the cases, the momentum for reforming prison systems through the courts has been slowed, but not entirely stopped, following two cases in which the Supreme Court partly reverted to the 'hands-off' position of regarding courts as being ill-equipped to intervene with problems of prison administration.[99] *Bell* v. *Wolfish* dealt with gross overcrowding and related complaints in the Metropolitan Correctional Centre which in 1975 had replaced the infamous Tombs jail in Manhattan. The jail was described by the Court of Appeal as representing '. . . the architectural embodiment of the best and most progressive penological planning'. Although most of the cells were designed for single occupancy, population pressures quickly led to double-bunking. The suit was initiated only a few months after the jail was opened. The Supreme Court ruled there was no minimum standard on crowding, 'lurking in the due process clause of the Eighth Amendment'.[100] Lower federal courts had held a series of practices, including double-celling in 75 square foot cells, to be unconstitutional.

The Supreme Court, however, in a majority decision in 1979, reversed these rulings and held that restrictions placed on pretrial detainees that are reasonably related to legitimate, non-punitive objectives do not deprive detainees of liberty without due process. The Supreme Court observed: '. . . in addition to ensuring the detainee's presence at trial, the effective management of the detention facility, once the individual is confined is a valid objective that may justify imposition of conditions and restrictions of pretrial detention and dispel any inference that such restrictions are intended as punishment.' It is important to note that the court, in reversing the decision by lower courts, took account of the fact that detainees were confined to their cells only at night and for very few did their stay exceed 60 days. Subsequent to this ruling, several lower court decisions continued to suggest modest ground for optimism that litigation might be a vehicle for reform and for making prison systems more accountable.[101]

However, this optimism may have been blunted by the Supreme Court's ruling in *Rhodes* v. *Chapman* which dealt with the maximum security prison at Lucasville, Ohio, opened in 1972, which at the time of the trial housed 38 per cent more prisoners than its design capacity. The Supreme Court held that double-celling, as practised at Lucasville (prisoners sharing 63 square feet but, in most cases, with access to dayrooms) did not violate the Eighth Amendment's prescription on cruel and unusual punishment, and stated: '. . . conditions that cannot be said to be cruel and unusual under contemporary standards are not unconstitutional. To the extent that such conditions are restrictive and even harsh, they are part of the penalty the criminal offenders pay for their offences against society.'[102] Although these two cases may signal a reluctance by the courts to extend the interventionist stance of the early 1970s, it remains to be seen whether the high influential watchdog role over prisons which the courts have assumed will be reduced.

In most European countries, the courts have displayed reticence in intervening in the administration of prison systems. In West Germany, however, a fairly considerable case law on prison administration has developed since the early 1960s. West German cases have been heard dealing with a variety of issues including solitary confinement, home leave, conjugal visiting, cell-sharing, censorship of correspondence with lawyers and access to newspapers and magazines.[103] Prior to the Prison Act of 1976, prisoners were only able to petition the supreme court of their own state, but these courts were reluctant to interfere in most cases. The Prisons Act, which took effect on 1 January 1977, provided for special courts to deal with prisoners' grievances and specified the rights of prisoners over several areas of activity. While considerable problems remain to be overcome in the implementation of this legislation, the Act at least provides a framework for more active intervention by the courts.

In Britain the situation is less satisfactory. There is no such legislative framework upon which the courts can act. Instead the Prison Rules, which are a statutory instrument, are regarded by the courts as administrative instructions and not as a statement of rights enjoyed by prisoners.[104] In *Williams* v. *Home Office*, although the judge accepted that Prison Rules had been infringed in 1974 by placing Williams in a control unit for a period in excess of what was permissible under Prison Rules, the suit for false imprisonment was dismissed.[105] This case and the events which followed starkly illustrate the absence of public accountability within the English prison system. In April 1980, a full-page story appeared in *The Guardian* under the headline, 'How Ministry hardliners had their way over control units.'[106] The story, by David Leigh, was based upon discovery of documents made available by the plaintiff's solicitor, Harriet Harman, and which had been read out in open court. The article summarized the efforts made by officials to reduce public knowledge of control units. For example, '. . . the circular to governors setting up the regime was to be kept secret, even from MPs. A draft circular warned governors that there were bound to be pressures to modify its severities and censorship must be rigid.' An official is quoted as observing: 'Only circular instructions which modify standing orders are sent to the House of Commons Library. This one will not, therefore, go to the House of Commons.'[107]

Detailing in a national newspaper the decision-making processes that set up and later abandoned control units was not to the liking of the Home Office. Ms Harman was subsequently successfully sued for contempt of court with costs awarded against her. In dismissing her appeal, Lord Denning stated: 'I can see no public interest whatever in having these highly confidential documents made public . . . It was in the public interest that these documents should be kept confidential. They should not be exposed to the ravages of outsiders.'[108]

Standard-setting Organizations

In the United States, between 1931 and 1973, a number of national commissions and associations issued recommendations for upgrading conditions in prisons and jails.[109] The early standards used rather general phraseology and in tone were aspirational rather than mandatory. Since the mid-1970s there has been some movement towards minimum standards with the focus upon implementation. Largely in response to intervention by the courts, prison systems have become interested in the articulation of standards and the establishment of accreditation machinery. One of the most important sets of standards are those of the American Correctional Association. For example, with regard to accommodation the A.C.A. standards call for a minimum of 60 square feet of floor space when confinement does not exceed ten hours per day; and at least 70 square feet in jails, and 80 square feet in prisons, when prisoners are confined for more than ten hours per day. The standards state that prisoners be housed singly and that new construction not contain units designed for multiple occupancy. To receive accreditation, the correctional agency must comply with 90 per cent of all 'essential' standards, 80 per cent of all 'important' standards and 70 per cent of all 'desirable' standards. The minimum square footage standards have been classed as 'important' but not 'essential', which is a temporary classification designed to allow time for refurbishing to take place.

By March 1981, 500 prison and parole agencies were under contract to participate in the accreditation process and 115 agencies had been accredited. Federal funds have been made available in some instances to assist agencies in reaching the required standards. Additionally, standards have been developed by various professional groups such as the American Bar Association and the American Medical Association.[110] These activities also have received considerable federal funding.

These various efforts have formed the basis of the *Federal Standards for Prisons and Jails* produced in 1978 by the U. S. Department of Justice for use by the Federal Bureau of Prisons and to assist divisions of the Justice Department in dealings with state and local prison systems. A recent study, however, made the timely comment that, '. . . the proliferation of guidelines might confuse rather than strengthen efforts to achieve a consensus on minimum standards of institutional operations.'[111] There is little doubt, however, that minimum standards provide a crucial complement to the interventionist role of the courts.

Outside the United States there have been a number of standard-setting exercises, mostly of an aspirational nature and sufficiently imprecise in their requirements to allow prison systems to fairly easily claim compliance. The United Nations Standard Minimum Rules, adopted in 1955, were little more than a revised version of standards first agreed to by the League of Nations in 1934. Even so, many governments did not claim compliance with a substantial number of the rules in a survey conducted in 1975. European Standard Minimum Rules were formulated by the Council of Europe in 1973 and are essentially an adaptation of those set forth by the United Nations. The European Convention on Human Rights is a considerably more potent institution, serving as an instrument for applying pressure on member countries to upgrade their prison systems; although with a few exceptions this can only operate in those countries which allow individuals the right to apply to the European Commission on Human Rights. Article 3 holds: 'No one shall be subject to torture or inhuman or degrading treatment or punishment.'

A few European countries have gone some way towards incorporating minimum standards into legislation. The West German Prison Act of 1976 provides that, with respect to prisons opened since 1976, each prisoner should have an individual cell for non-waking hours. The same Act authorizes the federal minister of justice to lay down minimum requirements concerning air volume, ventilation, heating, and floor and window space. Although no such action has yet been taken at the federal level, the Act has prompted states which are responsible for prison administration to agree to a set of standards addressed to these physical requirements. As noted earlier, in the Netherlands since 1947 there has been a statutory proscription on placing more than one prisoner to a cell. In England, the Home Office announced, in 1982, that consideration was being given to a white paper on minimum standards but it is doubtful, even if such standards become official policy, that they will be justiciable.[112]

Conclusion

There is a variety of pressures exerted on prison systems which contribute to deteriorating conditions. The assumption can safely be made that without extraordinary resources and concerted efforts the quality of prison life will decline rather than improve. This vastly depressing state of affairs is all the more likely to exist where the prison system is set on an expansionist course. There is a powerful tradition which insists that persons in prison are less eligible than others. This tradition helps to ensure that increased expenditure on prison systems is not channeled towards improving the conditions of prison life but is likely to be absorbed mainly by staffing within prisons and the administrative structure of the prison system. A crucial feature of the inertia to ameliorate conditions is the insularity and low visibility of prison systems. Prison administrators have largely been successful in avoiding the attentions of the media and the enquiring eyes of independent inspection and research. The most substantial challenge, although still rather tentative in most jurisdictions, has taken the form of civil action through the courts. Litigation against prison systems has complemented efforts to fashion standards defining minimum prison conditions. The important feature of the new standards movement is the promise of enforceability. The intent is less to sketch a vision of the utopian prison system than to effect substantive and reasonably rapid improvements.

In the late eighteenth century the spread of gaol fever prompted reform partly from considerations of self-interest; it was recognized that the fever could not be contained within the prisons and threatened the general community. Three centuries later many prison systems are in the grip of a new gaol fever, which in many countries has every appearance of being endemic. The new gaol fever can be challenged only through a reversal of expansionist policy. It is this challenge to which the remaining chapters are addressed.

References

1 Stephen Shaw, *Paying the Penalty, An Analysis of the Cost of Penal Sanctions*, NACRO, 1980, p. 5.
2 *Report of the Committee of Inquiry into the United Kingdom Prison Services*, Cmnd 7673, London: HMSO, 1979, p. 149.
3 National Institute of Justice, *American Prisons and Jails*, vol. III, Washington D.C.: Government Printing Office, 1981, p. 117.
4 Research project on American Prisons and Jails, working notes.
5 *Swedish Code of Statutes*, 1974, p. 203.
6 David A. Ward, 'Inmate Rights and Prison Reform in Sweden and Denmark', *Journal of Criminal Law and Criminology and Police Science*, **63**, pp. 244–5.

7 Ulla Bondesson, Fången i fångsamshället, Malmo: P.A. Norstedt and Soners Forlag, 1974.
See also, Ulla Bondesson, 'A Critical Survey of Correctional Treatment Studies in Scandinavia, 1945–1974', in *Crime Deterrence and Offender Career Project*, ed. Ernst van den Haag and Robert Martinson, report prepared under a grant from the US Office of Economic Opportunity, New York, 1975.

8 Cited by David A. Ward in 'Sweden: The Middle Way to Prison Reform', in *Prisons: Present and Possible*, ed. Marvin E. Wolfgang, Lexington, Massachusetts: Lexington, 1979, p. 143. Nils Christie discusses efforts to humanize Scandinavian prisons in the context of the demise of treatment ideology. 'Protagonists of treatment in countries that have been through the stages of treatment ideology do often these days scold their Scandinavian colleagues for letting them down. They have attempted to humanize their penal systems by pointing to treatment in Scandinavia. In the meantime, the Scandinavians declare treatment dead, and thus make it completely impossible to modify old fashioned unkind penal systems.' Nils Christie, *Limits to Pain*, Oxford: Martin Robertson, 1982, p. 48. Christie makes the important point that for all its defects, the treatment ideology has, 'its own vital, but often hidden, message of compassion, relief, care and goodness . . .', ibid., p. 47.

9 John Howard, *The State of the Prisons*, London: Dent, 1929, p. xxi.

10 *Hanging, Not Punishment Enough, for Murderers, Highway Men and House-Breakers. Offered for the Consideration of the House of Parliament.* Anon., London, 1701.

11 Jeremy Bentham, 'Panopticon or the Inspection House: Postscript Part II' 4, *Works*, 1843, p. 122.

12 *Yorkshire Post*, 16 October, 1980.

13 G. Rusche and O. Kirchheimer, *Punishment and Social Structure*. New York: Russell and Russell, 1968, pp. 187–8.

14 David A. Ward, op. cit., note 8, p. 155.

15 ibid., p. 149.

16 *H.C. Deb.* Sixth series, vol. 1, col. 575, 20 March 1981 (Mr Tom Benyon).

17 *Home Office, statement on the background, circumstances and action taken subsequently relative to the disturbance in 'D' wing at H.M. Prison Wormwood Scrubs on 31 August 1979; together with the Report of an Inquiry by the Regional Director of the South East Region of the Prison Department.* H.C. 199, London: HMSO, 1982, p. 39.

18 John Irwin, *Prisons in Turmoil*, Boston and Toronto: Little Brown, 1980, pp. 127–8.

19 See, e.g. J. Dollard, *Caste and Class in a Southern Town*, New Haven: Yale University Press, 1937; and, Tom J. Scheff, 'Control over policy by attendants in a mental hospital', *Journal of Health and Human Behaviour*, 2, 1961, pp. 93–105.

20 Donald R. Cressey, 'Prison Organisations', in *Handbook of Organisations*, ed. J. G. Marsh, Chicago: Rand McNally, 1975, p. 1045.

21 ibid., p. 1047.

22 See, F. E. Emery, *Freedom and Justice within Walls; The Bristol Prison Experiment*, London: Tavistock, 1970.

23 Evidence of Central Departments to the May Committee, vol. III, London: Home Office 1979, p. 16.

24 Report of H.M. Chief Inspector of Prisons, Gartree, London: Home Office, 1981: p. 5. This report cites the quotation from a Prison Department inspectorate report on Gartree prison, 1975.

25 Evidence of Central Departments, op. cit., note 23, p. 16.

26 May Report, op. cit., note 2, p. 120.

27 ibid., p. 122.

28 *Ruiz* v. *Estelle*, 503 F. Supp. 1292, (E.D. Tex., 1980).

29 ibid., p. 1294.

30 Ian Dunbar, unpublished paper, 1981, p. 4.

31 *Deinstitutionalisation: Out of Their Beds and Into The Street*, American Federation of State, County and Municipal Employees, 1975.

32 Between 1960 and 1982 governor grade positions increased from 250 to 541, but many of these were at the lowest level and, despite appearances, promotion prospects to senior governor positions declined.

33 Evidence of Home Office to May Committee, vol. I, 1979, London: Home Office,

p. 116; see also debate on Criminal Justice Bill in House of Lords, 22 June 1982, H.L. Debates, vol. 431, cols 1001–1010. During the debate the Home Office Minister, Lord Elton, remarked: '. . . because of population pressures the CNA serves as an index rather than a limit to the capacity of population. It is a sort of Plimsoll Line and sometimes we sail rather deep.' ibid., at col. 1007.

34 See e.g. Roy D. King and Rod Morgan, *The Future of the Prison System*. Farnborough: Gower, 1980, p. 116; Lord Avebury in House of Lords debate, 22 June 1982, H.L. Deb., vol. 431, col. 1004.

35 *American Prisons and Jails*, vol. III, op. cit., note 3, p. 59.

36 ibid., p. 81.

37 In England and with respect to the national aggregate of state systems in the United States in 1978, two out of every five cells designed for one person held more than one person.

38 Bert Hallstrom, 'Some Questions Concerning the English Prison System', unpublished paper, 1982. The author is grateful to Mr. Hallstrom for permission to quote this extract and to Gunnar Marnell for the translation.

39 Michael Ignatieff, *A Just Measure of Pain*, London: Macmillan, 1978, p. 168.

40 Sidney and Beatrice Webb, *English Prisons Under Local Government*, London: Longmans, Green and Co., 1922, p. 195.

41 *Prison Act*, 1865, 28 and 29 Vict. c.126, section 17(1).

42 Derived from Seán McConville, *A History of English Prison Administration*, vol. 1, 1750–1877, London: Routledge and Kegan Paul, 1981, p. 337.

43 *American Prisons and Jails*, op. cit., note 3, p. 46.

44 McConville, op. cit., note 42. p. 365.

45 Sidney and Beatrice Webb, op. cit., note 40, p. 215.

46 *Report of the Departmental Committee on Prisons*, Chairman Herbert Gladstone, C.7702, LVI,1. London: HMSO, 1895, *Minutes of Evidence*, pp. 100–101, p. 529.

47 *Prison Act*, 1952 s. 14(1).

48 *The Prison Rules*, 1964, Statutory Instrument, 1964, No. 388, Rule 23.

49 *Prison Department Report for 1964*, 1965, p. 12.

50 *Report of the Committee on Homosexual Offences and Prostitution*. Chairman, Sir John Wolfenden, Cmnd. 247, London: HMSO, 1957.

51 Roy D. King and Rodney Morgan, op. cit., note 34, p. 120.

52 John McCarthy, letter to *The Times*, 19 November 1981. A letter on rather similar lines was sent to *The Daily Telegraph* by Norman Brown, governor of Strangeways prison, Manchester, on 30 November 1981. John McCarthy resigned from the English prison system in December 1982. In an interview he commented: 'The Home Office wants to make the prison service system into something it can understand, control and defend. It's got nothing to do with punishment or rehabilitation. It's to do with people coming in, getting looked after in defensible conditions and going out again.' *The Guardian*, December 31, 1982.

53 H.M. Chief Inspector of Prisons, report on *Gloucester Prison*, London: Home Office, 1982, p. 11.

54 H.M. Chief Inspector of Prisons, report on *Leeds Prison*, London: Home Office, 1982, p. 11.

55 ibid., p. 6.

56 Home Office, *Report of Her Majesty's Chief Inspector of Prisons for England and Wales, 1981*, Cmnd. 8532, London: HMSO, 1982, p. 18. The following year the Chief Inspector reported no improvement in the state of overcrowding and estimated, on the basis of Home Office forecasts, that the situation by the end of the decade would worsen still further. Home Office, *Report of Her Majesty's Chief Inspector of Prisons, 1982*. H.C. 260, London: HMSO, 1983, pp. 4–9.

57 Rod Caird, *A Good and Useful Life, Imprisonment in Britain Today*, London: Hart-Davis, MacGibbon, 1974, pp. 24–6.

58 *Pugh* v. *Locke*, 406 F.Supp. 321 (M.D. Ala., 1976). On overcrowding in American prisons, see generally, *Overcrowded Time: Why Prisons Are So Crowded and What Can Be Done*, New York: Edna McConnell Clark Foundation, 1982.

59 *Ruiz* v. *Estelle*, op. cit., note 28, p. 1277.

60 ibid., p. 1278.

61 ibid., p. 1279.
62 ibid., p. 1282.
63 *Gates* v. *Collier*, 349 F.Supp. 881 (N.D. Miss. 1972), aff'd 501 F. 2nd 1291 (5th Cir. 1974).
64 See, e.g. *Johnson* v. *Levine*, 450 F.Supp. 648 (D.Md. 1978), where the Maryland state prison system was ordered to remove about 1,000 prisoners from maximum and medium security institutions.
65 *Prison Overcrowding Emergency Powers Act, Public Act 519 of 1980*. The Michigan legislation took effect on 26 January 1981 and on 14 May 1981 the Michigan Supreme Court ruled that the statute was constitutional (overturning a ruling by the Court of Appeal). The state governor issued declarations of states of emergency in May 1981 (ended August 1981) and again in May 1982. On both these occasions prison population exceeded the rated capacity of the prison system. The governor is required to declare a state of emergency if prison population exceeds rated capacity for 30 consecutive days. The effect of the emergency declaration is to reduce by 90 days the minimum sentences of all prisoners with established minimum sentences (life sentence prisoners are excluded). If this reduction does not result in population being reduced to 95 per cent of rated capacity within 90 days of the declaration of the state of emergency, minimum sentences would again be reduced by 90 days. Details set out in memoranda prepared by the Michigan Prison Overcrowding Project, 1982.
66 See, note, '"Mastering" Intervention in Prisons', *Yale Law Journal*, **88**, 1979, p. 1081.
67 *Ruiz* v. *Estelle*, op. cit., note 28, p. 1284.
68 Stephen Hobhouse and A. Fenner Brockway (eds.), *English Prisons Today*, London: Longman, Green & Co., 1922, p. 64.
69 Sidney and Beatrice Webb, op. cit., note 40, p. 235.
70 Lionel W. Fox, *The English Prison and Borstal Systems*, London: Routledge and Kegan Paul, 1952, pp. 83–4.
71 Denis Trevelyan, Director General in *Prison Department Annual Report for 1980*, Cmnd. 8228, London: HMSO, 1981, p. 2.
72 The press reported the confidential memorandum as saying: 'If a Governor, like any official, feels compelled to enter into any political controversy on a matter within his official sphere of responsibility, his proper course of action would be to resign first.' *The Guardian*, 17 December 1981.
73 Tom Wicker, *A Time To Die*, New York: Quadrangle, 1975. See generally, Ira P. Robbins, 'Legal Aspects of Prison Riots', *Harvard Civil Rights – Civil Liberties Review*, **16**, 1982, pp. 769–72. The media played a key role in the peaceful resolution of the hostage-taking incident at Sing Sing prison in January 1983, see *The Times*, 12 January 1983.
74 Malcolm Dean, 'The News Media's Influence in Penal Policy', in *Penal Policy-Making in England*, ed. Nigel Walker, Cambridge: University of Cambridge Institute of Criminology, 1977, pp. 25–36.
75 Gladstone Report, op. cit., note 46, section 115–16.
76 The appointment of H.M. Chief Inspectors of Prisons for England and Wales and for Scotland, was recommended in 1979 by the May Committee. See, May Committee, op. cit., note 2, pp. 95–6.
77 An inspectorate was also established for the Scottish prison system and located in the Scottish Office.
78 Leon Radzinowicz, 'John Howard', in *Prisons, Past and Future*, ed. John C. Freeman, London: Heinemann, 1978, pp. 7–13.
79 Stanley Cohen and Laurie Taylor, *Psychological Survival: The Experience of Long-Term Imprisonment*, Harmondsworth: Penguin, 1972; Cohen and Taylor noted, '. . . eventually the Home Office rejected our ideas for research. Fortunately, we were able to reply that most of the work had already been done', ibid., p. 39.
80 Charles Goring, *Statistical Study of the English Convict*, London: HMSO, 1913. Also Cesare Lombrozo, *L'uomo delinquente*, Milan 1876.
81 Donald Clemmer, *The Prison Community*, Boston: Christopher Publishing House, 1940; the first British study in this tradition was Terence and Pauline Morris, *Pentonville: A Sociological Study of an English Prison*, London: Routledge and Kegan Paul, 1963.
82 See, e.g., Gene Kassebaum, David Ward and Daniel Wilner, *Prison Treatment*

and Parole Survival, New York: John Wiley; 1971; and, A. E. Bottoms and F. H. McClintock, Criminals Coming of Age: *A Study of Institutional Adaptation in the Treatment of Adolescent Offenders*, London: Heinemann, 1973.

83   Richard H. McCleery, 'Communication Patterns as Bases of Systems of Authority and Power' in *Theoretical Studies in Social Organisation of the Prison*, eds. Richard A. Cloward *et al.*, New York: Social Science Research Council, 1960, pp. 49–110. In this tradition are James B. Jacobs, *Stateville: The Penitentiary in Mass Society*, Chicago: The University of Chicago Press, 1977; and an English study, Roy D. King and Kenneth W. Elliott, *Albany: Birth of a Prison: End of an Era*, London: Routledge and Kegan Paul, 1978.

84   Important exceptions are Lloyd E. Ohlin, 'Conflicting Interests in Correctional Objectives' in *Theoretical Studies in Social Organisation of the Prison*, eds. Richard A. Cloward *et al.*, op. cit., note 1, pp. 111–29; and Thomas Mathiesen, *Across the Boundaries of Organisations: An Exploratory Study of Communication Patterns in the Penal Institutions*, Berkeley, California: Glendessary Press, 1971. For a history of the California state prison system 1944–61 see, Joseph W. Eaton, *Stone Walls Not a Prison Make: The Anatomy of Planned Administrative Change*, Springfield, Illinois: Charles C. Thomas, 1962.

85   *Becker* v. *Home Office* (1972), 2 Q.B. 407, 418.

86   The term 'hands off' in this context was first used in Comment, 'Beyond the Ken of the Courts: a Critique of Judicial Refusal to Review the Complaints of Convicts.' *Yale Law Journal*, **72**, 1963, p. 506; it is of interest to compare this article with the situation twenty years later in England. See, e.g. G. Zellick, 'The Prison Rules and the Court', *Criminal Law Review*, 1981, pp. 602–16.

87   *Ruffin* v. *Commonwealth* 62, Va. (21 Gratt.) 790, 796 (1871).

88   Such actions could be brought for First Amendment violations, *Cooper* v. *Pate*, 378 U.S. 546, (1964).

89   A further twelve states were facing litigation on prison crowding in 1980.

90   *Pugh* v. *Locke*, op. cit., note 58.

91   *Hutto* v. *Finney*, U.S. 90 U.S. 2565 (1978).

92   An early ruling by the Supreme Court referred to the 'cry of horror' at punishment that is 'so foul, so inhuman and so violative of basic concepts of decency'. *Robinson* v. *California*, 370 U.S. 660, 676 (1962).

93   Cases are cited in *American Prisons and Jails*, vol. III, op. cit., note 3, p. 169.

94   *Holt* v. *Sarver*, 309 F.Supp. 362 (E.D. Ark, 1970).

95   *Pugh* v. *Locke*, op. cit., note 58. For a detailed assessment of *Pugh* v. *Locke* with reference to the 'totality of conditions' approach to the Eighth Amendment, see Ira P. Robbins and Michael B. Buser, 'Punitive Conditions of Prison Confinement: An Analysis of *Pugh* v. *Locke* and Federal Court Supervision of State Penal Administration Under the Eighth Amendment', *Stanford Law Review*, **29**, 1977, pp. 893–930.

96   *Ruiz* v. *Estelle*, op. cit., note 28, pp. 1383–4.

97   Ira P. Robbins and Michael B. Buser, op. cit., note 95, p. 915.

98   The State of Texas engaged a major law firm to deal with just one item of the court order.

99   *Bell* v. *Wolfish*, 441 U.S. 520 (1979), and *Rhodes* v. *Chapman*, 452 U.S. 337 (1981).

100   *Bell* v. *Wolfish*, ibid., p. 462.

101   Ira P. Robbins, 'The Cry of Wolfish in the Federal Courts: The future of federal judicial intervention in prison administration'. *J. Criminal Law and Criminology*, **71**, 1980, p. 225.

102   *Rhodes* v. *Chapman*, op. cit., note 99, p. 69.

103   See, Barbara Huber, 'Safeguarding of Prisoners' Rights under the New West German Prison Act', *South African Journal of Criminal Law and Criminology*, **2**, 1978, pp. 229–38. The overcrowding case arose in Nordrhein-Westfalen. As a consequence of severe overcrowding, there was a decision by the Oberlandesgericht Hamm in 1967 stopping the practice of placing three or more prisoners in cells designed for only one. Olg Hamm, *Neue Juridstische Wochenschrift*, 1967, p. 2024.

        Professor Johannes Feest kindly provided the author with this summary of the case: 'The court acted upon a complaint from a prisoner, who had found himself placed (together with two others) in a cell-room of 23 cubic meters air space. The cell-room furnishing included a toilet, but there were no partitioning walls to hide the toilet from view and/or smell. The cell-room was originally designated for only one prisoner. The court took notice that according to prison rules (at the time, 1966) one-person-cells were supposed to have at least 11 cubic meters of air space. There were no standards available for two- or three-person-cells. The court ruled that punishment should be carried out within the confines of 'human dignity' (as laid down by Art. 1 of the German Constitution). 'If a sentenced prisoner together with two other prisoners is placed in a one-person-cell of about 23.45 cubic meters air space with a toilet lacking a 'modesty partition' (Schamwand), this kind of correction violates Art. 1 of the Grundgesetz (i.e. the Constitution)'. According to the court, overcrowding cannot legitimate violations of these standards: 'If the number of sentenced prisoners surpasses the capacity of a prison, overcrowding may be prevented by a temporary halt in receptions with respect to short-term prisoners'. This was exactly what the administration did, thereby reducing drastically the prisoners admitted to prisons in Nordrhein-Westfalen.' (Personal communication to author, 9 September 1982.)

104   The Prison Rules, Statutory Instruments, 1964, No. 388. See Graham Zellick, 'Prison Rules and The Courts', *Criminal Law Review*, 1981, pp. 605–11.

105   *Williams* v. *The Home Office*, (1981), All E.R. 1211. The case centred on false imprisonment; counsel made no attempt to rely on a breach of Prison Rules. The appeal was rejected; (1982) 2 All E.R. 564. See, Graham Zellick, 'The Prison Rules and the Courts: A Postscript', *Criminal Law Review*, Sept. 1982, pp. 575–6.

106   *The Guardian*, April 8 1980.

107   ibid.

108   Home Office v. *Harman*, 1981, 1Q.B. 557.

109   The major reports are the U.S. National Commission on Law Observance and Enforcement (1931), the National Commission on Criminal Justice Standards and Goals (1973). Mention should also be made of the American Prison Association's Declaration of Principles (1870).

110   American Bar Association, *Standards for Criminal Justice*, (17 volumes) and *Legal Rights of Prisoners* (1977), American Medical Association, *Standards for the Accreditation of Medical Care and Health Services in Correctional Institutions* (1976); by National Clearinghouse for Criminal Justice Planning and Architecture. See, e.g. *Guidelines for the Planning and Design of Regional and Community Correctional Centres for Adults*, (1971).

111   *American Prisons and Jails*, vol. 3, op. cit., note 3, p. 7. For a preliminary attempt to standardize data so as to provide an overall assessment of a prison or prison system by means of a prison environment index, see Lawrence A. Greenfeld, 'Assessing Prison Environment: A Comparative Approach', unpublished paper, (Washington D.C.) National Institute of Justice.

112   Much of the initiative for the interest in standards in England has come from the Prison and Borstal Governors' Branch of the Society of Civil Servants.

Part Three

Reduction

6   Tactics for Reduction

In introducing the reductionist alternative, this chapter presents case studies of three prison systems which have taken a reductionist direction. Some of the tactics and strategies described may be transferable to other jurisdictions, but of crucial significance is the demonstration that reductionist policy can be implemented successfully. In the late 1960s and early 1970s much use was made of the notion of decarceration. Articles were published and papers presented at seminars; but it was actual events in Massachusetts which were, around 1972, to gain most attention in and beyond the United States.[1] As Commissioner of the Department of Youth Services, Jerome Miller was able to show that huge reductions in institutional populations could be achieved and sustained. Although it was not possible to replicate the particular reductionist tactics used in Massachusetts, Miller's achievement gave an urgency to efforts elsewhere to cut back the scope of incarceration.[2]

The three case studies portray substantial reductions in prison population size which were sustained at the new low level. The first case study deals with the thirty-year period in England which ended with the Second World War. England's prison population rate, at about 30 per 100,000 inhabitants in the mid-1930s, had become one of the lowest in Europe. By comparison, in the Netherlands at this time, the prison population rate was 52 per 100,000, not very different from the rates of 56 and 61 achieved by France and Belgium respectively.[3]

The other two cases of reductionist tactics described in this chapter are the national prison systems of Japan and the Netherlands over the period 1950–1975. It is instructive to compare the shifts in prison population size of these two prison systems with that of England over this period, shown in Table 6.1.

In considering these three reductionist case studies, it must be re-emphasized that the level of recorded crime is a most unreliable indicator of the direction of prison population size. Of paramount significance, as was noted in Chapter 3, is the impact of various intervening strategies which shield the criminal justice process from the impact of crime.

Level of crime

Recorded serious crime for Japan, the Netherlands and for England for the period 1950–78 is displayed alongside prison population rates, in Table 6.2.

Table 6.1
Prison population size 1950–75 (1950 = 100)

	1950	1955	1960	1965	1970	1975
England	100	103	132	148	190	194
Japan	100	79	76	61	48	44
Netherlands	100	60	51	46	36	35

Source: cross-national study

Table 6.2
Recorded serious crime and prison populations, shown as rates per 100,000 inhabitants, 1950–78, England, Japan and the Netherlands

	England		Japan		Netherlands	
	Crime	Prison popul.	Crime	Prison popul.	Crime	Prison popul.
1950	1,051	47	1,515	123	902	66
1955	952	48	1,457	91	826	38
1960	1,613	59	1,312	83	1,048	30
1965	2,397	64	1,216	64	1,277	25
1970	3,228	80	1,140	47	1,959	19
1975	4,297	81	1,040	40	3,270	17
1978	4,869	85	1,107	43	3,670	24

The same data are shown below expressed as 1950 = 100

	England		Japan		Netherlands	
1950	100	100	100	100	100	100
1955	80	102	96	74	91	57
1960	153	125	87	67	116	45
1965	228	136	80	52	141	38
1970	307	170	75	38	217	29
1975	408	172	67	32	362	26
1978	453	180	73	35	406	36

Note: serious crime is defined as: Japan – non-traffic penal code offences
Netherlands – penal code offences
England – indictable offences

Source: abstracted from cross-national study files

In the concluding section of the chapter some general considerations arising from the case studies are discussed together with a brief review of the tactics used to generate and sustain reductionist policies.

England 1908–38

England experienced a remarkable drop in prison population size during the period of 1908–20 and sustained this lower level throughout the inter-war years. The English experience attracted attention overseas, exemplified in the United States in a detailed analysis by the American criminologist Edwin Sutherland who began his article: 'Prisons are being demolished and sold in England because the supply of prisoners is not large enough to fill them.' Sutherland described the events as being, '. . . part of a great social movement which has been underway in England and other countries for at least a century'.[4] During the fifteen year period, 1908–23, the size of the English prison population was halved, falling to around 11,000. At a rate per 100,000 inhabitants, the decline over this period, as shown in Table 6.3, was from 62 to 30, and for the next fifteen years the rate remained one of the lowest in Europe.

Table 6.3
Prison population and rate per 100,000 inhabitants, 1908–38

	Total prison population	Rate per 100,000
1908	22,029	63
1913	18,155	50
1918	9,196	25
1923	11,148	29
1928	11,109	28
1933	12,986	32
1938	11,086	30

Source: based on figures abstracted from the annual Reports of Prison Commissioners, England and Wales

Note: the years 1908 to 1923 refer to year beginning 1st April, above and in subsequent tables

In 1908 the English prison system as a national entity had been in operation for thirty years, having been established by the Prison Act of 1877 which amalgamated the centralized convict prisons with jails which were the responsibility of local government. The size of the convict system had grown from 6,000 prisoners in 1850 to 10,000 prisoners housed in thirteen prisons by 1878. The Act of 1877, which took effect on 1 April, 1878, at a stroke added to the central government's prison system some 112 local prisons holding a little over 20,000 prisoners. The total prison population of almost 31,000 represented a rate of 118 per 100,000 inhabitants. Once the national prison system was established there followed a phase of considerable rationalization, achieved mostly by prison closures. In 1878, 44 prisons were immediately closed, a further nine were closed by 1887 and six more prior to 1914. By 1888, the size of the prison population had declined to 21,200 and to 17,600 by 1898. However, over the next decade the prison population increased by 25 per cent and in 1908 stood at 22,000, only marginally below the certified capacity of the prison system. There was overcrowding in some local prisons and the Prison Commissioners referred to, 'a great strain on the cellular accommodation'.[5]

A principal feature of the English prison system in 1908 was the magnitude of throughput of prisoners, in excess, excluding remand prisoners, of 200,000 persons annually. The profile of prisoners received into the prison system in 1908 was one of very large numbers of petty offenders. Three out of every four prisoners received were either sentenced for a non-indictable offence or imprisoned as fine defaulters. Less than fifteen per cent of receptions had been sentenced for indictable offences. By 1910 there was a determination within the Home Office to effect a reductionist policy, and the principal initiative in setting this direction was taken by Winston Churchill during his brief tenure as Home Secretary between February 1910 and October 1911. Churchill displayed considerable scepticism as to what might be achieved through the prison system, and he quickly came to believe that imprisonment was greatly over-used. He corresponded with John Galsworthy on the need to reduce solitary confinement, he used his powers of executive clemency more frequently than was customary;[6] and, of most significance, he set about framing legislative proposals to reduce severely the number of persons entering the prison system.

In a memorandum to the Prime Minister in September 1910, Churchill described the main problem as being, 'the immense number of committals of petty offenders to prison on short sentences'. He noted that two-thirds of sentenced prisoners were sentenced to two weeks or less. He described the situation as being, 'a terrible and purposeless waste of public money and human character'. The concern led to specific proposals in order to 'break in upon this volume of petty sentences for trifling offences from several different directions with a view to effecting a substantial and permanent reduction in them'. Churchill listed four possible strategies:

- to extend the use of probation for young adult offenders;
- to abolish imprisonment for debt;
- to allow time for persons to pay fines;
- to give courts the powers to suspend sentences, for petty offences, of up to one month.

Churchill's target was to reduce the number of short prison sentences by 'at least a third, perhaps much more' and to achieve a reduction of 10 to 15 per cent in the average daily prison population. In his reply to Churchill, the Prime Minister, Herbert Asquith, himself a former Home Secretary, anticipated particular difficulties with respect to abolishing imprisonment for debt but nonetheless promised general support. Churchill redrafted his memorandum and submitted it as a confidential paper to Cabinet under the heading 'Abatement of Imprisonment'.[7] Twelve months later, Churchill was moved to the Admiralty but left behind a momentum for reforming legislation. The Prison Commissioners publicly stressed the need for legislative action, and in 1913 commented: 'Of the many social problems now demanding the attention of Parliament, we believe the question of unnecessary commitment to prison to be one of the most urgent, and we similarly trust that the Secretary of State will be able to press forward legislation with a view to dealing with this matter.'[8] Two important statutes were enacted immediately prior to the outbreak of War, aimed to divert mentally retarded persons from prison sentences, and requiring magistrates to allow time for the payment of fines unless there were exceptional reasons for not so doing.[9]

Winston Churchill played a crucial role in creating the political climate for change. Upon the accession of King George V, remission was granted to all convicted prisoners in England and Wales who, on May 23, 1910, had still to serve more than one month of their prison sentence. The following formula was used:

> One week remission: persons with one month or more to serve;
> one month remission: persons with one year or more to serve;
> two months remission: persons with three years or more to serve;
> three months remission: persons with five years or more to serve.[10]

In July 1910, shortly before dispatching his legislative proposals on reducing the scale of imprisonment, Churchill described to the House of Commons the action which had already been taken to reduce the prison population:

> 'When His Majesty came to the Throne one of the very first wishes which he was pleased to express was the desire that at a time when all hearts were stirred, and when everyone felt anxious to lay aside old quarrels, the wretched prison population of the country should not stand outside that movement in the national mind.
>
> 'On similar previous occasions the proposal has always been to release a certain number of prisoners definitely. I think we have found a much better way, and that is not to release individuals, but to make a general *pro rata* reduction of sentences over the whole are of the prison population. The remissions which were granted on this occasion affected 11,000 prisoners, and at a stroke struck 500 years of imprisonment and penal servitude from the prison population. I am glad to be able to tell the House that no evil results of any kind have followed from this. It is not at all true to say that a number of the men released have already returned to gaol.'[11]

Churchill continued his speech with an eloquent summary of his penal philosophy:

> 'We must not allow optimism or hope, or benevolence in these matters to carry us too far. We must not forget that when every material

improvement has been effected in prisons, when the temperature has been rightly adjusted, when the proper food to maintain health and strength has been given, when the doctors, chaplains, and prison visitors have come and gone, the convict stands deprived of everything that a free man calls life. We must not forget that all these improvements, which are sometimes salves to our consciences do not change that position. The mood and temper of the public in regard to the treatment of crime and criminals is one of the most unfailing tests of the civilization of any country. A calm and dispassionate recognition of the rights of the accused against the State, and even of convicted criminals against the State, a constant heart-searching by all charged with the duty of punishment, a desire and eagerness to rehabilitate in the world of industry all those who have paid their dues in the hard coinage of punishment, tireless efforts towards the discovery of curative and regenerating processes, and an unfaltering faith that there is a treasure, if you can only find it, in the heart of every man – these are the symbols which in the treatment of crime and criminals mark and measure the stored-up strength of a nation, and are the sign and proof of the living virtue in it.'[12]

The new legislation of 1913–14, together with shifts in sentencing practice, arising from the new mood for change and the upheavals of the First World War, had immediate effects on the English prison population, both in terms of size and throughput. The drop in the number of fine defaulters entering prison was especially sharp, falling by 80 per cent between 1908 and 1923. In 1908 fine defaulters accounted for half of all sentenced receptions into prison compared with one third in 1923. In their annual reports, the Prison Commissioners stressed that the downward trend of the prison population had preceded the War and was, 'due to many social causes operating in different directions, but due also to a very considerable degree, to the legislation of 1908 (Children Act, which excluded under 16-year-olds from prison) and 1914 (Criminal Justice Administration Act, which extended time to pay fines).'[13] The Commissioners emphasized that the reduction was not the result of a decrease in crime but reflected a shift in sentencing practice.

Time to pay fines, new developments in probation, and the screening out of some mentally defective offenders were among the significant specific shifts of practice. However, Sir Evelyn Ruggles-Brise, head of the prison system, drew from the decline in prison population lessons for prison reform which he turned upon his critics, perhaps in particular, the Prison System Enquiry Committee which had been set up in 1919. 'The real solution to the penal problem is to be found, not in fanciful suggestions and devices preferred by advocates of so-called prison reform, but by the great political considerations which determine trade and the consumption of alcohol.'[14]

In the early post-war years the Commissioners, with an eye to the general economic situation, anticipated an increase in prison population size but concluded that this would be countered by unemployment benefits. By 1922 the prison population exceeded 12,000 but then, instead of increasing further as the Commissioners expected, it dropped to around 11,000. The Commissioners were quick to note that their forecast of increased prison population was misplaced, and took an early opportunity to pay tribute to the courts. 'Unforeseen events may falsify any forecast, especially in prison matters, but present circumstances and the history of the past few years give us reason to hope that prison population will not only not increase in the near future; but will show a steady, if slow, decline. No general remarks on this subject would be complete without a tribute to the increasing care which is being shown by Courts of Justice in investigating the circumstance of offenders and avoiding unnecessary committals to prison.'[15]

The prison population remained at around 12,000 prisoners until the early 1940s. The sceptical mood as to the efficacy of the prison system, which had been created by Churchill and others, was revived in the years immediately following the First World War. Two books published in 1922 as companion volumes helped consolidate the mood of scepticism about the prison system during the inter-war years. *English Prisons Under Local Government* by Sidney and Beatrice Webb, while dealing mainly with local prison administration prior to 1878, contained an epilogue sharply critical of several aspects of contemporary prison administration, especially its cloak of secrecy. While noting with approval the shift away from custody in sentencing practice, the Webbs maintained that magistrates, in particular, continued: '. . . almost recklessly to commit to prison offenders who would otherwise be spared this demoralising and dangerous experience.'[16] They noted geographic variations in sentencing practice and recommended the compilation of comparative court statistics so that central government could '. . . bring home to the minds of those judicial authorities who were making the most extravagant use of the device of imprisonment that they were falling behind the more enlightened of their colleagues'.[17] The Webbs concluded that the 'most practical of all prison reforms is to keep people out of prison altogether'.[18] *English Prisons Today*, edited by Stephen Hobhouse and Fenner Brockway, was addressed directly to the existing prison system.

The Prison System Enquiry Committee had been set up in 1919 by the Labour Party's research department but two years later broke its official association with the Labour Party. The committee included persons who, like Hobhouse and Brockway, had themselves been imprisoned as conscientious objectors during the War. It was this direct experience of the English prison system which prompted the study. The result was a carefully documented indictment of the Ruggles-Brise administration, concluding that, 'imprisonment actually creates or perpetuates rather than abates crime in those upon whom it is inflicted'.[19] Furthermore, despite the reductions in prison committals which had occurred over the previous decade, it was forcefully argued by Hobhouse and Brockway that fine defaulters were still being imprisoned unnecessarily, that probation was insufficiently used and that restitution provisions made available in 1907 were largely ignored.[20]

The new scepticism did not permit the progress that had been achieved to stave off further criticism. In particular, Hobhouse and Brockway held that the Prison Commission was hidebound, lacking both 'an inside experience that has enthusiasm and initiative, and an outside enthusiasm that is based on correct knowledge'.[21] In 1921, the Howard Association became the Howard League for Penal Reform and quickly became identified with the need for alternatives to imprisonment.[22] The following year, a further significant event was the appointment of Alexander Paterson to the Prison Commission. Paterson served as a Prison Commissioner until retiring in 1946, and although he never became chairman his influence inside and beyond the English prison system was immense. In his writings, Paterson did not shirk from highlighting the negative aspects of imprisonment, although he firmly believed that rehabilitative results could be achieved under some circumstances. Paterson wrote: 'What is easy is always dangerous. The Court has attached to it, as a ready handmaid for its use, a state or provincial prison. Once guilt is ascertained, the easiest method for the disposal of the prisoner is a sentence of imprisonment. It may or may not be the best method of disposal on psychological grounds, or on those of economy and common sense.'[23] The mood of doubt and scepticism about the prison system, initiated by Churchill and others in the years just prior to the First World War, was carried forward into the 1920s and beyond. It is against this background that sentencing practice for the period is considered.

Table 6.4
Prison receptions (excluding remand prisoners) 1908–38

	Civil prisoners	Fine defaulters	Prison sentences	Total receptions (1908 = 100)	
1908	20,315	95,686	89,215	205,216	100
1913	14,761	74,461	61,963	151,185	74
1918	1,903	5,264	20,786	27,953	14
1923	11,837	15,261	30,874	57,972	28
1928	13,562	13,260	27,189	54,011	26
1933	12,054	11,615	27,066	50,735	25
1938	8,205	7,936	24,289	40,430	20

Source: abstracted from annual reports of Prison Commissioners for England and Wales

As can be seen from Table 6.4, there was a reduction in the number of persons received into the English prison system immediately prior to and during the First World War. In 1923, the number of receptions into English prisons was less than one third of what it had been fifteen years before. This trend reflected a distinct shift in sentencing practice. In 1908, of all indictable offences dealt with by the courts, 49 per cent received imprisonment compared with 25 per cent in 1923 and 19 per cent in 1938. As is evident from Table 6.5, there was also much less use made of prison by the courts with respect to non-indictable offences. The movement away from custody by the courts occurred in the context of comparative stability followed by gradual growth in the number of guilt findings. In the period 1908–1923, indictable guilt findings increased by an annual rate of growth of 0.2 per cent, and non-indictable guilt findings had an average decline of 0.3 per cent. During the second fifteen year period, 1923–1938, there was an average annual growth in indictable guilt findings of 1.3 per cent and in non-indictable guilt findings of 2.4 per cent.

Table 6.5
Sentencing practice, 1908, 1923 and 1938

Indictable offences
Percentage of total guilt findings

	Total guilt findings	Prison	Juvenile institutions	Fine	Dismissal recognisance	Probation	Other
1908	59,052	49	3	16	17	7	8
1923	60,711	25	2	19	19	24	11
1938	78,463	19	4	18	24	31	4

Non-Indictable Offences
Percentage of total guilt findings

1908	649,243	13	1	75	8	1	2
1923	520,790	3	—	83	11	1	1
1938	709,019	1	—	87	10	1	3

Source: based on figures abstracted from the relevant volume of *Criminal Statistics, England and Wales*

It is important to note that the reduction in prison population and subsequent stability took place against a background of a gradual increase in indictable offences recorded by the police. Table 6.6 sets out recorded crime, convictions for indictable offences and prison population size. The gap between recorded offences and guilt findings widened very considerably over this period. As a later study of crime statistics pointed out, this was the consequence not of a declining conviction rate, but of the falling clear-up rate by the police over the period.[24]

Table 6.6
Recorded crime, guilt findings and persons received into the English prison system, 1908, 1923 and 1938

| | Indictable offences | | | Prison receptions | | Average |
	Recorded by police	Guilt findings	Fine defaulters	Prison sentences Non-indictable	Indictable	daily population
1908	105,279	55,966	95,600	63,400	28,972	22,029
1923	110,200	60,711	15,261	16,758	15,092	11,148
1938	283,000	78,000	7,936	9,824	14,570	11,086

Source: based on figures abstracted from relevant volume of *Criminal Statistics, England and Wales,* and *Reports of Prison Commissioners*

The result was that the total number of persons found guilty for indictable offences was only 33 per cent more than it had been in 1908 despite an increase of about 160 per cent in the level of recorded indictable crime.

The data displayed in Table 6.6 underline the importance of the decline in persons sentenced to prison for non-indictable offences and, as noted earlier, received by the prison system in default of payment for fines. The pattern of receptions into the English prison system between 1908–1938 is displayed in Table 6.7.

Table 6.7
Receptions into the English prison system 1908, 1923 and 1938 (shown as percentage of total receptions*)

| | | | Prison Sentences | |
	Civil prisoners	Fine defaulters	Non-indictable	Indictable
1908	10	46	30	14
1923	20	26	28	26
1938	20	20	24	36

*Note: the totals on which these percentages are based exclude remand prisoners, and differ slightly from those in Table 6.6 for 1908 and 1923 due to use of financial year by Prison Commissioners and the calendar year for Criminal Statistics.

Source: based on figures abstracted from relevant volumes of *Criminal Statistics, England and Wales* and *Reports of Prison Commissioners*

Edwin Sutherland, in his 1934 article on the decrease in the English prison population, drew particular attention to the decline in public intoxication and of the change in sentencing practice of persons convicted of drinking offences. He suggested that, 'a considerable part of the reduction in commitments to prison is due to the decrease in intoxication and this decrease has not been off-set by increases in other important types of non-indictable offences'.[25] Sutherland also noted that crime rates over this period, as measured by indictable offences recorded by the police, were not related to the trends in sentences to prison.

The estate and personnel of the prison system during this period showed no signs of growth. Indeed, between 1914 and 1929, twenty-five local prisons were closed. There was virtually no new capacity added to the system with the exception of borstal institutions. In 1930, the English prison system consisted of 22 prisons and seven borstals, two of which were part of adult prisons. Total capacity, as measured by certified normal accommodation, was 19,600.[26] The decline in capacity over the period 1878–1938 is shown in Table 6.8.

Table 6.8
Capacity of the English prison system, 1878–1938

1878	37,771
1908	22,872
1923	21,386
1938	15,778

Source: abstracted from relevant volumes of *Reports of the Prison Commissioners*

In 1901 there were 2,993 officers in the prison system and by 1909 this number had increased to 3,330.[27] However, staff numbers substantially declined over the next fifteen years. In 1923 there were 2144 staff of officer grade and a further 351 persons working in prisons and borstals.[28] There was no regional structure and the number of staff at headquarters over the period remained small.[29]

The Criminal Justice Bill, introduced into Parliament in 1938, sought to consolidate the emphasis of policy away from the use of custody. In particular, the Bill had the intention of extending the use of probation and restricting the imprisonment of persons under the age of 21. New facilities to be introduced included attendance centres for persons aged 12–20 and residential hostels, to be known as Howard Houses, for persons aged between 16 and 20. The Bill was in Committee stage when War was declared, and in November 1939 it was abandoned. It was not until 1947 that criminal justice legislation was again considered, but by this time the mood of the country had hardened on law and order; and the prison population had already increased by almost 80 per cent over the pre-war level.

Japan, 1950–75

In recent years, Japan has attracted considerable attention as a result of a sharp decline in the level of recorded crime. Over the same period, prison population size was substantially reduced. The physical capacity of the prison system and the number of personnel remained stable. In 1935 there were some 55,000 sentenced prisoners in Japan,[30] representing a rate of 56 per 100,000 inhabitants.[31] Ten years later, at the conclusion of the Second

World War, the total prison population was a little under 54,000. During the five-year period, 1945–1950, the prison population in Japan increased by 92 per cent.

As shown in Table 6.1, over the next two decades there was a period of steady decline, and by 1968 the prison population had returned to its 1945 level. Between 1970 and 1975 the decline continued, although at a reduced rate, and in 1975 the prison population rate per 100,000 inhabitants had fallen to 40, one of the lowest rates in the western world. The Japanese prison population rate in 1975 was half the size of the rate in England and almost one fifth of the rate in the United States.[32] The rate of decline of sentenced and unsentenced prisoners over the period was similar, with unsentenced prisoners remaining about seventeen per cent of the total. The declining prison population size was accompanied by a reduction in the number of persons received by the prison system on sentence, as shown in Table 6.9.

Table 6.9
Prison population and persons received on sentence, Japan 1950–75

| | Prison population | | Persons received on sentence* | |
	Total	Rate per 100,000 inhabitants	(1950 = 100)	
1950	103,170	123	65,860	100
1955	81,868	91	68,153	104
1960	78,521	83	54,399	83
1965	63,515	64	48,299	73
1970	49,209	47	35,370	54
1975	45,690	40	34,133	52

*includes fine defaulters and all other receptions of sentenced prisoners

Source: figures abstracted from cross-national study files

The decline in serious crime recorded by the police between 1950 and 1975 is displayed in Table 6.2 alongside the prison population, as rates per 100,000 inhabitants. Between 1945 and 1950 recorded serious crime had risen sharply and has been accounted for by Japanese commentators on criminal justice in terms of the damaged economic system and the shattered social order brought about by the military defeat in 1945. Since the mid-1950s most people in Japan have benefited from the rapid economic growth, with average individual incomes rising fourfold in real terms between 1955 and 1978. During this period the number of more serious offences such as those involving violence declined.

An official statement on crime in Japan cites four explanatory factors as to why Japan has differed from other industrial nations with respect to its relatively lower level of recorded crime. These factors are first, the existence of informal social controls, strengthened by a homogeneity of culture, ethnic origin and language; second, a fair and efficient criminal justice process which receives general public support, and whose goals are shared with non-criminal justice agencies; third, the efficient control of weapons and drugs; fourth, the relative affluence of Japanese citizens and the relatively equitable distribution of wealth across all social groups.[33] A possible fifth factor stressed by David Bayley, an authority on policing practice in Japan, is the natural deference displayed by the Japanese to authority.[34] Bayley places the Japanese recorded crime rates in a comparative context by noting that, taken overall with respect to serious crime, the rate per population in the United States is four times as great than in Japan, and for certain offences very much higher. The robbery rate, for example, is more than 100 times higher in the United States than in Japan.

Changes in the Japanese prison population size cannot simply be accounted for in terms of recorded levels of crime. As shown in Table 6.2, the prison population fell more sharply than the level of recorded serious crime between 1950 and 1975. It is important, therefore, to consider how criminal events and offenders were dealt with at the different stages of the criminal justice process.

Diversion by Prosecutors
The police in Japan enjoy unusually high clear-up rates. In 1979 the overall clear-up rate for non-traffic penal code offences was 59 per cent. The clear-up rate for robbery was 88 per cent, for rape 89 per cent and 55 per cent for theft. All criminal cases investigated by the police are referred to the public prosecutor, who exercises discretion as to whether or not to take the case to court in the light of personal circumstances or considerations with regards to the offence. Prosecutorial discretion to dismiss minor offences dates from 1885 and was formally authorized in the 1922 Code of Criminal Procedure. In 1978 43 per cent of adults found by public prosecutors to have committed non-traffic penal code offences were granted suspension of prosecution. The rate of prosecutorial suspension varies considerably between offences. For example, in 1978, 64 per cent of embezzlement cases were suspended, compared with nine per cent of robberies. An official Japanese statement refers to prosecutorial dismissals as contributing significantly '. . . to the speedy disposition of vast numbers of criminal cases and a consequent reduction of criminal court dockets . . . prompt recognition can be given to expression of contrition even in relatively serious cases without exacting the price of a criminal conviction; restitution and expressions of apology to victims can be required without a necessity for extended criminal proceedings.'[35]

Sentencing Practice
Courts in Japan are able to exercise broad discretion in sentencing practice. Of particular importance are powers to suspend prison sentences which

were introduced in 1905 and, subsequent to the 1922 Code of Criminal Procedure, suspended sentences accounted for some ten per cent of all sentences of imprisonment. The Penal Code permits sentences of imprisonment of three years or less to be suspended for a period of one to five years. The revocation rate for suspended sentences of imprisonment in 1978 of persons sentenced in 1975 was 14 per cent, rather higher than earlier years for which data are available. It is, however, important to note that breach does not necessarily involve imprisonment; where there are extenuating circumstances and the suspension did not involve supervision, a new prison sentence, if not over one year in length, can again be suspended. Suspension of imprisonment varies by offence; and in 1978 the variation was from 57 per cent for theft, 44 per cent for fraud, 33 per cent for robbery involving violence and 28 per cent for homicide.[36]

Powers to fine were much expanded in the 1907 Penal Code, and in 1978 fines accounted for about 85 per cent of all penal code sentences. Defaulting is quite unusual and such persons in 1978 made up less than 0.2 per cent of the total prison population. Defaults accounted for about 0.1 per cent of all persons fined.[37]

Probation supervision arises with respect to some sentences of imprisonment which have been suspended. The court has discretion regarding cases where no previous suspended sentence has been made, but must order probation supervision where a second suspended sentence is imposed. In 1978 some 8,500 persons were placed under probation supervision.

Prison Population Throughput
A striking feature of Japan's prison system is the relatively low throughput of prisoners. The length of sentences imposed in Japan are relatively long as can be seen in Table 6.10. Less than twenty per cent of those released in 1978 served under six months compared with over 65 per cent in England. Comparative data on time served by prisoners for the two countries are displayed in Table 6.11.

Table 6.10

Length of prison sentences, Japan 1976

	Number sentenced	Per cent of total
One year or less	15,309	53.4
Over one year to three years	10,731	37.4
Over three years to five years	1,815	6.3
Over five years to ten years	654	2.2
Over ten years	108	0.3
Life sentence	30	0.1
Total	28,647	100

Source: cross-national study

Table 6.11

Time served (months) by releasees in England and Japan, 1978

Months	under 6	6–11	12–23	24–47	48+	Total releasees
England	66.3	20.6	10.3	2.4	0.4	72,077
Japan	19.2	31.5	29.9	11.6	2.1	28,123

Source: cross-national study

Regulation of prison population size

Parole availability in Japan for prisoners who have served one third of a fixed term dates from the latter part of the nineteenth century, but for many years has been used sparingly, not exceeding about ten per cent of all released prisoners. With the sharp increase in the size of the prison population after the Second World War, parole became an important instrument of reductionist policy. In 1949, 80 per cent of all releasees were paroled. As an official report put in, '. . . this reflected severe prison overcrowding brought about by the socio–economic chaos of the immediate post-war era'.[38] Without the pressures arising from prison overcrowding the parole rate fell and in 1978 was 51 per cent. During the first half of this century pardons were frequently used; and mass amnesties have been promulgated more than twenty times to mark national occasions, most recently in 1956 on the occasion of Japan joining the United Nations.[39]

Prison System Capacity and Personnel

The drop in prison population size in Japan between 1950 and 1975 was not matched a reduction in the physical capacity and numbers of prison system personnel. As shown in Table 6.12 total capacity has remained at around 60,000 since 1945, and since 1970 there has been a margin of about 20 per cent excess capacity.[40] Old prisons have been replaced by new construction without adding to total capacity, but there has been no attempt to reduce the prison system's overall physical estate. In 1980 the Japanese prison system consisted of 189 prisons.

Similarly, total staff numbers remained fairly constant between 1950 and 1975. In 1975 there were 13,500 custodial staff and 1,100 administrative and clerical staff. Given the sharp drop in prison population the custodial officer-to-prisoner ratio increased from 1:7 to 1:3 over this period. It is important to recognize that despite the fact that prison population was more than halved and although capacity and personnel were held steady, total operating costs substantially increased. Between 1950 and 1978 operating costs increased in real terms by 260 per cent and on a per prisoner basis, given the fall in prison population size, by 430 per cent. The Japanese experience illustrates that even during a phase of prison population reduction there is a tendency for costs to escalate.

Table 6.12

Capacity of Japan's prison system and occupation factor, 1945–78

	Capacity	Occupation factor
1945	60,483	0.88
1950	66,941	1.54
1955	66,056	1.22
1960	56,955	1.37
1965	62,220	1.02
1970	63,581	0.77
1975	62,273	0.73
1978	61,986	0.80

Source: abstracted from cross-national study files

In 1975 the decline in Japan's prison population came to an end, and between 1975 and 1978 prison population increased by nine per cent. This growth was due largely to an increase of 11 per cent in the number of sentenced prisoners entering the prison system over this period. Between 1970 and 1975 there had been a decline in guilt-findings for non-traffic penal code offences but a slight increase in the proportion receiving immediate prison sentences. Between 1975 and 1978 guilt-findings increased, but the proportion receiving immediate prison sentences declined. But for this shift in sentencing policy away from custody, the recent increase in the size of the Japanese prison population would have been greater. In part, the prison population growth is a result of an increase in convictions for drug offences from 8,200 to 18,000 between 1975 and 1978. In 1978, persons imprisoned for alcohol or drug offences constituted fifteen per cent of the total sentenced prison population compared with two per cent in 1960. The Japanese prison system is geared for moderate expansion during the 1980s. The prison system has forecasted that the prison population will increase over the decade by between three and ten per cent. This simple linear prediction is based upon recent trends in prisoner numbers, especially with respect to drug offences. In line with the projected increase in prison population the Japanese prison system is planning to increase physical capacity.

The Netherlands, 1950–75

Between 1950 and 1975 the prison population in the Netherlands fell from over 6,500 to under 2,500. In terms of the rate per 100,000 inhabitants, the reduction was from 66 to 17. The United Nations International survey of prison populations, prepared for the Fifth United Nations Congress on the Prevention of Crime and the Treatment of Offenders held in 1975, reported no other Western country with a rate under 30.[41] The reductionist policy, which has been successfully pursued in the Netherlands, has attracted extensive international attention.[42] The dramatic drop in the Netherlands prison population, unlike the situation in Japan over the same period, was accompanied by an increase in reported crime. The reduction in prison population is associated with the relative mildness of Dutch criminal justice, typified by measures which filter offenders out of the criminal justice process. The mildness of criminal justice in the Netherlands has long been commented upon by both Dutch and foreign observers. As early as 1750, the situation in the Netherlands was favourably contrasted with that in England in the following terms: '. . . more criminals are executed in London in a year than have been in all Holland for twenty years.'[43] Two centuries later, Herman Bianchi observed: 'Any survey of radical success in the field of social control would probably show that the Netherlands has one of the least inhuman systems in the world.'[44]

The decline in prison population size in the Netherlands since the end of the Second World War has been spectacular. On the last day of 1947 the prison population was 12,836, and this total was to drop by two thousand over each of the next two years. Table 6.13 sets out the subsequent decline which took place between 1950 and 1975.

Table 6.13

Prison population in the Netherlands, 1950–75

	Total	Rate per 100,000 inhabitants
1950	6,730	66
1955	4,075	38
1960	3,449	30
1965	3,105	25
1970	2,433	19
1975	2,356	17

Source: cross-national study

The decline in the Dutch prison population, at least since 1955 for which more complete data are available, has been almost entirely with respect to sentenced prisoners. The number of remand prisoners in custody fluctuated over this period, with remand prisoners increasing as a proportion of the total prison population from 36 per cent in 1955 to 46 per cent in 1975 and rising further to 60 per cent by 1980. The proportion of remand prisoners in the Netherlands is very much higher than in most other national prison systems. In most other European countries, the remand population constitutes about one-fifth of the total. The details for the Netherlands are set out in Table 6.14.

Between 1955 and 1975 the remand population fell by 26 per cent compared with a drop of 51 per cent in sentenced population. Efforts to sustain a reduction in the remand population have not been successful. For example, an act of January 1974 had the purpose of reducing the extent to

Table 6.14

Remand and sentenced prison population, Netherlands, 1955–80

	Remand	Sentenced	Total	Remand prisoners as percentage of total
1955	1,479	2,596	4,075	36
1960	1,510	1,939	3,449	43
1965	1,460	1,645	3,105	47
1970	1,350	1,083	2,435	55
1975	1,094	1,262	2,356	46
1980	1,921	1,282	3,203	60

Source: cross-national study

which powers of remand in custody were used. The act appears to have had an effect for some offences. For example, the remand in custody rate for burglary fell from 50 per cent in 1972 to 38 per cent in 1975, and to 32 per cent in 1977.[45] However, as noted above, the Dutch prison population increased between 1975 and 1980; and this growth is almost entirely accounted for by increases in the remand population, which rose by 75 per cent compared with virtually no change in the sentenced prison population.

The reason for the increase in the population of unconvicted prisoners has do with an increase of numbers and not length of stay on remand. Average length of stay on remand remained throughout the 1970s at about 70 days. The details are set out in Table 6.15.

Table 6.15

Time spent in custody on remand, Netherlands

	Total remands in custody	Percentage of total			
		up to 42 days	43–103 days	103–192 days	192 days
1970	6,761	24	46	26	NIL
1974	6,452	34	41	20	NIL
1979	7,164	38	36	20	6

Source: cross-national study

Average time in custody on remand is very much longer than time in custody after sentence. In 1977 the average time in custody for all prisoners, remand and sentenced, was 41 days; and Dato Steenhuis reports that the average number of days for remand prisoners was about 70 days.[46] Calculating the balance for sentenced prisoners shows an average length of stay for sentenced prisoners of 33 days, less than half the average time spent in custody by unconvicted prisoners.[47]

The decline in prison population size between 1950 and 1975 was in large part the result of shielding the criminal justice process from rising levels of reported crime over this period, for which the annual rate of growth was

11 per cent, as detailed in Table 6.2. Shielding criminal justice from crime events can occur in a number of ways which may or may not represent intended policy. The following overview of practice in the Netherlands takes recorded crime as the starting point and examines four stages in the criminal justice process where there is significant filtering of persons from deeper penetration into the criminal justice process. These stages are police investigation, prosecutorial screening, judicial sentencing and the calling-up of prisoners by the prison system.

Detection of crime

The proportion of all offences detected by the Dutch police between 1970 and 1980 fell from 41 to 30 per cent.[48] The apparent decline in police efficiency may, as was suggested in a recent study, be related partly to the high dismissal rate by prosecutors. 'The police undertake a certain pre-selection from economic considerations. The involvement of the machinery of criminal law is limited by them to cases which appear prosecutable in principle.'[49]

Prosecutorial diversion

Since at least 1960 there has been an increasing tendency by public prosecutors to dismiss cases rather than to proceed with prosecution through the courts. In 1960, of all prosecutorial dismissals and guilt findings combined, 30 per cent were dismissed by prosecutors compared with 44 per cent in 1975.[50] The upward trend in dismissals of cases by public prosecutors is also evident with respect to certain more serious offences. Between 1960 and 1975, of all rape cases handled by public prosecutors, the percentage dismissed increased from 40 to 53 per cent. In the case of robbery and burglary offences, the increased dismissal rate was quite dramatic, up from 20 to 43 per cent and from 31 to 50 per cent respectively.[51] By 1978 the percentage dismissed by public prosecutors for rape, robbery and burglary had further increased to 53, 48 and 59 per cent respectively.[52] The discretion exercised by public prosecutors in the Netherlands plays a crucial part in determining both the volume and composition of cases dealt with by the courts.

Sentencing practice

Despite the decline in clear-up rates and the increase in prosecutorial dismissals, the total number of persons found guilty by the courts between 1950 and 1975 increased by 54 per cent, as displayed in Table 6.16. Over the same period the proportion of offenders receiving immediate imprisonment (unconditional or partly conditional prison sentences) remained fairly constant, at between 27 and 29 per cent. In fact it was not until after 1975 that the use of immediate prison sentences, as a proportion of all guilt findings, began to decline.

Table 6.16

Sentencing practice, 1938–79 shown as percentage of total sentenced

		Prison sentences			Fine	Other
		(i)	(ii)	(iii)	(iv)		
	Total sentenced	Per cent suspended prison	Per cent partially suspended	Unconditional prison	Immediate prison (ii + iii)		
1938	23,329	14	3	29	32	42	12
1947	60,040	9	4	25	29	58	4
1950	35,129	10	5	22	27	58	6
1955	34,401	7	7	19	26	55	12
1960	36,550	6	10	17	27	59	7
1965	40,167	4	10	19	29	53	13
1970	45,334	4	10	18	28	64	3
1975	54,230	4	9	20	29	65	3
1979	69,497	4	8	13	21	72	4

Source: abstracted from relevant volumes of *Statistical Yearbook of the Netherlands*, 1951 to 1979

The length of unconditional prison sentences increased during the 1970s. In 1979 eight per cent of unconditional prison sentences were for periods of one year or more compared with three per cent in 1970. Additionally, the percentage of unconditional prison sentences which were for periods of under six months fell from 90 to 86. This shift towards longer prison sentences, in part, was the consequence of a more severe approach to narcotics offences. In particular the Opium Act of 1975 increased prison terms for heroin dealing. On the other hand there was, as noted below, a shift from imprisonment to fines with respect to offences of drunken driving which contributed to the decline in the proportion of very short prison sentences.

Researchers in the Ministry of Justice have argued that it is instructive to compare penal practice in the Netherlands and elsewhere not only in terms of the prison population rate but also with respect to the extent to which imprisonment is used as a sanction. Dato Steenhuis and colleagues suggest that more use is made of imprisonment in the Netherlands than in Sweden and West Germany.[53] However, account has to be taken of differences in decision-making prior to the sentencing stage. The relatively lower level of prosecutorial diversion by prosecutors in West Germany is, as Steenhuis acknowledges, of crucial significance. Furthermore, it is possible that less resort is made to the criminal justice process in Holland across a wide spectrum of events. Any firm conclusion on prison usage across different countries would need to take account of these considerations. The Steenhuis study, however, usefully draws attention to total numbers of persons passing through the prison system, emphasizing that this measure is as important as prison population rate.

The main sentencing alternatives to custody in the Netherlands are suspended sentences and fines. Suspended sentencing powers were introduced in 1915 and were extended in 1929. Most forms of judicial sentence, including fines, can be suspended. Sentences can be fully or partially suspended, and since the mid-1950s courts have preferred the partially- over the fully-suspended sentence. Of particular importance, breach of a suspended sentence, as in Japan, is not usually dealt with by custody. This may explain why use of the suspended sentence in these two countries has not had the unintended consequence experienced in England of increasing pressure on the prison system. In the Netherlands it is a complicated process to invoke the suspended sentence, and the Commission on Alternative Sanctions has recommended that additional conditions be first satisfied. As a result the suspended sentence mainly has a symbolic function.

The fine is by far the most frequently used penal sanction. Courts were empowered to impose fines on a wide scale as alternatives to custody in 1925. Between 1950 and 1975 fines were used increasingly by the courts, rising from 58 per cent of all sentences in 1950 to 65 per cent in 1975. Between 1975 and 1979 the use of fines increased to 72 per cent. The Netherlands has not adopted the day fine approach of matching the fine to the offender's income, but the individual's income in practice sets the ceiling. The decline in the proportion of custodial sentences during these four years reflected this increased use of the fine. In the early 1980s, the deliberations of the Commission on Property Sanctions appear to have had an important impact on prosecutorial and sentencing practice even though legislation still has to take effect. Reports of the Commission were widely distributed and these may have been especially influential with respect to drunken driving offences, where the use of fines increased from 16 to 80 per cent between 1968 and 1978. This shift away from custody in sentencing drunken driving offences was in part due to a campaign by the Coornhert League, an influential pressure group on criminal justice issues.

Probation agencies in the Netherlands date back to the 1820s. These agencies are non-governmental and, in the main, are organized by Protestant, Catholic and non-religious organizations. The work of these agencies is largely at the pre-sentencing stage, with probation supervision being most often initiated as a consequence of a prosecutorial dismissal rather than a sentence of the court.[54] In fact, probation supervision as a court sentence has declined since 1965 when it was used in two per cent of cases. In 1975 it was used in only one per cent of cases and by 1979 even less frequently. Probation in the Netherlands has the task of helping to befriend the offender, but also has the broader purpose of influencing the criminal justice process and public opinion.

The Prison Waiting List

A customary aspect of Continental criminal procedure is to delay the start of a prison sentence where the offender was not remanded in custody up to the time of sentence.[55] In the Netherlands this procedure has been developed and manipulated by the prison system so as to reduce pressure of numbers on prison capacity. Table 6.17 shows the increase in the size of the waiting list for prison places, sometimes referred to as 'running sentences'.

Table 6.17

The prison waiting list, 1965–75, the Netherlands

	Total immediate imprisonment	Waiting list	Total per cent waiting
1965	11,872	7,934	67
1970	12,954	9,261	71
1975	14,316	10,627	74

Source: see reference 51

The waiting list process has been described by the head of the Netherlands prison system as follows: 'An important measure, which underlines the independence of the inmate and moreover may stimulate his co-operative attitude, is the system of calling people up to serve their sentences. Persons sentenced to imprisonment are divided into two categories: those remanded in custody who have to serve their sentence following the remand in custody, who number about 6,000 a year, and those sentenced to imprisonment without being remanded in custody, of whom there are about 10,000 a year. The latter are not arrested at the trial but are sent a letter inviting them to report on a certain date at a specified prison. If a person responds to the call-up, security measures against escape are considered to be superfluous. Therefore, they serve their sentence in a semi-open institution, that is to say, one without walls or fences designed to prevent escape. Moreover, on the site of the institution these prisoners are allowed almost unlimited freedom of movement.'[56]

The waiting list arrangement is a centralized system to allocate prison space by deferring the start of a sentence, which is granted on reasonable grounds. Of those called up, usually about 40 per cent report immediately, and 40–45 per cent after requesting deferment; approximately 15 to 20 per cent do not answer and have to be arrested by the police.[57] Delays of a year or more may occur but the average waiting period is about three months.[58] A build-up in the waiting list resulted from a decline in capacity in 1971 and enactment of legislation which expanded indictments for driving under the influence of alcohol, together with an increase in drug-related convictions, many of which involve imprisonment. In 1975 an attempt was made to reduce the size of the waiting list by means of a mass pardon, especially for sentences of up to fourteen days. The relief provided by this measure was only brief, and a second mass pardon was rejected by the government which feared judicial opposition. During the late 1970s the Ministry of Justice reviewed the problem of reducing the waiting list which at that time amounted to some 11,000 cases. Of this number it was estimated that only 3,300 formed an avoidable backlog with the balance being persons whose cases were being processed.[59] The call-up process has the consequence of locating the pressure point outside rather than inside the prison system. Whereas in England and parts of the United States pressure from the courts has resulted in severely overcrowded prisons, in the Netherlands overcrowding has been avoided. The use of the waiting list and call-up process in the Netherlands complements the statutory prohibition on cell-sharing.

The Prison System Estate, Personnel and Budget

The large-scale reduction in the size of the Dutch prison population was accompanied by some reduction in the physical capacity of the prison system estate, but also by a marked increase in personnel. The prison system's capacity hovered at around 4,300–4,500 between 1960 and 1967, then gradually declined to 3,100 by 1975. Since then it has increased slightly.

Sixteen prisons were closed between 1949 and 1973, but, as shown in Table 6.18, capacity began to increase in 1975, in part due to the opening of two new remand prisons. In 1975 the Maastricht local prison with 228 places was opened, followed in 1978 by the largest prison in the Netherlands, the Amsterdam local prison with 622 places. Louk Hulsman's observations on the background to this new prison construction are of considerable interest. He notes that the van Hattum Commission, reporting in 1977, recommended that contrary to the prison system's original plans further prison construction was not required. As a consequence of changes in the national economy, a number of projects conceived in the 1960s were reinstated including the Maastricht and Amsterdam institutions. Hulsman notes: 'As the implementation of such construction plans did not fall under the principal jurisdiction of the Ministry of Justice, the Ministry and the Justice Committee of Parliament were not informed at first of the Amsterdam project. The outcry which greeted the news of the project's implementation caused Parliament to adopt a motion of opposition. The Ministry of Justice however, decided that the project was too far advanced to be stopped. Therefore, the Amsterdam project is still underway and the Maastricht project has been completed. Two of the most important projects conceived since the War are thus in contradiction to the principles of officially adopted criminal policy.'[60]

After citing a study showing fairly constant prison capacity in the

Table 6.18

Capacity of the Dutch prison system 1960–78

	Capacity	Occupation factor
1960	4,546	0.75
1965	4,241	0.73
1970	3,770	0.77
1975	3,127	0.75
1978	3,555	0.94

Source: abstracted from cross-national files

Netherlands since the 1840s, David Downes poses the crucial question as to why the Dutch should regard capacity as a constant.[61] Despite the two jails constructed in the 1970s, national policy has eschewed prison building programmes. Furthermore, enshrined by statute since 1950, the one-prisoner-to-a-cell rule in the Netherlands has enabled existing capacity to impose a ceiling on prison population size.

As shown in Table 6.19, the number of prison system employees increased by 40 per cent between 1960 and 1978, and the custody staff-to-prisoner ratio in 1976 was 1:1.3 compared with 1:2.2 in 1960.

Table 6.19

Prison employees, Netherlands, 1960–76

	1960	1965	1970	1976
Custody staff	1,560	1,425	1,640	2,246
Total	2,826	2,973	3,293	3,964
Ratio of custody staff to prisoners	1:2.2	1:2.1	1:1.5	1:1.3

Source: abstracted from cross-national files

A relatively high percentage, about 30 per cent, of prison system personnel are involved in the provision of services.[62] Efforts are made by staff to keep prisoners in touch with the wider society. However, despite this heavy investment in staff and the strivings made to humanize the prison regime, the emphases of the prison system remain on the goals of security and control. Louk Hulsman claims that no real progress has been made in terms of improving the legal status of prisoners. Furthermore, Hulsman concludes that, overall, the quality of life within Dutch prisons worsened during the 1970s.[63]

Associated with the steady growth of manpower there has been a substantial increase in the prison system's budget. Between 1960 and 1978, total operating costs rose in real terms by 360 per cent. Given the decline in the prison population over this period, operating costs per head increased even more sharply, rising by over 500 per cent. As in Japan over the same period, the financial costs of the prison system rose sharply despite the significant reductions in prison population size. That prison personnel should have risen so sharply is of interest given the low numbers in the Netherlands of criminal justice personnel generally. The ratio of police to population, for example, is relatively low at 178 per 100,000 inhabitants in 1980.[64] There are only 200 public prosecutors and 700 judges who also handle civil cases and some 600 social workers involved in the criminal justice process. As Louk Hulsman comments, the imposition of an immediate custodial sentence consumes more time of criminal justice officials than do other solutions. 'The system's reduced capacity in this sense results in a strong self-limiting tendency.'[65]

The reduction in prison population size in the Netherlands between 1950 and 1975 was less the result of articulated policy than a combination of factors within and beyond the criminal justice process. In addition to citing the relatively low capacity of the criminal justice process, Louk Hulsman points to the importance of a well-developed system of social security, the extensive network of social services which is less treatment oriented than is generally the case elsewhere, and the relatively mild and informal coverage of crime issues by the media. Although there has been some increase in the remand population since 1975 there are no indications that the prison system in the Netherlands is likely to depart from its reductionist course.

Conclusion

Three examples have been described of prison populations being reduced and sustained at a new low level. Two general conditions have emerged. In each of the three countries, key decision-makers shared a profound scepticism as to what benefits, if any, derive from imprisonment. This viewpoint is exemplified by an official statement of the Japanese government in 1980, which held that although imprisonment, '. . . may achieve the correctional aims advanced to justify it, the disadvantages suffered by those undergoing imprisonment must not be overlooked. Indeed, the adverse effects are not limited to loss of liberty during confinement; imprisonment affects prisoners' social life after release, an aftermath from which their families are not exempt. Moreover, incarceration, particularly over a long period of time, weakens the ability of offenders to adapt themselves to society following release and destroys the foundation of free community life experience indispensible to reintegration into society. This in turn strongly enhances the likelihood that they will recidivate. It should also be stressed that indiscriminate and widespread use of imprisonment as a sanction against criminal conduct that is not truly serious not only imposes an un-needed financial burden on the community, but also dilutes the deterrent impact of imprisonment generally in potential criminals and thus may promote rather than hinder the commission of heinous or serious offences.'[66]

In the Netherlands widespread doubts as to the utility of prisons are expressed by many leading criminal justice practitioners who are well versed as to the negative research findings on imprisonment. One student of the Dutch penal scene has concluded: '. . . the judiciary in the Netherlands have evolved a distinctive occupational culture, central to which is the strongly negative value placed upon imprisonment, which is viewed as at best a necessary evil, and at least as a process likely to inflict progressive damage on a person's capacity to re-enter the community.'[67]

Likewise, in England between 1908 and 1938 there was considerable questioning of the prison system. This mood was set during the vigorous stewardship of the Home Office exercised by Winston Churchill between 1910 and 1911. In 1922, in the preface to the Webbs' *English Prisons Under Local Government*, George Bernard Shaw wrote: 'Imprisonment as it exists today . . . is a worse crime than any of those committed by its victims; for no single criminal can be as powerful for evil, or as unrestrained in its excercise, as an organised nation.'[68] The companion volume by Stephen Hobhouse and Fenner Brockway concluded: '. . . our prison system, while it sometimes makes good prisoners, does almost nothing to make good citizens. It fails to restore the weak will or to encourage initiative; it reduces energy by the harshness of its routine and adds depression to the depressed . . . The influences of the prison system are, therefore, not only anti-individual but anti-social as well; in both directions it debases the currency of human feeling. That debasement is its fundamental defect; and in so far as this stands proved against it, it must necessarily be judged as a failure. And the more the system costs the community, the more highly it is organized, the more monumental must that failure be.'[69]

The second general conclusion to emerge from the three case examples is that the crucial factor in understanding changes in prison population is less the level of recorded crime or known offenders but, more significant, the responses to crime by officials engaged throughout the criminal justice process. Of particular importance, in the Netherlands and Japan the criminal courts have been insulated from the impact of increasing numbers of offenders as a consequence of action taken by public prosecutors. Prosecutorial decisions to dismiss charges have been one of the most important mechanisms for achieving and sustaining reductions in prison population size. In England, during the inter-war period, total numbers of persons dealt with by the courts remained fairly stable, but this was due to fewer offences cleared up by the police rather than shifts in prosecutorial practice. The critical intervening tactic was the movement away from custody in sentencing practice by the courts. In 1908, of all offences, indictable and non-indictable combined, 16 per cent received prison sentences compared with three per cent in 1938.

A further crucial component of the sustained low level of imprisonment in the Netherlands and Japan is a profound intolerance of overcrowding in prisons. In the Netherlands, since 1950 there has been a statutory prohibition on more than one prisoner being placed in a cell designed for one person. Under these circumstances, capacity acts as a powerful constraint on prison population growth and, in the absence of new construction, places a ceiling on prison population size. In Japan in the late 1940s there was also revulsion at the level of overcrowding which then existed. Total capacity of the prison system in Japan remained constant during the subsequent period of prison population decline, and by the mid-1960s there was much excess capacity.

By contrast, in England during the inter-war years capacity declined alongside a reduction in prison population size. Average daily prison population fell from 22,000 to 11,100 between 1908 and 1938, and capacity declined from 22,600 to 15,700. There was virtually no prison construction during this period, and indeed some 25 prisons were closed. In the English case, however, it is doubtful that capacity would at that time have acted as a brake in population growth. There was overcrowding at various times during the nineteenth century and first decade of the twentieth century, and excess capacity in the period up to the Second World War. Once prison population expansion got underway soon after the Second World War, overcrowding quickly reappeared. The high tolerance for crowding in England played an important part in the expansionist phase which began after 1945. It is crucial to understand why tolerance for prison overcrowding should differ so markedly from one country to another.

The experiences of the three prison systems examined in this chapter demonstrate that although reductionist policies can be pursued successfully there remain powerful tendencies towards expansion. The thirty-year reductionist phase of the English prison system was followed by a phase of relentless expansion which has persisted for over forty years. As a rate per 100,000 inhabitants the prison population is rapidly approaching what it was at its earlier zenith of the mid-nineteenth century. The contrast of two phases of the English prison system, 1908–1938 and the period since 1945, provides a sober reminder of the inherent problem of sustaining reductionist initiatives. Similarly, in the Netherlands and Japan, in the period since 1975 there have been pressures threatening to reverse reductionist gains made over the preceding twenty-five years. In the Netherlands the size of the prison estate has slightly increased along with the number of unsentenced prisoners. Despite these pressures there are no indications of a political willingness in the Netherlands to adopt an expansionist course. In Japan prison building plans exist which anticipate an increase in prison population during the 1980s. In both the Netherlands and Japan contemporary strains on the prison system in part reflect new criminal justice concerns such as the increased processing of drug-related offences. The availability of the prison system makes it especially vulnerable to new uses and serves to discourage inventive thinking as to alternative resolution. Policy and practice on the prison system dictates the scope and substance of alternatives to imprisonment. The strategic significance of alternatives to imprisonment is the focus of the next chapter.

References

1 For accounts of the events in Massachusetts see, Andrew Rutherford, *The Dissolution of the Training Schools in Massachusetts*, Columbus, Ohio: Academy for Contemporary Problems, 1974; and Lloyd Ohlin, Robert B. Coates and Allen D. Miller, 'Radical Correctional Reform: A Case Study of the Massachusetts Youth Correctional System.' *Harvard Educational Review*, **44**, 1974, pp. 74–111.

2 See, e.g. *Report of Working Party on Children and Young Persons in Custody*, Chairman, Peter Jay. NACRO, Chichester and London: Barry Rose, 1977, pp. 49–54.

3 Howard League for Penal Reform, *The Prisoner Population of the World*, London, 1936.

4 Edwin H. Sutherland, 'The Decreasing Prison Population of England', *Journal of Criminal Law and Criminology*, **24**, 1934, p. 800.

5 *Report of Prison Commissioners, England and Wales for 1908–09*, Cd 4847, 1909.

6 For a description of Churchill as Home Secretary, with particular reference to the use of executive clemency, see Leon Radzinowicz and Roger Hood, 'Judicial Discretion and Sentencing Standards: Victorian attempts to solve a perennial problem', *University of Pennysylvania Law Review*, **127**, 1979, pp. 1288–1349.

7 See, Memorandum from Winston S. Churchill to H. H. Asquith, 26 September 1910, included in Randolph S. Churchill, *Winston S. Churchill*, Volume 11, Companion, Part 2, 1907–1911, London: Heinemann, 1969, pp. 1198–1203, and p. 1204. No action was taken at that time on civil prisoners. See generally, *Report of the Abatement of Imprisonment Committee*, a confidential Home Office document prepared in 1911 and setting out for Churchill the legislative options. PRO, HO 45/10613/194534.

8 *Report of the Prison Commissioners, England and Wales for 1911–12*, Cmnd 6406, 1913, p. 8. However, not all Home Office officials shared Churchill's views. In early 1911 the Criminal Statistics for 1909 were published with an introduction by H. B. Simpson of the Home Office (writing, as the Permanent Under-Secretary noted in the forward, in a personal capacity). After making a number of general observations on the rising trend of recorded crime since 1900, Simpson went on to note an increase in the proportion of fines which defaulted. Of all fines imposed, the percentage resulting in default had increased from 15 per cent in 1900 to 20 per cent in 1909. Simpson observed: 'It may be that prison is losing the terror it once had; that imprisonment is coming to be regarded more as a misfortune than a disgrace, and that, consequently, convicted offenders are less likely than once they were, to make pecuniary sacrifice in order to escape it'. *Introduction to Judicial Statistics for England and Wales, Part 1, Criminal Statistics*, Cd 5473 1911, p. 15.

    Churchill retorted: 'the publication of the Criminal Statistics for 1909, including as they do, Mr Simpson's Memorandum, is exceedingly ill-timed, and will improbably cause me embarrassment and trouble. I regret that none of those privy to my confidential plans of Prison Reform thought fit to consult me before making this inopportune and injudicious publication'. Memorandum by Winston S. Churchill, 3 February 1911, included in Randolph S. Churchill, op. cit., note 7, p. 1245.

9 The Mental Deficiency Act of 1913 and the Criminal Justice Administration Act of 1914.

10 *Judicial Statistics, Part 1, Criminal Statistics 1910*. Cd 6071, 1912, p. 164. Although this royal amnesty did not result in the immediate release of a large number of prisoners, it did impact upon the numbers released on 'special grounds' as can be seen from the following data:

Prisoners discharged on special grounds for year ending:

1910	287
1911	1,128
1912	674
1913	296

Source: abstracted from the relevant annual reports of the Commissioners of Prisons and the Directors of Convict Prisons.

11 Home Office Supply (Report), H.C. Debates, 5th Series, vol. 19, cols. 1353–4, 20 July 1910.

12 ibid., col. 1354.

13 *Report of the Prison Commissioners for 1916–1917.* Cd 8342, p. 19. The following year the Prison Commissioners speculated as to whether the 30 per cent depletion in the number of police officers, with the outbreak of war, might have been a factor in the prison population decline.

14 *Report of the Prison Commissioners for 1918–19*, Cmd 374, 1920, p. 6. In fact, the conclusions as to the declining prison population reached by the Prison System Enquiry committee were similar to those of the Commissioners. 'The great drop between 1914–18 was due principally to war conditions – to full employment, to liquor restrictions, and to the induction of a large proportion of the male population in the army'. Hobhouse and Brockway, op. cit., p. 3.

15 *Report of Prison Commissioners for 1923–24*, Cmd 2307, 1925, pp. 6–7.

16 Sidney and Beatrice Webb, *English Prisons under Local Government*, London: Longmans, Green, 1922, p. 249.

17 ibid., p. 250. This notion was developed half a century later by Radical Alternatives to Imprisonment, with the annual 'Ball and Chain Award' to the locality making most use of custodial sentences.

18 ibid., p. 248.

19 Stephen Hobhouse and A. Fenner Brockway, *English Prisons Today, Being the Report of the Prison System Enquiry Committee*, London: Longmans, Green, 1922, p. 593.

20 ibid., pp. 49–51.

21 ibid., p. 66.

22 See, Gordon Rose, *The Struggle for Penal Reform, the Howard League and its Predecessors*, London: Stevens & Sons, 1961, p. 113. In 1933, E. Roy and Theodora Calvert, who were closely associated with the Howard League, argued, on the basis of 1930 data, that total receptions, including remand prisoners, could be reduced by 60 per cent. E. Roy Calvert and Theodora Calvert, *The Lawbreaker*, London: George Routledge, 1933, p. 145.

23 Alexander Paterson, paper prepared in 1934, included in *Paterson on Prisons*, ed. S. K. Ruck, London: Frederick Muller, 1951, p. 157.

24 F. H. McClintock and N. Howard Avison, *Crime in England and Wales*, London: Heinemann, 1968, pp. 149–52.

25 Sutherland, op. cit., note 4, p. 894.
The decline in convictions for drunkenness was indeed dramatic, as can be seen below:

1913	188,877
1923	77,094
1937	46,757

Abstracted from Herman Mannheim, *Social Aspects of Crime Between the Wars*, London: George Allen and Unwin, 1940, p. 165.

26 *Report of the Prison Commissioners for 1930*, Cmnd 4151, 1932.

27 PRO HO 45/10606/191265

28 *Report of the Committee Appointed to Inquire into the Pay and Conditions of Service at the Prisons and Borstals in England and Scotland and at Broadmoor Lunatic Asylum*, Chairman, The Earl of Stanhope. Cmd 1959, London: HMSO, 1923.

29 The turnover in heads of the English prison system was greater during this period than it had been earlier. There were two chairmen of the Prison Commission during its first four decades, between 1878 and 1921. Over the next two decades, 1921–42 there were five chairmen.

30 It might be noted that in 1885 the prison population rate in Japan was 165 per 100,000.

31 Howard League for Penal Reform, *The Prisoner Population of the World*, 1936.

32 In making cross-national comparisons, differences as to the age jurisdiction of the respective prison systems should be kept in mind. In Japan the age cut-off point between adult and juvenile justice is the 20th birthday and it is unusual for juveniles to be held by the prison system. In 1978 there were 50 under-20-year-olds held by the prison system; there were some 3,270, however, held in training schools. If these training school juveniles are included in the total population of Japan's prison population, the rate per 100,000 inhabitants increases only marginally in 1978 from 43 to 46. However, in previous years when the training school population was larger, the contribution of juveniles to the national prison population rate would have been greater, for example, in 1960 up from 83 to 94, and in 1970 up from 47 to 52.

33 *Crime Prevention and the Quality of Life*, National Statement of Japan to the Sixth United Nations Congress on the Prevention of Crime and the Treatment of Offenders, Tokyo, 1980, p. 4.

34 David H. Bayley, *Forces of Order, Police Behaviour in Japan and the United States*, Los Angeles: University of California Press, 1976.

35 *Crime Prevention and the Quality of Life*, op. cit., note 33, pp. 12–13.

36 ibid., p. 65.

37 ibid., p. 27.

38 ibid., p. 28.

39 ibid., p. 63.

40 An important consideration arising with reference to rated capacity in the Japanese prison system is whether the prisoner uses a Japanese style bed called 'Futon' (roll-away) or a western-style bed. In the case of the former for single occupancy cells, 3.77 square metres (41 sq. ft.) is required compared with 5.52 (59 sq. ft.) for the latter. Where cells are shared, the requirements are 2.6 square metres (28 sq. ft.) and 4.2 square metres (45 sq. ft.) per person, respectively. These two types of bed provide prison administrators in Japan with some flexibility in determining capacity of the prison system.

41 Working paper prepared for the Secretariat, Fifth United Nations Congress on the Prevention of Crime and the Treatment of Offenders, A/CONF. 56/6, New York, 1975, p. 67.

42 See, for example, Polly D. Smith, 'It Can Happen Here: Reflections on the Dutch System', *Prison Journal*, **58**, 1978, pp. 31–7; David Downes, 'The Origins and Consequences of Dutch Penal Policy since 1945', *British Journal of Criminology*, **22**, 1982, pp. 325–62.
    The May Committee briefly considered the reductionist path followed in the Netherlands, but did not draw any clear-cut conclusions for practice in the United Kingdom. See, *Report of the Inquiry into the United Kingdom Prison Services*, Cmnd 7673, London: HMSO, 1979, p. 44–7.

43 *Gentleman's Magazine*, May 1750, p. 235.

44 Herman Bianchi, 'Social Control and Deviance in the Netherlands' in *Deviance and Control in Europe*, ed. H. Bianchi *et al.*, London: Wiley, 1975, p. 51. See also, L. H. C. Hulsman, 'The relative mildness of the Dutch criminal justice system: an attempt at analysis', in *Introduction to Dutch Law for Foreign Lawyers*, eds. D. C. Fokkema, W. Chorus, E. H. Hundius, *et al.*, Deventer: Kluwer, 1978, pp. 373–77.

45 D. W. Steenhuis, unpublished paper for cross-national study.

46 ibid.

47 A more detailed analysis would need to take account of time on remand which counts against the length of time served by sentenced prisoners.

48 This calculation is based upon data abstracted from Netherlands Central Bureau of Statistics, *Statistical Yearbook of the Netherlands, 1981*, The Hague, 1982, Table 24; the declining detention rate appears to date from at least 1960 when Downes states it was 60 per cent. Downes, op. cit., note 42, p. 331.

49 J. J. M. van Dijk and C. H. D. Steinmetz, *The ROC Victim Surveys, 1974–1979*, The Hague: Ministry of Justice, 1980, p. 68.

50 Derived from data abstracted from *Statistical Yearbook of the Netherlands* (for 1978 and 1979), and from cross-national study files. Cases may be dismissed by prosecutors

for varying reasons, but the published statistics do not go much beyond the data given here.

51 David Downes, op. cit., note 42, p. 330.
52 ibid.
53 Dato W. Steenhuis, L. C. M. Tigges and J. J. A. Essers, 'The Penal Climate in the Netherlands: Sunny or Cloudy', *British Journal of Criminology*, **23**, 1983, pp. 1–16.
54 However, a study of a new initiative in early intervention by a probation agency achieved its intention of reducing remands in custody to only a limited extent. See, E. G. M. Nuyten-Edelbroek and L. C. M. Tigges, 'Early Intervention by a Probation Agency: A Netherlands Experiment', *Howard Journal*, **1**, 1980, pp. 42–51.
55 For example, in Sweden the waiting time for persons sentenced to imprisonment, on bail at the time of sentence, is about four months. Ekhart Kuhlhorn, draft report for cross-national study.
56 Hans Tulkens, *Some Developments in Penal Policy and Practice in Holland*, London: NACRO, 1979, p. 9.
57 ibid.
58 Downes, op. cit., note 42, p. 332.
59 'Policy problems in the penological scene', Discussion paper by the Minister of Justice, Houses of Parliament, The Hague, 1976–7.
60 L. H. C. Hulsman, 'The Evolution of Imprisonment in the Netherlands', *Revue de Droit pénal et de criminologie*, (Belgium), **57**, 1977, p. 48.
61 Downes, op. cit., note 42, pp. 337–9.
62 Cross-national study data file.
63 Hulsman, op. cit., note 60, p. 52.
64 *Statistical Yearbook of the Netherlands, 1981*, 378. It is of interest, however, to note that the number of police officers and prison personnel increased at the same rate between 1965 and 1976, by 33 per cent in both cases.
65 Hulsman, op. cit., note 60, p. 47.
66 *Crime Prevention and the Quality of Life*, op. cit., note 33, p. 62.
67 Downes, op. cit., note 44, p. 345.
68 George Bernard Shaw, preface to Sidney and Beatrice Webb, op. cit., note 16, p. vii.
69 Hobhouse and Brockway, op. cit., note 19, p. 585.

7 Punishment Without Custody

Despite the development of non-custodial sanctions during most of this century, and particularly since 1950, prison populations in many countries have continued to increase. Nowhere is this paradox more painfully visible than in England. A complex and unresolved problem facing policy-makers is the setting up and implemention of non-custodial sanctions so that they actually serve as alternatives to imprisonment. The lessons from English experience highlight a number of important considerations in any search for more effective strategies aimed at reducing prison populations.

In England the most significant non-custodial developments were the introduction of the probation order in 1907 and broad extension of powers to fine in 1948. The probation order represented a direct attempt to allow for the individualization of sentencing, and the growth of the probation service for the first sixty years of this century reflected in large measure the increased importance attached to notions of rehabilitation. The extension of the fine by the Criminal Justice Act of 1948 to cover most serious offences was designed to provide an alternative punishment to short sentences of imprisonment. In 1938 just over one quarter of all adults sentenced for indictable offences were fined. Following the 1948 Act, the fine became the most often used sanction for dealing with serious offences in England, accounting for about half of all sentences for serious offences, although, as shown in Table 7.1, the percentage had fallen to 45 in 1981.

Since the early 1960s a central theme of Home Office policy has been the widening of the powers of courts through the provision of new sanctions intended to be used as alternatives to imprisonment. Most of the new sanctions emerged as a consequence of initiatives taken by the Home Office. A particularly important role was played by the Home Secretary's Advisory Council on the Penal System, and the community service order was one of several new sanctions proposed by the Council. Other measures, such as the suspended prison sentence, resulted from initiatives outside the Home Office. The Criminal Justice Act of 1972 specifies that the suspended sentence should only be used when imprisonment would otherwise be imposed. Similar statutory guidance has not been provided with regard to other sentencing options. Even the community service order, which came into being as an alternative to custody, is not so defined by statute, although its use is limited to imprisonable offences. This *laissez-faire* approach to sentencing legislation underscores the reluctance of Parliament to restrict the discretion of the courts by going beyond the provision of general principles.

The fine, although its use declined slightly during the late 1970s, occupies the central position in the contemporary English punishment structure. Table 7.1 shows that the fine is the most frequently used sanction for all serious offences except robbery. The income generated for the government by fines in 1980–81 exceeded £100 million. After taking account of the costs of fine enforcement, including the imprisonment of fine defaulters, the net revenue produced by fines approximates the total expenditure on magistrates' courts[1] The fine and the prison system are closely interlocked with the use of imprisonment to deal with non-payment of fines. Just under one quarter of all sentenced persons received by the Prison Department in 1981 were fine defaulters, and the proportion of persons imprisoned for default of persons fined has risen since 1974. The average length of stay in prison by fine defaulters is around one month, reduced somewhat by the Criminal Law Act of 1977 which lowered the maximum sentence available to the court for a given amount of unpaid fines. There has been little support within the Home Office for removal of powers to imprison fine defaulters, and an amendment to this effect was not incorporated into the Criminal Justice Act of 1982.

One of the most striking features of sentencing practice in England between 1970 and 1980 was the steady decline in the use of probation orders, despite a 70 per cent increase in expenditure in real terms on the probation and after-care service. In fact, during the 1970s spending on the probation and after-care service rose at a faster rate than any other area of criminal justice expenditure. Over the decade the number of probation officers increased by nearly 2,000, an increase of about 60 per cent on the 1970 establishment. Despite this investment in the probation service, the number and proportion of persons placed on probation steadily fell. This decline in the use of probation has been greatest for seventeen- to twenty-year-old males. In 1970, twelve per cent of all young adult males sentenced for indictable offences were placed on probation. By 1978 this percentage had fallen to six per cent (rising to eight per cent in 1981) despite special attention directed to this age group by the Advisory Council on the Penal System which, in the Younger Report of 1974, urged '. . . the encouragement of treatment of an increasing proportion of young adults in the community, and the necessary swith of resources within the penal system in order to implement this change of policy to the benefit of public and offenders alike'.[2] In particular, the Advisory Council envisaged a greater

Table 7.1

Sentencing practice – England and Wales, 1981
(shown as percentage by total of offence type)

Indictable offence type	Discharge	Fine	Probation	Community service	Suspended prison	Immediate custody	Other	Total (000's)
Violence against person	14	48	6	4	8	14	6	50.7
Sexual offence	12	41	16	1	9	18	3	6.9
Robbery	3	3	6	3	5	73	6	4.1
Burglary	10	22	14	8	8	28	10	75.6
Theft and handling stolen goods	14	48	12	5	6	10	4	232.9
Motoring offences	4	67	2	6	9	8	0	28
Total indictable offences (including other indictable offence types)	12	45	10	5	7	15	5	464.7

Note: Discharge includes absolute and conditional discharges; probation includes supervision order against juveniles

Source: Criminal Statistics, England and Wales, 1981, pp. 164–7

proportion of young adults being dealt with under the supervision of probation officers.

The specific proposal for a new supervision and control order was never adopted, in part because of opposition by probation officers, but it remained, nonetheless, government policy to reduce the number of young persons receiving custodial sentences by greater use of the probation order. Why was government policy in this respect so singularly unsuccessful? At least four considerations are important. First, the Younger doctrine that resources be shifted from custody to the community was dismissed and later repudiated. Three years after the Younger Report, the Home Office issued the following caution: 'The possibility of financing an increase in probation-based facilities through a major shift of resources from the prison service is unrealistic; it overlooks the need for new resources to be made available to the probation service until substantial enough inroads have been made into the prison population to allow compensatory savings to be made from the prison budget. For the time being, therefore, it will not be possible as it has been previously to make the central feature of policies for the reduction of the prison population the development of facilities for the offender to be dealt with in the community, where fresh resources are required.'[3] The Home Office refused to adopt the common-sense view that short-term additional expenditure was required in order to secure long-term economies.

The later repudiation of the Younger doctrine was delivered by the May Committee report on United Kingdom prison systems in 1979: 'There has been a natural reluctance to invest in penal institutions and a preference for developing more attractive, community-based alternatives in partnership with the burgeoning social work profession . . . (which has) . . . relatively, diverted resources away from penal institutions and the staff trying to run them.'[4] The May Committee also delivered the following extraordinary admonition: 'Although we urge the very strongest support for the development of non-custodial alternatives, any notion that their development can justify an inadequate allocation of resources to penal establishments is wholly misconceived. In so far as there has been any tendency to starve the services of resources on the grounds that developing alternatives will make those resources unnecessary, then that tendency must be stifled.'[5]

The second factor associated with the failure of government policy was the gradual demise of the rehabilitative ideal during the 1970s. In particular, the results of a Home Office study of intensive probation supervision were widely disseminated. This evaluation found that offenders with moderate or high criminal tendencies and average or few personal problems fared significantly worse under intensive supervision than under normal probation supervision.[6] The consequence of these findings on the morale of probation officers appears to have been considerable, making, for example, probation officers more exclusive as to the composition of their caseloads.

As the 1970s drew to a close, more direct challenges to the rehabilitation basis of traditional probation practice took hold. One key commentary suggested, with reference to social enquiry reports prepared for the courts, that '. . . the use of treatment concepts by probation officers can actually encourage a greater use of custody', and went on to argue that probation officers should abandon treatment concepts in recommendations contained in social enquiry reports for court, cease to recommend custodial sentences and be more imaginative in putting forward alternatives to custody.[7]

The other two factors associated with the failure of government policy to boost probation at the expense of custody can be described more briefly. There was a shift of emphasis from probation order supervision towards parole supervision and other after-care activities. In 1974 the average probation order supervision caseload per officer was twenty and the after-care caseload twelve. By 1981 average caseload sizes were, respectively, sixteen and fourteen. During this same period, the number of probation officers seconded to work inside prisons increased by 25 per cent to 465 officers. Finally, the probation order has been used less as other non-custodial sanctions such as the community service order have been introduced.

Since their first appearance in 1974, community service orders have experienced a dramatically increased use. Although over 28,000 orders were made in 1981, their administration occupied less than 200 probation officers, three per cent of total probation officer strength, together with ancillary workers. The total cost of community service orders was about seven per cent of the probation budget. Community service orders are popular with the courts because of the additional sting provided by the sanction, and since 1980 have been imposed more frequently on young adult males than probation orders. In fact, rather more than half of all community service orders made involve young adults. Most community service work takes place at week-ends, and in many parts of the country involves the individual working alone rather than in a group placement. It is likely that persons with more serious offence histories will be placed in group situations.

Settings used for community service orders include community centres, youth clubs, homes for the mentally handicapped, old people's homes and projects for offenders. A report on one scheme for the years 1975–81 concluded: 'Over 150,000 hours of work have now been successfully completed by offenders under the scheme, and this unpaid effort has contributed to the quality of life of young and old, able bodied and disabled, in town and country alike.'[8] The appeal of reparation as a component of punishment cuts across widely differing philosophical positions, and there is a considerable interest in British experience with community service orders in the United States and elsewhere.

Mention should also be made of two other new non-custodial sanctions.

The Criminal Justice Acts of 1972 and 1982 made financial compensation much more readily available; courts may make an order requiring that compensation be paid for any personal injury, loss or damage resulting from the offence. In 1981 compensation orders were made in 130,000 cases, about 15 per cent of the total number of sentences, excluding motoring offences. Although courts are disinclined to combine compensation with custody, it is not apparent that the introduction of compensation orders has had an appreciable impact on the use of custodial sentences.

Since 1968 courts have been able to suspend sentences of imprisonment but not youth custody or detention centre orders. Courts were quick to make use of the suspended sentence, and in 1981 this power was used in over 38,000 cases, 43 per cent of immediate and suspended imprisonment combined. The Court of Appeal in 1969 and the Criminal Justice Act of 1972 attempted to establish the principle that the suspended sentence be used only after all other non-custodial penalties are rejected as inappropriate.[9] However, as discussed below, there are considerable doubts as to whether the suspended sentence is being used in this way.

Problems

Non-custodial sanctions are not necessarily intended by the legislature to be used as alternatives to custody, and even when so intended it does not necessarily follow that sentencers will use them in this way. Furthermore, there is disturbing evidence that sanctions which are supposedly alternatives to custody have the result of supplementing rather than replacing custody. A major and largely unresolved policy problem is how to develop alternative sanctions without the unintended consequence of widening the scope of criminal justice.[10] Furthermore, the development of non-custodial penalties may lead to insidious controls over the personal liberties of an increasing number of citizens. One sociologist has suggested that '. . . the prison is being restored into the community, in which the cracks in the solid walls of the nineteenth century prisons are allowing new forms of social control to percolate into the community with little scrutiny or public accountability'.[11] This analysis, in part, rests upon the curious premise that contemporary prison systems are being dismantled. The reality is that prisons systems, far from being in decline, are expanding and, ironically, this is taking place alongside an extension of community-based sanctions.

An obstacle to the development of non-custodial sanctions is that the prison system provides an exceptionally convenient dumping place. Imprisonment reduces pressure to be vigorous and creative in consideration of alternative sanctions by sentencers and persons making recommendations to the courts, such as probation officers, hostel wardens and others. Indeed, the very availability of the prison system encourages persons responsible for non-custodial programmes to be highly selective in their clientele. In many cases, the factor leading to custody is not the offence but the personal circumstances and 'hard-to-place' characteristics of the offender. The prison system takes the individual immediately and completely, thereby effectively stifling incentives to seek less drastic forms of intervention.

Given that getting someone into prison is absurdly easy, it is hardly remarkable that prison overcrowding often coexists with under-utilized alternatives, such as hostels administered by the probation service. Much of the difficulty arises from the selective filters created by persons responsible for the administration of alternative sanctions. Those offenders who are regarded as likely to be unresponsive to social work methods receive custodial sentences by default. Similarly, persons who present serious social or personal problems, such as homelessness, may find themselves in prison. Custody provides an immediate but short-term relief to irritants experienced by social workers and probation officers. Given its availability, the temptation to use it is often irresistable.

Even when persons are sentenced to a non-custodial punishment, they may finish up in prison as a result of breaches of the conditions imposed. A critique of the Community Treatment Project in California concluded that this intensive supervision scheme, intended as an alternative to custody for young offenders, increased rather than decreased the use of custody. This occurred because supervisors had, under this scheme, the power to impose temporary custody as a sanction and made widespread use of it; and because intensive supervision uncovered a high number of violations which returned the offender to court.[12] Several English studies have also revealed that some of the new non-custodial sanctions have had similar unintended consequences.

A Home Office study suggested that the suspended sentence was being used to replace a sentence of imprisonment in only 40 to 50 per cent of cases.[13] Furthermore, as a consequence of the imposition of a consecutive sentence, if the suspended sentence is breached, the suspended sentence has had the result of increasing pressure on the English prison system. An analysis by Tony Bottoms of the first ten years of the suspended sentence concluded: '. . . those who are anxious to reduce the prison population cannot afford to ignore the role of the suspended sentence in helping indirectly to contribute to the total number of people incarcerated.'[14] Rather similar conclusions have been reached with regard to the use of the community service order, with most studies estimating that community service orders serve as alternatives to custody in 45 to 50 per cent of cases. Ken Pease has argued that the community service order may have been placed too high on the penal sanctions ladder and proposed a two-tier scheme of community service where only community service orders exceeding 100 hours be regarded as alternatives to custody, with the number of hours ordered to match prison sentence lengths.[15] This proposal may give weight to arguments for raising the existing 240 hour maximum for community service orders so that greater equivalence with custodial terms is available.

Reform of the suspended sentence is less viable, and the case for its removal in England is very powerful. However, as noted in Chapter 6, the suspended sentence has not had these negative consequences in the Netherlands and Japan where, indeed, it has played a part in the reductionist policies which have been successfully pursued. In large measure, the difference has to do with the consequences of any breach of suspended imprisonment. In the Netherlands and Japan, where breach only rarely leads to imprisonment, the suspended sentence has contributed to stretching the punishment tariff. In England, it has had the reverse effect.

Ways Forward

The English experience of new non-custodial sanctions exemplifies the immense problems of developing rational sentencing practice. There is no reason to expect sentencing practice to match statutory intent. New sanctions will not replace custody unless more is done than merely espousing that intent. Four strategies are discussed, and these should be viewed not as mutually exclusive but representing a continuum.

Packaging Alternative Sanctions

The growth of community service orders in England suggests that if alternatives to custody are to be seriously considered, intermediate sanctions with sting are likely to have most appeal to sentencers. This might be achieved by legislating new sentencing powers or, within the existing framework, by encouraging courts to accept recommendations which meet the requirements of a specific sentencing situation. One or two English probation areas have taken tentative steps towards this tailoring or packaging concept, but resistance has been encountered from probation officers. This resistance arose perhaps, in part, because there was no built-in provision that extra resources would be available to match the additional work entailed. One study concluded that apart from the project organizer and staff at headquarters, few others had much desire for change.[16]

Since 1979, the National Center for Institutions and Alternatives in Washington D.C., under the leadership of Jerome Miller, has been working with defence counsel preparing sentencing packages in cases where a prison sentence seems likely. This fee-paying service has developed independently of probation services, although a probation officer usually assumes responsibility for subsequent oversight of the court's order. One case involved three 19-year-old youths who set fire to their former school in Virginia, causing over $4 million worth of damage. With the prosecution demanding long prison terms, the defence attorneys called in the National Center, and an alternative proposal was submitted to the court. In the case of one of the youths, the sentencing package consisted of repayment of $10,000 over the next ten years, 3,000 hours of unpaid community service (six hours per day for five days per week for a minimum of two years) as an aide to severly mentally handicapped persons, and agreement to undergo alcohol abuse counselling. It was agreed that the court would be furnished with monthly progress reports. The youth also received two years imprisonment, one of which was suspended but, as he had been held in jail for nearly a year since the offence, he was released to commence the alternative sanction. This project has expanded beyond the Washington D.C. area, involving courts at both the state and federal level.

Behaviour Modification of Sentencers by Fiscal Incentives
The packaging of alternative sanctions is an extension of the approach followed through the 1970s of enhancing the choices available to courts. Its appeal is its individualization, but this also represents a principal shortcoming for purposes of general usage. An alternative strategy is to bring powerful influences to bear on sentencing practice. One tactic, attempted primarily in the United States, has been to shape sentencing decisions by means of financial incentives and disincentives. In 1967 California introduced a probation subsidy scheme by which the legislature sought to reduce committals to state prisons and youth institutions. Essentially, the aim was to encourage county government to retain responsibility for a larger proportion of sentenced offenders by paying counties a subsidy for probation agencies where a reduction in the committal rate to state institutions was achieved.

The scheme, which remained operational until 1978, had mixed results. State adult and youth custodial populations fell sharply, and the counties participating in the scheme received considerable revenues for their probation services, amounting to $200 million. In 1968, when the subsidy scheme commenced, the California state prison population was about 23,500. By 1975 the prison population had declined to 16,300 but over the next five years it returned to almost the pre-subsidy scheme level. During this latter period prison sentences as a proportion of all sentences also rose sharply. Almost from its inception the subsidy scheme was under strong attack from police chiefs and others who blamed it for rising rates of recorded crime. The legislature failed to adjust the funding formula to take account of inflation, and the scheme lost potency.[17] In 1978, new legislation was enacted allowing subsidy funds to be distributed across criminal justice agencies. However, the state agencies were allowed discretion as to whether to withhold subsidies from counties which increased committals, and the revised scheme had little impact and was to be overtaken by other events.

Minnesota took the subsidy approach a stage further with the Community Corrections Act of 1973. The Minnesota formula provides a state subsidy for the development of community-based correctional programming by participating counties, and a charge is imposed on participating counties for commitals to state institutions in cases which the Act aims to divert. Underlying the legislation was the view that greater efficiency and economy would be achieved by a shift of resources from institutions to community-based programmes and from state to county government. Each participating county is obliged to establish a Corrections Advisory Board, serving as a forum in which information can be exchanged and local corrections policy discussed, and involving representatives from criminal justice, social welfare, education, county government and the general public. By July 1978, 25 counties constituting 60 per cent of the state population had chosen to come under the Act.

Preliminary studies of the impact of the Minnesota Community Corrections Act suggest rather mixed results. Research undertaken by the state prison system concluded that some persons being sent to residential community correction centres would probably have been placed on probation in the absence of the centre and would not have been sent to prison.[18] On the other hand, a study funded by the federal government found that participating counties sentenced significantly fewer offenders to state prison than did non-participating counties. For the three years after the legislation, release decisions had a greater impact on prison population size and accounted for the increase which took place.[19]

The California and Minnesota subsidy schemes should be regarded as tentative steps in search of mechanisms which reverse the trend towards increased centralization of criminal justice. While research findings point to the inherent dangers of widening the criminal justice net, there is a powerful case for shifting responsibility for criminal justice from central to local goverment. When the high financial costs of imprisonment are borne by local government, it seems likely that more sparing use will be made of prison. This point is reinforced by the consideration that the key decision-makers at the front of the criminal process are largely local rather than central government officials. Localized delivery of punishment would, in Nils Christie's phrase, be more vulnerable and would therefore be more controllable.[20]

Legislative restrictions on sentencers
These two examples of state governments in the United States attempting to regulate the size of prison populations highlight the complexity of the task of influencing the wide spectrum of decision-makers within criminal justice. The examples serve as reminders that experience from one jurisdiction is not always easily applied elsewhere. Account has to be taken of varied sets of prevailing conditions and circumstances.

A third strategy for legislative action goes a stage further and would seek to curb sentencing powers of the courts. Legislation might, for example, be introduced to make more offences non-imprisonable beyond the existing number which are largely regulatory offences. Yet this strategy may have little impact. For example, in England the offence of being drunk and disorderly was, in 1978, made non-imprisonable.[21] However, persons fined for this offence have continued to be imprisoned in default of payment of fines, as can be seen from Table 7.2 below. If this strategy is to be successful, the principle of making petty offences non-imprisonable must apply also to default on sanctions such as fines.

Table 7.2

Adult males received by the English prison system for drunkenness under sentence or in default of fine payment, 1977–81

	Immediate imprisonment	In default of fine payment	Total
1977	381	2,097	2,478
1978	23	2,465	2,488
1979	NIL	2,791	2,791
1980	1	2,304	2,305
1981	1	2,048	2,049

Source: based on figures abstracted from the relevant volumes of Prison Statistics, England and Wales, 1977–81

Recent experience in the United States prompts caution as to the efficacy of legislative reform. A study of the impact of new sentencing statutes on prison and jail populations in five states concluded: '. . . that when any system is confronted with legislative changes in procedure, capability or sanction, the behaviour of key actors probably changes as little as necessary to comply and as much as possible to mediate the perceived disruption of the change.'[22] Sentencing is not a discrete act located in the courtroom, but should be seen as a composite of decisions commencing with arrest. A statute widening the scope of non-imprisonable offences may simply be nullified at the prosecutorial stage by changes in charging practice.

The significance of prison capacity and structural sentencing
Alternatives to custodial sentences are unlikely to emerge without reductions in prison capacity. There is some evidence that the amalgam of decisions which constitute the sentencing process are influenced by perceptions of available custodial capacity. It was noted in the previous chapter that the Netherlands is by statute bound to the rule of one man per cell, thereby fixing a ceiling on prison system population and prompting the extensive use of tactics such as the waiting list. The industrial dispute by prison officers in England during the winter of 1980–81 also demonstrated

that prison population size could be reduced by a refusal to allow population to exceed certified capacity. During the last quarter of 1980, the prison population fell from 44,000 to just below 40,000, including persons held in army camp accommodation and police cells. The impact was greatest with respect to remand prisoners and persons serving short sentences including fine defaulters. The dispute was settled in mid-January 1981 and by the end of March the prison population had returned to around 44,000.[23] Even allowing for seasonal factors, the decrease in prison population size over these few months was the most significant to occur since 1945.

Reductionist policies need to acknowledge the informal nature of much of the decision-making at the various stages of the criminal justice process. In particular, such policies are likely to be successful only if it is recognized that sentencing practice is unlikely to match rational design. A ceiling on custodial capacity encourages informal processes to produce results not too far removed from the intended direction.

It is essential to consider the strategic role of alternative sanctions in reducing the use of imprisonment. In England, Parliament has ducked the difficult task of articulating the principles from which a jurisprudence of sentencing might emerge. Indeed in some respects, legislation has moved in the contrary direction and has increased discretion without providing sentencers with guidance. For example, the Theft Act of 1968 consolidated eleven varieties of larceny, each with its own maximum penalty, into one statutory definition of theft, with a maximum penalty of ten years. This trend in the drafting of criminal law statute is in contrast to the elaborate Continental penal codes which were developed in the mid-nineteenth century. The scene in England was decried as early as 1836 by the Criminal Law Commissioners, who observed: 'The scarcity of distinctions defining the gradations of guilt and annexing commensurate penalties constitutes a remarkable characteristic of the Criminal Law of this country. Offences, bearing little moral resemblance to each other, are by sweeping definitions, frequently classed together without discrimination as to penal consequences.'[24] Attempts during the remainder of the nineteenth century to fashion penal codes which went in the direction of confining sentencing discretion were repeatedly blocked by the judiciary and their supporters. Even after the Consolidation Act of 1861, the discretionary powers of the courts remained as wide as ever. Parliament bowed to pressure and set its face against a grand design.[25]

Reluctance by legislators to develop sentencing principles has been evident throughout the twentieth century. Not only has consolidation of criminal statutes widened judicial sentencing discretion, but new types of sentences have been added without legislative guidance as to how these measures relate to existing sanctions. These developments have greatly added to the complexity of the sentencing task. Andrew Ashworth has noted that much of the proliferation of new sentences has occurred in the crucial area of deciding between a custodial and non-custodial sentence with, 'precious little guidance on their use as an integrated set of alternatives'.[26]

Only in the case of the suspended sentence has Parliament attempted to locate its position on the tariff but, as reviewed earlier, sentencers have often used the suspended sentence in ways not intended by the legislature. If a new sanction is intended to provide an alternative to imprisonment, the question must be put as to whether its effect is likely to stretch or contract the tariff. Louk Hulsman has raised this issue with respect to proposals in the Netherlands to introduce the community service order. 'It goes without saying that by introducing a new method of dealing with offenders, such as community service, a real danger is created that the new methods will be applied to cases other than those which are now covered by custodial sentences. Considering that community service encroaches quite deeply into the life of those involved, such a development could increase the total impact and intervention of the criminal justice system instead of decreasing it. This would not be acceptable. An important criterion for judging the desirability of introducing any new penalty is thus whether reasonable guarantees can be created that such a development will not occur.'[27]

In England, it might have been expected that the Court of Appeal would have generated a rich case law on the decision to imprison. This the Court of Appeal has failed to do, preferring to articulate the tariff in terms of lengths of custodial sentences.[28] Since the early 1980s the Court of Appeal has attempted more actively to reduce the length of prison sentences, but in doing so it has attached importance to what David Thomas has described as the 'clang of the gates' principle. This principle holds that petty property offenders benefit from the shock of a brief period in custody. If magistrates courts were to apply this principle more diligently in cases similar to those endorsed by the Court of Appeal the number of custodial sentences would in fact increase. The 'clang of the gates' principle bears some resemblance to the concept of 'shock probation' in the United States which involves a brief taste of custody prior to probation supervision. The use of custody for shock purposes is consistent with the dualistic function of the prison system, described in Chapter 3, to accommodate both serious and petty offenders.

A more direct approach towards structuring sentencing decisions developed in the United States during the 1970s under the term 'sentencing guidelines'. In large part, the impetus for sentencing guidelines has been concern regarding disparities in sentencing practice rather than any need to establish basic principles. In several states the new sentencing statutes have sought to achieve mandatory minimum prison terms for a range of offences. Legislation of this type was vetoed by the governor of Minnesota because of a drafting oversight, providing the opportunity for consideration to be given to a different approach. The statute of 1978 established a Sentencing Guidelines Commission which is entrusted with the task of structuring judicial discretion by setting guidelines for the use and length of prison sentences.[29] The state legislature delegated to the Commission the complex considerations and questions concerning punishment.

The Minnesota Sentencing Guidelines Commission has described its mission as follows: 'The purpose of the sentencing guidelines is to establish rational and consistent sentencing standards which reduce sentencing disparity and ensure that sanctions following conviction of a felony are proportionate to the severity of the offence of conviction and the extent of the offender's criminal history.'[30] Judges may sentence outside the recommended guideline if written reasons are provided. Several factors are specified by the Commission as not constituting appropriate reasons, and these include race, sex, educational attainment, employment and marital status.

As can be seen from the sentencing guidelines displayed in Table 7.3, offences are placed into one of ten categories, the exception being first degree murder which carries a mandatory life sentence. The primary factor is the immediate offence on which a conviction has been obtained with secondary weight given to criminal history. The Minnesota guidelines, unlike related developments in other states, did not avoid difficult values questions. 'Our information on sentencing practices and sentencing disparity lead us to conclude that the guidelines must produce substantial changes in past sentencing and releasing practices if significant reductions in disparity were to be achieved.'

Research by the Commission found that the majority of violent offenders with low criminal histories were not committed to state prisons, despite the fact that they were convicted of crimes involving a weapon, and, therefore, subject to mandatory imprisonment provisions; and a large number of property offenders, generally with moderate or longer criminal histories, were being committed to state prisons despite the legislative policies embodied in the Community Corrections Act. As can be seen from the grid, the guidelines recommend that imprisonment be presumptive for persons convicted of offences of aggravated robbery, assault in the first degree and other more serious violent offences. On the other hand, for the great majority of less serious crimes the presumption is for non-custodial sentences, such as fines, restitution, community service and probation. However, it should be noted that probation may be imposed concurrently with periods of confinement in local jails.

The Minnesota legislation specifies that sentencing guidelines be implemented in a manner consistent with the resources of the prison system.[31] The Commission noted that sentencing reforms elsewhere had resulted in, '. . . massive increases in prison populations. Most of the population increases have been attributed to changes in sentencing behaviour and very

Table 7.3
Minnesota sentencing guidelines grid

(presumptive sentence length shown in months; italicised numbers within the grid denote the range within which a judge may sentence without the sentence being deemed a departure.)

Criminal History Score

Severity Levels of Conviction Offense		0	1	2	3	4	5	6 or more
Unauthorized Use of Motor Vehicle Possession of Marijuana	I	12*	12*	12*	15	18	21	24 23-25
Theft Related Crimes ($150-$2500) Sale of Marijuana	II	12*	12*	14	17	20	23	27 25-29
Theft Crimes ($150-2500)	III	12*	13	16	19	22 21-23	27 25-29	32 30-34
Burglary-Felony Intent Receiving Stolen Goods ($150-$2500)	IV	12*	15	18	21	25 24-26	32 30-34	41 37-45
Simple Robbery	V	18	23	27	30 29-31	38 36-40	46 43-49	54 50-58
Assault 2nd Degree	VI	21	26	30	34 33-35	44 42-46	54 50-58	65 60-70
Aggravated Robbery	VII	24 23-25	32 30-34	41 38-44	49 45-53	65 60-70	81 75-87	97 90-104
Assault 1st Degree Criminal Sexual Conduct, 1st Degree	VIII	43 41-45	54 50-58	65 60-70	76 71-81	95 89-101	113 106-120	132 124-140
Murder, 3rd Degree	IX	97 94-100	119 116-122	127 124-130	149 143-155	176 168-184	205 195-215	230 218-242
Murder, 2nd Degree	X	116 111-121	140 133-147	162 153-171	203 192-214	243 231-255	284 270-298	324 309-339

1st Degree Murder is excluded from the guidelines by law and continues to have a mandatory life sentence.

*one year and one day

Note: Cells *below* heavy line receive a presumptive prison sentence. Cells *above* the heavy line receive a presumptive non-prison sentence (and the numbers in those cells refer only to duration of confinement if non-prison sentence is revoked).

'The Commission urges judges to utilize the least restrictive conditions of stayed sentences that are consistent with the objectives of the sanction. When rehabilitation is an important objective of a stayed sentence, judges are urged to make full use of local programs and resources available to accomplish the rehabilitative objectives. The absence of a rehabilitative resource, in general, should not be a basis for enhancing the retributive objective in sentencing and, in particular, should not be the basis for more extensive use of incarceration than is justified on other grounds. The Commission urges judges to make expanded use of restitution and community work orders as conditions of a stayed sentence, especially for persons with short criminal histories who are convicted of property crimes, although the use of such conditions in other cases may be appropriate. Supervised probation should continue as a primary condition of stayed sentences. To the extent that fines are used the Commission urges the expanded use of day fines which standardizes the financial impact of the sanction among offenders with different income levels.'[32]

little appears to be attributed to changes in crime rates. The sentencing guidelines were developed so that the state prison capacity of 2,072 beds will not be exceeded as a result of changes in sentencing.' The intention was not to increase the state prison population but to alter its composition by increasing the proportion of violent offenders and reducing that of property offenders. The guidelines became operational in 1981 and apply only to felons and do not as yet extend to sentences other than state imprisonment.[33] The jail population in Minnesota has been increasing since 1973, but it is difficult to estimate what proportion, if any, of the increase which took place since 1980 can be attributed to the use of sentencing guidelines. It is important to note that the Minnesota guidelines have served a standstill rather than a reductionist policy. Given the conservative political climate of the early 1980s, even in Minnesota, a standstill policy was probably the best that could be achieved; and the legislation is unlikely to have been enacted had it been presented in reductionist terms. Compared with the sharp increases in state prison populations elsewhere, the Minnesota sentencing guidelines can be credited with a considerable achievement.

The developments in Minnesota are of particular relevance to jurisdictions which articulate the issue in these terms: is it possible to develop a sentencing process focused on the offence rather than the offender and insisting on justice and fairness which does not lead to an increase in the prison population? Sweden, for example, has established a commission to examine non-custodial penalties with the purpose of finding new ways of stretching the tariff. The strategic problem is holding on to recidivists in community programmes given that traditional probation supervision appears ill-equipped for this task. Options being considered by the Swedish Commission include intensive probation supervision and the community service order.[34] The Commission is also examining, in the context of a discredited rehabilitative ideal, sentencing guidelines as a means of standardizing sentencing practice. A central concern in Sweden about fairness in sentencing practice arises with reference to the disposition of persons convicted of drunken driving. Most drunken drivers in Sweden can expect on conviction to be sentenced to prison, usually for one month; but if the individual is involved in other offences rehabilitative criteria are taken into account, and the sentence may well be probation.

Swedish commentators on criminal justice problems describe the main policy thrust as being neo-classicist, by which is meant a return to giving primary consideration to the seriousness of the offence but with important modifications. In particular, the general deterrent function of the penal code is stressed, so that the relative severity of criminal offences is articulated. Sentencing guidelines provide one means of doing this. Whereas in Minnesota a higher premium is placed on violent offences, in Sweden it is drug-dealing offences which are likely to be accorded greater severity.[35]

Conclusion

It should be re-emphasized that there is always a danger that alternatives to custody will supplement rather than replace existing custodial arrangements. In introducing a new non-custodial sanction, careful attention has to be given to where this sanction fits into the existing sentencing tariff. Of importance also are the consequences of further offending while the non-custodial sanction is in force. Practice with the suspended sentence in England has almost certainly contributed to an increase in the number and length of prison sentences. If alternatives to prison fail to replace the prison sentence, the result is to widen the criminal justice net.

An associated danger has to do with the nature of the non-custodial penalties themselves. Very intensive forms of supervision may be so highly restrictive of individual freedom that they threaten the basic values of democratic society. House arrest, for example, may be less restrictive than imprisonment, but contradicts assumptions about individual freedom. Modified forms of house arrest, such as curfews as a penal sanction, raise similar questions. Intermittent custody, for example, week-end imprisonment, fudges the distinction between custody and alternative sanctions. If custody is to be regarded as a last resort, boundaries must be clearly defined. If the essential feature of imprisonment, the deprivation of liberty, is blurred, custody may be used even more widely. This is not to argue for the bastille prison, but to emphasize that the distinction between prison and its alternatives should be drawn with precision.

A critical problem remains to devise means by which non-custodial sanctions might be used to reduce the scale of the prison system and to avoid expansion of non-custodial sanctions alongside an expanding prison system. For reductionist policy to be effective, the sequence of reform strategies may be crucial. Pouring resources into alternative programmes is unlikely by itself to make a significant dent on the prison population size. The alternative sanctions simply may not be used, or, as is more likely, they will be used, but for persons already being dealt with outside the prison system.

Reductionist policy must aim to restrict not only the prison system, but the scope of criminal justice. For these objectives to be achieved, the sequence of the reform agenda would seem to be clear. To use a phrase associated with the closure of custodial institutions for youth in Massachusetts, 'a deep-end strategy' is likely to be most effective. By this is meant attention is given first to contracting the size of the prison system, the deep-end of the criminal justice process. Only after steps have been taken in this direction do alternative sanctions serve a strategic role. The deep-end strategy reverses the conventional wisdom regarding alternative sanctions which is that when these are made available, less use will be made of custody. There is sufficient experience available to be confident that this is an unlikely outcome. For alternative sanctions to replace custody, it is necessary that such sanctions be used not as a pre-condition, but as a consequence to contraction of the prison system. In Chapter 8, this and related issues concerning the reductionist agenda are explored.

References

1 Stephen Shaw, *Paying the Penalty: An Analysis of the Cost of Penal Sanctions*, London: NACRO, 1980, pp. 37–9. On fines generally, see, Rod Morgan and Roger Bowles, 'Fines: The Case for Review', *Criminal Law Review*, 1981, pp. 203–14.

2 Advisory Council on the Penal System, *Young Adult Offenders*, Chairman, Sir Kenneth Younger, London: HMSO, 1974, pp. 56–7.

3 *Home Office, A Review of Criminal Justice Policy, 1976*, London: HMSO, 1977, p. 7. This view was elaborated upon by a senior Home Office official. '. . . a policy of transferring *x* prisoners to treatment of some sort in the community would be supported by many. But resources for their treatment would have to be additional resources. The allocation of resources to the custodial side could not be reduced in anticipation of a drop in demand; nor indeed, unless *x* was a very large number of prisoners, would even their departure free substantial resources, given the degree of overcrowding of buildings and over-stretch of staff. Hence, it is difficult to avoid a frozen system, with little possibility even of changes that would in the longer term make it cheaper or more efficient'. Michael Moriarty, 'The Policy-Making Process: How it is seen from the Home Office', in *Penal Policy-Making in England*, Cambridge: Institute of Criminology, 1977, p. 141.

4 *Report of the Inquiry into the United Kingdom Prison Services*, Chairman, Mr. Justice May, Cmnd 7673, London: HMSO, 1979, pp. 59–60.

5 ibid., p. 152.

6 M. S. Folkard, D. E. Smith and D. D. Smith, *IMPACT, Intensive Matched Probation and After-Care Treatment*, Home Office Research Unit Report No. 36, London: HMSO, 1976.

7 A. E. Bottoms and William McWilliams, 'A Non-Treatment Paradigm for Probation Practice', *British Journal of Social Work*, **9**, 1979, pp. 179–87.

8 Hampshire Probation and After-Care Service, *Community Service By Offenders In Hampshire – Planning for the Future*, Winchester, 1981, p. 16; it should be noted that community service orders involve a maximum of 240 hours and a minimum of 40 hours.

9 *R. v. O'Keefe* (1969) 2 Q.B. 29.

10 The Scandinavian prisoners' rights movements challenged the conventional way in which alternatives to imprisonment were considered. For example, in opposing the introduction of British-style detention centres into Norway, KROM learned that this could successfully be accomplished without putting forward alternatives, which essentially served the same function. See, Thomas Mathiesen, *The Politics of Abolition*, London: Martin Robertson, 1974, pp. 86–90.

11 Stanley Cohen, 'Prisons and the Future of Control Systems: From Concentration to Dispersal' in *Welfare in Action*, ed. M. Fitzgerald *et al.*, London: Routledge and Kegan Paul, 1977, pp. 217–28.

12 Paul Lerman, *Community Treatment and Social Control*, Chicago: University of Chicago Press, 1975.

13 E. Oatham and F. Simon, 'Are Suspended Sentences Working?', *New Society*, **21**, 1972, pp. 233–5.

14 A. E. Bottoms, 'The Suspended Sentence in England, 1967–1978', *British Journal of Criminology*, **21**, 1981, p. 25.

15 Ken Pease, 'Community Service and the Tariff', *Criminal Law Review*, 1978, pp. 269–75.

16 Colin Eden and Stephen Fineman, 'A Fitting Role', *Community Care*, **287**, 1979, pp. 20–21.

17 For early descriptions of the California Probation Subsidy Scheme, see Robert H. Smith, *A Quiet Revolution – Probation Subsidy*, Washington D.C.: U.S. Dept of Health, Education and Welfare, 1971; and Andrew Rutherford, 'The California Probation Subsidy Scheme', *British Journal of Criminology*, **12**, 1972, pp. 186–8. A critical analysis is provided by Paul Lerman, op. cit., note 12.

18 Minnesota Department of Corrections, *The Effect of the Availability of Community Residential Alternatives to State Incarceration on Sentencing Practices: The Social Control Issue*, St Paul, Minnesota, 1977.

19 National Institute of Justice, *American Prisons and Jails*, Volume IV: Supplemental Report, Case Studies of New Legislation Governing Sentencing and Release, Washington D.C.: Government Printing Office, 1981, pp. 91–105.

20 Nils Christie, *Limits to Pain*, Oxford: Martin Robertson, 1982, pp. 85–8.

21 By means of Section 91 of the Criminal Justice Act of 1967, brought into effect on 1 February 1978.

22 *American Prisons and Jails*, Vol. IV, op. cit., note 19, p. 126.

23 Home Office Statistical Bulletin, 12, *Changes in the prison population during the industrial action by the POA*, 1981.

24 Second Report of His Majesty's Commissioners on Criminal Law, 1836, cited by Leon Radzinowicz and Roger Hood, 'Judicial Discretion and Sentencing Standards, Victorian attempts to solve a perennial problem'. *University of Pennysylvania Law Reform*, **127**, 1979, p. 1293.

25 ibid., p. 1304.

26 A. J. Ashworth, 'Judicial Independence and Sentencing Reform', paper presented to Cambridge Criminology Conference, 1979, p. 14.

27 L. H. C. Hulsman, 'Penal Reform in the Netherlands: Part II – Criteria for deciding alternatives to imprisonment'. *Howard Journal*, **1**, 1982, p. 36.

28 The Court of Appeal has, however, attempted to develop guidelines with respect to the partly suspended sentence, see *R*. v. *Clarke*, *Criminal Law Review*, 1982, pp. 464–7.

29 For an account of the legislative history, see Dale G. Parent, 'Minnesota's New Sentencing Guidelines Legislation', *Hennepin Lawyer*, Sept.–Oct. 1978, pp. 14–17.

30 Minnesota Sentencing Guidelines and Commentary, August 1981, p. 1. The enactment of sentencing guidelines in Minnesota has overtaken earlier reform initiatives in that state such as the community corrections subsidy scheme reviewed earlier.

31 The statute states that the Sentencing Guidelines Commission take account of '. . . correctional resources including but not limited to the capacities of local and state correctional facilities' (Ch. 723, Section 9). This section of the statute was inserted at the request of the state prison system.

32 Minnesota Sentencing Guidelines, op. cit., note 30, p. 31; the grid is shown on p. 27.

33 The Commission has noted that about 80 per cent of convicted felons in Minnesota receive non-state prison sentences. Guidelines to cover these cases which were, 'developed without adequate consideration to policy and resources implications, could create unintended disruptions in current practices and cause serious resource problems'. Minnesota Sentencing Guidelines and Commentary, ibid., p. 26.

34 There is little enthusiasm in Sweden for an extension of day fines as this would run counter to assumptions regarding basic welfare provision. Information concerning the Commission on Non-Custodial Penalties was provided by Professor Eckhart Kuhlhorn of the University of Stockholm.

35 For a review of sentencing policy and practice, with respect to narcotics offences, see, Jan Andersson and Artur Solarz, *Drug Criminality and Drug Abuse in Sweden*, 1969–1981, Stockholm: The National Swedish Council for Crime Prevention, Report No. 10, 1982, pp. 35–44.

8 The Reductionist Agenda

Most contemporary prison systems are expanding through a combination of drift and design. Criminal justice administrators perpetuate the myth that the prison system is swept along by forces beyond their control or influence. The convenient conclusion is announced that, given increased rates of reported crime and court workloads, it inevitably follows that there is no alternative other than for the prison system to expand further. Strategies which might shield the prison system from increases in persons processed by criminal justice have been disregarded and administrators have preferred to proceed as though policy choices do not exist. In large part, criminal justice administrators are the architects of the crisis with which they are now confronted.

Reductionist policy has as its underlying premise that the prison system should deal only with persons sentenced or remanded in connection with serious crime. As a starting point, reductionist policy recognizes that most prison systems are bogged down in dealing with relatively minor offenders. Indeed minor offenders are the staple fodder from which the expanding prison system feeds. The reductionist alternative seeks strategies aimed at barring the entry of minor offenders from the prison system and, if such persons do enter, of effecting their expeditious removal.

Some prison systems are proactively expanionist and pursue growth by design. Most typically, expansion occurs in the absence of coherent policy and takes a reactive stance to perceived demands made by other segments of the criminal justice process or by various interest groups. In England since the early 1980s prison system policy has followed an expansionist course and has displayed both reactive and proactive elements. The view that an alternative policy direction is urgently required has been expressed in a series of reports by Parliamentary and other committees.[1] Most of these reports, however, have proposed what amounts to standstill policy. For example, although the Home Affairs Committee of the House of Commons concluded that the public interest would not suffer from a diminished use of imprisonment and went on to recommend a number of strategies by which the size of the English prison population might be reduced, its report remained firmly within the standstill frame of reference. 'We would emphasize that we do not regard the provision of additional resources for the prison system and the reduction of the prison system as alternatives; the two are complementary, and both are necessary to a resolution of the present crisis.'[2]

This viewpoint echoes the official theme, articulated by prison system administrators, of aligning the supply of resources and the demand for prison places. Standstill policy is not in the long term a viable alternative to expanding prison systems; at best short-term relief from population pressures is provided. Furthermore, standstill policy fails to take account of the extent to which the size of the prison population is determined by the capacity of the prison system and of the criminal justice process as a whole. A supply-led view of the criminal justice process should be accompanied by profound caution before resources are increased to match actual or forecasted increases in crime.

Crises which would undermine the foundations of most other organizations tend, instead, to generate yet further resources for the prison system. In the mid-1960s the English prison system was gravely shaken by embarrassing lapses of security. The result of the Mountbatten Inquiry was the injection of greatly increased manpower and capital resources. Twelve years later there were signs indicating that management had lost control of English prisons to local branches of the Prison Officers' Association. The result was a recommendation by the May Committee to further escalate prison system expenditure. Just as rationales change for increasing resources for the prison system so do the justifications for imprisonment. Notions of general deterrence gave way to those of rehabilitation which, in turn, have been superseded by the language of selective incapacitation and individual deterrence. The new expansionist phase in England leans most heavily upon two justifications: the incapacitation of serious offenders and individual deterrence for minor offenders. This dualistic approach to prison purposes, if given full expression in penal practice, will ensure prison population growth in excess of that forecasted by the Home Office.

By the early 1980s, standstill policy regarding the English prison system had been abandoned for reactive expansionism. The Home Secretary declared, to the applause of his political colleagues, that room would be found in the prison system for all persons whom the courts wished to send. Home Office forecasts of prison population during the 1980s were revised upwards to take account of modified assumptions about 'demand'. For example, the forecast published in March 1982 concerning the size of the English prison population in 1984 increased by ten per cent the projection made a year before. The anticipated total of 47,000 prisoners first published by the Home Office in 1978 for 1987 had by 1982 been brought forward to 1984.[3]

Forecasting prison population size does not occur in a political vacuum and is usually closely related to the allocation of public funds.[4] Prison population forecasting plays a crucial part in expansionist policy-making, and it is insufficiently appreciated that it is not possible to forecast prison population size accurately, even over the short-term. A forecasted prison population is no more than a set of assumptions, particularly in relation to prosecution and sentencing practice. If the forecast turns out to be accurate, it may well be by chance. In England, as in America, where expansionist prison system policies reign, the forecasting method is to present a single scenario of the future. Single scenario forecasting assumes that the size of the population is determined by external forces and that these are largely beyond regulation.[5] Although caveats may be made as to reliability, especially with reference to long-term forecasts, the multiple scenario method is eschewed. Multiple scenarios of the future highlight the point which expansionist administrators prefer to obscure, namely that policy choices on prison population size exist and need to be made.

The long-range Home Office forecast is for a prison population in England of about 52,000 by 1989. A prison population of this size represents a rate per 100,000 inhabitants of 110, close to the rate of 118 reached in 1878 when the English prison system was formally established.[6] From a reductionist standpoint, it is more appropriate to use the term 'target' rather than forecast. The Home Office target of over 52,000 by 1990 and the plans for increased expenditure to support it can be either accepted or rejected. If rejected, a new and much reduced target might be selected.

Targets of prison population size, at odds with Home Office forecasts, have in fact been specified by officials within the Home Office. The Chief Inspector of Prisons has suggested that 'the expectation should be that the prison system is capable of supporting in reasonable circumstances, a population of 37,000 prisoners'.[7] This target, representing a 14 per cent reduction on 1981 numbers, was reached by allowing a margin of five per cent on the existing physical capacity of the English prison system. However, given allocation policy as applied to local and training prisons within the English prison system, the reduction proposed by the Chief Inspector would make little impact on overcrowding which is largely located in local prisons. A more ambitious target has been proposed by the professional association of prison governors which has the aim of eliminating forced cell-sharing.[8] The target of 32,000 prisoners recommended by prison governors would, on 1981 numbers, involve a reduction of 25 per cent.

Both recommendations were developed on the basis of existing prison system physical capacity and neither goes far enough. A more far-reaching target would envisage a decrease in physical capacity together with a reduction in prison population size of greater proportions. In Chapter 6, three examples of reductionist prison system practice were described, each of which resulted in a reduction in prison population size of the order of 50 per cent. The reductionist target proposed here is that by 1990 the English prison population would be reduced, as it was in the early decades of this century, by 50 per cent. The reductionist target for the early 1990s should not be around 52,000 as planned by the Home Office, but 22,000 or, in terms of the prison population rate per 100,000 inhabitants, not 110 but in the region of 35.

In the three examples described in Chapter 6, reductionist practice was developed less in response to a specific prison target population than from a powerful realistic appreciation of the very limited utility of prison systems. This pessimistic stance on the prison is an integral aspect of the Bleak House perspective on criminal justice. As put by one Dutch commentator: 'The opinion that prison does not solve social problems, and that prison is rather such a social problem itself, and that it should be repudiated, is rather widely propagated in the Netherlands.'[9] Specifically targetting the scale of the reduction, however, does highlight an alternative to expansionist forecasts and also provides a benchmark against which results can be measured. Numerical targets for the prison population were, in fact, used by the reforming Home Secretary, Winston Churchill in 1910. Churchill's reductionist targets were not only met but were greatly exceeded.

Likewise, in Denmark and Sweden reductionist targetting has been a useful device. In the early 1970s with the Danish prison population rising, the situation was described by H. H. Brydensholt, the head of the prison system: 'We were in the situation of either having to secure more prison space or to change our criminal law so that imprisonment was used less frequently.'[10] A package of reforms, initiated in 1973, included the elimination of indeterminate sentencing. Legislation aimed to reduce both the use of prison and the length of sentences,[11] and to effect the transfer of resources from prisons to probation services. To facilitate this transfer of resources, prison and probation systems were placed under the same national agency. The result of these measures was to reduce prison population size by 15 per cent, with the aim of effecting a further reduction of similar proportions through early release schemes and new non-custodial sanctions. These changes in prison population size had no direct relationship with the level of recorded crime. Recorded crime rose both during the period of prison population increase and reduction. Mr Brydensholt commented: 'It may well be that we will achieve our goals (of crime reduction) only by looking outside the criminal justice system for the answers.'[12]

The absence of a direct relationship between the recorded crime rate and prison population size was also an important impetus for reductionist policy in Sweden. One Swedish official, Bo Svensson, has described developments in his country: 'In the early 1960s the National Prisons Board estimated that the average number of inmates in 1980 would be around

9,650. And in this context it might be recalled that former Minister of Justice, Lennart Geijer said that one of the goals of his efforts was to have a prison population of no more than around 600 inmates.'[13] The Swedish prison population, in fact, declined by 20 per cent between 1965 and 1975.[14] Svensson argued that the prison population size be reduced to 3,000, and he made the following observation: 'It would, in my opinion, be very interesting if the politicians would, for once, express their opinion as to how large a prison population they consider desirable and, in broad outline, what its composition should be in order to fulfil the goals indicated.'[15]

The reductionist approach to the prison system inevitably and necessarily overlaps with broader aspects of social and economic policy. In particular, policy and practice concerning education, mental health and the extent and distribution of poverty impinge upon directions set for the prison system. General policy issues of this sort are beyond the scope of this book, and the reductionist agenda outlined here is confined to the sphere of criminal justice. The reductionist agenda consists of nine items. While these items are reviewed primarily with reference to the situation in England, the general principles apply to expansionist systems elsewhere from Scotland to Texas. Although the items are not listed in a strict sequential order, there is merit in the view that action should commence with the prison system itself. The prison represents the deepest end of criminal justice, and strategies which restrict the availability of custody produce a ripple effect through other parts of the process. The classic example of criminal justice reform which focused at the deep-end was the abrupt closure in the early 1970s of most of the youth institutions in Massachusetts. This event had the consequence of forcing the development of procedures to ensure the highly selective allocation of the few available secure settings and also encouraging a wide range of alternative programmes in the community.[16]

The nine items on the reductionist agenda are as follows:

- The physical capacity of the prison system should be substantially reduced.
- There should be a precise statement of minimum standards as to the physical conditions of imprisonment and these should be legally enforceable.
- The optimal prison system staff-to-prisoner ratio should be determined and implemented.
- The prison system should have at its disposal early release mechanisms and use these to avoid overcrowding.
- Certain categories of persons sentenced to imprisonment should, if space be not immediately available, wait until called-up by the prison system.

- Sentencing discretion should be structured towards use of the least restrictive sanction.
- Breach or default of non-custodial sanctions should only exceptionally be dealt with by imprisonment.
- The range of non-imprisonable offences should be widened to include certain categories of theft.
- The scope of criminal law should be considerably narrowed.

The Physical Capacity of the Prison System should be Substantially Reduced
If the prison population in England is to be reduced to about 20,000, the required capacity, allowing a five per cent margin, would be 21,000. With reference to the existing penal estate, this implies a reduction in capacity of 18,000 places or about 45 per cent. The reduction of capacity has three central components:

– *A freeze on new prison construction.* In England this would mean cancellation of the prison building programme which in 1982 envisaged 5,000 new places by the end of the 1980s. The freeze would include so-called replacement prisons, which are more than likely to result in supplementation of the existing prison system. Even rebuilding projects on the existing site carries risks of this sort, as is evident at Holloway, the women's prison in London. The new Holloway prison is planned to have almost twice the certified accommodation of the original facility.

– *A phased programme of prison closures, amounting in England to, say, 12,500 places.* In England only five institutions, all open prisons and borstals, with a total capacity of about 800 have been closed since 1945.[17] There have been no closures of Victorian prisons during this period which, in the words of one Home Office official, are 'collapsing around our ears'.[18] The Home Office estimated in 1978 that four institutions with a total of 1,000 places were in such poor condition that they were not worth retaining for another decade.[19] Expansionist prison systems are highly resistant to closing prisons regardless of their physical conditions. In October 1979, the May Committee wrote of Dartmoor prison, '. . . what was permissible in a convict prison for the rigours of penal servitude on the reoccupied Napoleonic site of the 1850s, is nowadays simply against nature'.[20] On the day the May Report was published the Member of Parliament for the constituency which includes the prison within its boundaries expressed alarm in the House of Commons at, '. . . the possible closure of Dartmoor prison which would have very serious social implications for Princetown'. His fears were quickly put at rest. The Home Secretary replied that, in the present conditions of overcrowding, '. . . there is no question of closing down Dartmoor'.[21]

– *A refurbishment programme carried out in remaining prisons which will further reduce capacity.* The Home Office has estimated that provision of integral sanitation would eliminate 5,500 cells.[22] As noted in the next section, in the absence of further construction, adherence to minimum physical standards is likely to result in substantial reductions in total capacity.

There should be a Precise Statement of Minimum Standards Governing the Physical Conditions of Prison Systems, and These Standards should be Legally Enforceable

A central plank of reductionist policy is the articulation of and adherence to minimum standards. Minimum standards provide a basic floor, below which conditions should not be permitted to sink and should be differentiated from standards which are essentially aspirational in character. It is partly for this reason that some commentators prefer the concept of 'humane containment' to the elusive rhetoric of 'treatment and training'. King and Morgan have argued that '. . . the goal of humane containment is capable of being defined in ways which enable staff (and the public) to know when they are achieving it or when they are falling short'.[23]

There is, however, a reluctance within most prison systems to articulate basic standards. Officials prefer to be guided by lofty aspirations rather than measurable minimum standards. The former speak to good intentions which may remain beyond the grasp of the prison administrators who, claiming perseverance, remain absolved from blame. Measurable minimum standards provide criteria against which the prison administrator can be held accountable. Standards regarding physical space provide a linchpin of reductionist policy on the prison system. Minimum standards bring together the three strands of prison policy, namely population size, the level of capacity and the quality of conditions.[24]

In 1982 unsuccessful attempts were made to incorporate precise standards regarding prison accommodation into the Criminal Justice Bill. One amendment proposed no enforced cell sharing and a minimum of 60 square feet per person in dormitories when confined for ten hours or less per day, and a minimum of 80 square feet when confined for more than ten hours per day. As noted in Chapter 6, the Netherlands and West Germany have given statutory expression to some minimum standards. In the United States, although the Supreme Court has ruled in the contrary direction, lower courts have continued to find overcrowded conditions to be a crucial component in breaches of the cruel and unusual punishment provision of the Eighth Amendment. These considerations have prompted courts to order reductions of prison and jail populations.

By contrast, gross overcrowding continues to be tolerated in England. In 1973, the United Kingdom signed the Standard Minimum Rules for the Treatment of Prisoners, Rule 5(3), which sets forth the basic principle that: 'Deprivation of liberty shall be effected in material and conditions which ensure respect for human dignity.' As the Chief Inspector of Prisons has commented, conditions in English prisons certainly fall short of this standard. Unfortunately, the language of the European Rules lacks precision with respect to space and cell-sharing. Furthermore, while the Rules carry some moral force, they are not mandatory and lack enforcement machinery. The European Convention on Human Rights, on the other hand, does provide redress through the European Commission on Human Rights and the European Court. The key provision is Article 3 – 'No one should be subject to torture or inhuman or degrading treatment or punishment.' It is surprising that the European Court had not by the early 1980s been asked whether Article 3 is breached when three persons are crowded into a cell designed for one person, with no integral sanitation.[25] Eventually, pressure from the European Court may encourage British courts to take a more active position on this issue and the rights of prisoners generally. One legal commentator has written: 'To exempt from judicial control an administrative activity of the scale and importance of the prison system can have no justification either in principle or on grounds of expediency.'[26]

From the standpoint of reductionist policy, it is important that the penal scene does not become swamped with competing sets of standards, which is one of the difficulties facing reformers in the United States. What is required are a few tightly articulated central minimum standards which set the direction for action and provide a measure of its efficacy. It is also important to recognize the danger that minimum standards may also be used to secure increased resources and enhance expansionist policies. From the reductionist standpoint, minimum standards have the intrinsic virtue of imposing a population ceiling on existing prison system accommodation.

The Optimal Staff-to-Prisoner Ratio within the Prison System should be Determined and Implemented
Serious problems arise for the prison system if there are too few or too many staff. Most expansionist prison systems are characterized by considerable increases in manpower, often accompanied by extensive restrictive practices and huge amounts of overtime. Under these circumstances, manpower costs are likely to be met at the expense of conditions within the prison. Too many staff may be counter-productive in terms of effective control of prisoners but on the other hand some prison systems, notably in the United States, have rapidly expanded their prison populations while retaining low manpower levels. In these prison systems, control problems of alarming diminsions are commonplace. Despite the high financial costs of staffing, little is known about what constitutes appropriate manning levels and optimal staff-to-prisoner ratios. The crude nature of the staff-to-prisoner ratio has not been refined to take account of

considerations such as the security level of the prison, the extent to which prisoners are confined to their cells, staff tasks away from the prison, and the amount of overtime worked. Closely related to the optimal ratio is the important question of the morale of prison staff and the satisfaction they derive from their work.

The implications of reductionist policy for manpower needs vary according to the levels of staff to prisoners and the particular tasks of the prison. The experience in Japan and the Netherlands was that substantial reductions in prison populations were not accompanied by a decline in the number of custodial staff. In Japan, the number of prison officers remained static, whereas in the Netherlands manpower increased despite the decline in prison population. A fifty per cent reduction in the English prison population and no change in manpower would result in a prison officer-to-prisoner ratio of 1:1. This ratio is already achieved in English dispersal prisons and by the prison system of the Netherlands. Clearly formulated manning levels are an essential aspect of reductionist policy, and negotiations involving staff associations would need to take account of the interests of all grades of staff.

The Prison System should Have at its Disposal Early Release Mechanisms, and Use these to Avoid Overcrowding

Most prison systems are responsible for the use of remission or 'good-time' and, where parole exists, exercise at least some degree of influence on parole decisions.[27] In addition to these general powers, a prison system should have at its disposal various schemes of temporary and early release. Temporary release usually takes the form of home leave or other furloughs and is especially important in Sweden and West Germany. In West Germany following the Prison Act of 1976, the number of furloughs has more than doubled.[28] Early release can take various forms. The Republic of Ireland has since 1960 developed a scheme of 'full temporary release', under which selected short-term offenders (serving sentences of 12 months or less) are released, often shortly after committal, to serve their sentences in the community.[29] Intensive supervision is provided by the probation services, with the ratio of releasees to probation officers being about eight to one. The full temporary release scheme is occasionally used directly as a means of regulating prison population size. When numbers in the prisons become high, short-term offenders are granted full temporary release without supervision.[30]

Another method of early release is the amnesty. Amnesties are used fairly regularly to regulate prison population size in France, Israel and elsewhere.[31] While the amnesty provides reductions in prison population only over the short term, it is a useful tool for avoiding overcrowding. Powers exist under the Criminal Justice Act of 1982 to release specified categories of prisoners during the last six months of their sentence.[32]

Certain Categories of Persons Sentenced to Imprisonment Should, if No Space is Immediately Available, Wait until Called-up by the Prison System
In Continental law countries, where the person sentenced to prison is on bail at the time of sentence, or in other specified situations, a common procedure is for the person to await call-up by the prison system. For example, in the Netherlands at any one time, there are some 10,000 persons waiting for a prison place to become vacant. From the standpoint of the person sentenced to imprisonment the procedure, while not free from anxiety, does allow time for personal affairs to be attended to and perhaps flexibility as to when custody commences; from the standpoint of the prison system the call-up procedure permits an unhurried decision to be taken as to where the sentence will be served, and in particular forestalls overcrowded conditions. Of special importance, when there are increased demands on prison capacity, the procedure ensures that the pressure point is located outside rather than inside the prison system. A scheme along the Dutch lines was recommended by the Home Affairs Committee of the House of Commons in 1981 only to be rejected by the Government.[33]

Sentencing Discretion should be Structured towards Use of the Least Restrictive Sanction
The legislature should establish a commission with the task of determining sentencing guidelines. The purpose of these guidelines would be to structure sentencing decisions so that custody is regarded as the sanction of last resort. To the sentencing commission would be delegated the immensely complex task of weighing the value questions concerning offence types as well as directing attention to aggravating and mitigating circumstances. The guidelines would in particular address the decision to impose custody in addition to formulating a jurisprudence governing the use of non-custodial sanctions. Experience in England and elsewhere has amply demonstrated that exhortations to sentencers by the legislative and executive branches of government to be more sparing in the use of custody are likely to go unheeded. While the Court of Appeal has provided some guidance on the length of prison sentences, it has made very little progress in fashioning a coherent jurisprudence as to when imprisonment is appropriate.

The Sentencing Guidelines Commission in Minnesota, described in Chapter 7, is characterized by a gradual and evolutionary development. It is certainly to be expected that such a commission would vary in structure and style from one jurisdiction to another. A model for England was proposed in 1982 by Andrew Ashworth, not, it might be noted, to resounding cheers from either the Home Office or the judiciary.[34] Opposition to efforts to structure sentencing in part arise from constitutional conventions regarding the independence of the judiciary. As Andrew Ashworth comments: 'The judiciary seems to believe that it has the right to determine sentencing policy, and for that there is neither constitutional or pragmatic justification.'[35] The prerogative resides with the legislature which may decide to entrust the detailed work to a commission. Sentencing guidelines address both the decision of whether to imprison and the length of any custodial sentence that is imposed. The important consideration with respect to sentence length is less the maximum allowed by statute than the actual decision reached by the sentencer.[36] As to statutory maxima, the task of effecting reductions may be a political minefield. When in 1978 the Advisory Council on the Penal System sensibly proposed reductions to maximum terms of imprisonment, the report was howled down in derision by much of the popular press.[37]

The more viable reform strategy is to structure sentence length by means of a combination of guidelines and appelate review. The danger must always be guarded against that any reduction in sentence length may result in an increase in the total number of custodial sentences. When this occurs, the use of custody is likely to replace non-custodial sanctions. Sentencers may be impressed by opportunities to use the prison system to provide a taste of custody, since after allowance is made for remission and for time remanded in custody, the length of time to be served may be very brief. The personal consequences, however, are likely to be similar regardless of the period in custody. In particular, the individual has to deal with having a record of being in prison, the stigma of which is not reduced by reference to duration. Custody should be a sanction of last resort regardless of length of time to be served.

The Criminal Justice Act of 1982 provided courts with more rather than fewer opportunities to impose brief tastes of custody. In sentencing adults, the availability of the partly suspended sentence poses this danger.[38] Of greater significance, the new minimum three week detention centre sentence, which becomes two weeks after allowing for remission, promises a fourfold escalation of numbers of young men aged 14–20 passing through detention centres.[39] These considerations underline the crucial importance of structuring sentencing decisions with respect to the use of custody regardless of sentence length.

Breach of Default of Non-custodial Sanctions should Only Very Exceptionally be Dealt With by Imprisonment
The prison system should not, as a general rule, be available for persons in breach of non-custodial sanctions. The problem remains of fine defaulters coming into the English prison system despite a series of statutes intended to curb this practice. In fact, fine defaulters represent the most rapidly growing category of prison receptions, accounting in 1981 for 21,000 persons, or one in every four sentenced persons entering the English prison system.[40] Very exceptional circumstances might be specified where

custody be considered but generally other means of enforcement would be pursued. Resort to imprisonment often occurs because courts have not obtained adequate information about the individual and as a result of poorly developed enforcement procedures.

Existing legislation in England needs to be strengthened to ensure that courts satisfy specified conditions regarding information and enforcement procedures before prison for default can be considered.[41] As noted in Chapter 7, little advantage is gained from making an offence non-imprisonable if, as is the case with respect to the offence of being drunk and disorderly, imprisonment remains an option in the event of non-payment of a fine. When prison is regarded as inappropriate for the original offence it should not, in general, be available to enforce compliance with a lesser sanction.

The Range of Non-imprisonable Offences should be Widened to Include Certain Categories of Theft
Imprisonment is qualitatively different from non-custodial sanctions and should be used only when any lesser punishment would depreciate the seriousness of the offence. Few reformers of the penal system have urged the total abolition of the prison system and most would agree that prison be retained as the 'detestable solution' in dealing with persons convicted of serious offences. However, expanding prison systems have much to do with persons who are not serious offenders. From its earliest history, the prison system has served as a depository for persons involved in petty crime, much of which is little more than a social nuisance. While the prison system continues to provide this residual function, alternative means of responding to this type of behaviour are unlikely to emerge. The criminal justice process in general and the prison system in particular should not be a substitute for the delivery of welfare.[42]

The Criminal Justice Act of 1982 made one or two offences, such as sleeping rough and begging, non-imprisonable. Amendments to make other trivial offences non-imprisonable were defeated. Welcome as these proposals were, the arena for legislative action has to be considerably more ambitious. On pragmatic grounds, the impact on the size of the prison population will be very slight unless the reform thrust is extended to include at least some categories of theft and other property offences. Beyond these pragmatic considerations, however, there is the fundamental question of whether it is right to imprison persons for other than serious offences. On economic and philosophic grounds, property offences where the amount involved is less than, say £100, should be non-imprisonable. This approach is consistent with Andrew Ashworth's proposal for a rigorous ceiling, 'so that an offender who commits a modest theft for the fifth, tenth or fifteenth time should not be at risk of a custodial sentence'.[43] There may be more public support for avoiding imprisonment for property offenders, including burglary, than is sometimes supposed. An English public opinion poll on attitudes to crime and punishment found that more than half the respondents favoured a non-custodial sentence for burglary.[44]

Prosecutorial Discretion should be Structured Towards Restricting Entry into the Criminal Justice Process

Prosecutorial decision-making remains largely uncharted territory, and the significance of decisions by prosecutors for prison systems cannot be under-estimated. In the Netherlands and Japan, both countries with centrally administered systems of prosecution, discretion exercised not to prosecute has played a crucial part in the reduction of prison population size. Elsewhere, prosecutors have contributed to the mounting pressures on the courts and ultimately the prison system. Diversion by prosecutors is not without its dangers as a large body of research literature, mostly in the United States, has testified.[45] Unless the diversion strategy is pointed outside the criminal justice process, the probability exists that the scope of the criminal justice net will be widened and not narrowed. In England the complex task of structuring prosecutorial discretion is compounded by the absence of prosecuting agencies which are independent of the police. A preliminary step would be the establishment of Crown Prosecutors as recommended by the Royal Commission on Criminal Procedure.[46] Accepted in principle by the government in 1982 this proposal is a crucial component of coherent criminal justice policy. Efforts to structure decision-making in this area must take account of the inter-related nature of prosecution and sentencing. As attempts are made to formulate sentencing policy in a reductionist direction the probability exists that progress made will be counteracted by prosecutors. In Minnesota and other jurisdictions where sentencing guidelines are in use, attention is now being directed at decision-making which occurs earlier in the criminal justice process.

The Scope of the Criminal Law should be Narrowed

The criminal law extends across a broad and highly diverse canvas of events. In England more than seven thousand events are defined as criminal.[47] More than half these offences are of strict liability with no account taken of the individual's motivation. Compared to other forms of social control the administration of the criminal law is often slow, cumbersome and inefficient. For this and other reasons civil proceedings are often preferred. The Inland Revenue, for example, invokes informal rather than criminal procedures in virtually all cases of tax evasion, even when very large sums are involved. Most decriminalization has taken the de facto route, and this offers the most promising means to cutting back the scope of criminal justice.

Selective non-enforcement of the criminal law, however, carries dangers of serious inequities and disrespect for the rule of law. Legislative action is required on two fronts. Firstly, the temptation should be resisted to further widen the scope of criminal law. Wherever possible the legislature should be persuaded to provide for civil rather than criminal redress. This outcome, for example, was achieved in the area of racial discrimination following amendments to the Race Relations Bill.[48] Secondly, vigorous efforts should be made to achieve decriminalization by statute.[49] Louk Hulsman has urged the replacement of criminal by civil proceedings across a variety of problematic situations. Hulsman argues that the key question is how to promote better ways of tackling the very divergent problems labelled crime. By 'civilization', Hulsman refers to approaches by which the compensatory model of civil law replaces the blunt instrument of criminal law. Furthermore, Hulsman and others are finding growing support for the view that state resources should be directed primarily to the family, the school, the work setting and the neighbourhood, and that wherever possible the control of conflict and mediation be left to them.[50]

Existing policy and practice in many countries are geared for further massive expansion in prison systems throughout the remainder of the century. The myths of Great Expectations for criminal justice persist despite extensive knowledge regarding its inefficiency as a means of social control. The prison system represents the crude deep-end of society's control apparatus and growth by the prison system ultimately threatens the freedom of everyone. Unless expansionist policies are halted and reversed, the legacy for the twenty-first century will be a prison system archipelago of monstrous proportions. Reductionist policy options are available at each of the various stages of the criminal justice process. The starting point, however, must be the prison system itself. The urgent requirement is not for tentative steps at the margins, but for bold, decisive and sustained action at the penal epicentre.

References

1   See, e.g. Fifteenth Report from the Expenditure Committee, Session 1977–8, vol. 1, Report, *The Reduction of Pressure on the Prison System*, HC 662–1, HMSO, 1978, pp. xxxviii–xlix; Parliamentary All-Party Penal Affairs Group, *Too Many Prisoners, An Examination of Ways of Reducing the Prison Population*, Chichester and London: Barry Rose, 1980; Fourth Report from the Home Affairs Committee, session 1980/81. *The Prison Service*, vol. 1, House of Commons Paper 412–1, 1981, pp. xv–xxxix; Parliamentary All-Party Penal Affairs Group, *Still Too Many Prisoners, An Assessment of the Government's Response to the Report 'Too Many Prisoners' since June 1980*, 1981; see also, 'Prisons', Labour Party Discussion Document, London, 1982, pp. 6–7; and *A Time For Justice, A report on crime, prison and punishment*, Abingdon: Catholic Social Welfare Commission, 1982, pp. 17–19.
2   Fourth Report of the Home Affairs Committee, op. cit., p. xv.
3   At the request of the May Committee, the Home Office made available to them a longer-range forecast which the May Report summarizes in graphic form only. The

chart indicates a growth in average daily population commencing about 1985 and reaching 47,000 by 1987. No supportive documentation was provided by the Home Office for the long-range forecast. The May Committee commented: 'As the Home Office has pointed out to us, even the short-term forecasts are not precise and have a margin of error which increases the further ahead the forecast is being made. Indeed such considerations have led the Home Office to confine itself to publishing five-year forecasts only and not making – including initially also to us – the ten-year forecasts available publicly'. *Report of the Inquiry into the United Kingdom Prison Services*, Chairman Mr Justice May, Cmnd 7673, London: HMSO, 1979, p. 43.

4   For a description of the Home Office approach to prison population forecasting, see Memorandum submitted by the Home Office to the Home Affairs Committee, 'Projections of the Prison Population', Minutes of Evidence, 16 March 1981, pp. 217–18.

5   See generally, Andrew Rutherford *et al.*, *Prison Population and Policy Choices*, vol. 1, Preliminary Report to Congress, Washington D.C.: National Institute of Law Enforcement and Criminal Justice, 1977, pp. 131–245.

6   The peak for the English prison population rate was 142 per 100,000 inhabitants in the early 1830s. See Malcolm Ramsay, 'Two Centuries of Imprisonment', *Home Office Research Bulletin*, **14**, 1982, pp. 45–7.

7   Report of H.M. Chief Inspector of Prisons, 1981, Cmnd 8532, London: HMSO, 1982, p. 21.

8   Society of Civil Servants, Prison and Borstal Governors' Branch, paper on Prison Overcrowding, June 1982.

9   S. van Ruller, quoted by David Downes, 'The origins and consequences of Dutch penal policy', *British Journal of Criminology*, **22**, 1982, pp. 337–8.

10   H. H. Brydensholt, 'Crime Policy in Denmark', *Crime and Delinquency*, January 1980, p. 41.

11   For example, the maximum sentence for first-time property offenders, including burglary, was reduced from two years to one and a half years.

12   H. H. Brydensholt, op. cit., note 10, p. 41.

13   Bo Svensson, 'We can get by with 3,000 prisoners', unpublished paper, Stockholm, n.d., p. 10.

14   Information Bulletin of the National Swedish Council for Crime Prevention, No. 2, December 1981, p. 14.

15   Bo Svensson, op. cit., note 13, p. 17.

16   See Andrew Rutherford, 'Decarceration of Young Offenders in Massachusetts, The Events and their Aftermath', in N. Tutt (ed.), *Alternative Strategies for Coping With Crime*, Oxford: Blackwell, 1978, pp. 103–19.

17   Additionally, one other prison was closed in 1974, but reopened the following year with its capacity reduced by 230.

18   Home Affairs Committee, Minutes of Evidence, H.C. 412–2, 1981, p. 17.

19   May Report, op. cit., note 3, p. 143. In 1981 the Home Office provided the Home Affairs Committee with a list of twelve prisons which it wished to close. Home Affairs Committee, Minutes of Evidence, H.C. 412–2, 1981, p. 219.

20   May Report, op. cit., note 3, p. 125.

21   *H.C. Deb.*, vol. 972, col. 1239, 31 October 1979.

22   May Report, op. cit., note 3, p. 143.

23   Roy King and Rod Morgan, *The Future of the Prison System*, Farnborough: Gower, 1980, p. 27.

24   Minimum standards address a very much wider arena than physical space. In England, only very tentative steps have been taken to what these might be, and Home Office drafts of a white paper set forth some ideas for going some way further forward than existing Prison Rules. The Chief Inspector of prisons has drawn attention to particular parts of the European Standard Minimum Rules, for example on work (Rule 72(3)) and on education and training (Rules 66 and 67).

25   See, e.g. Michael Zander, Home Office Bicentenary Lecture, 1982, p. 14. The European Commission has had an impact in other areas, especially prisoners' rights regarding correspondence. See, e.g., *Silver and others against the United Kingdom, Report of the Commission*, Strasbourg, 11 October 1980. The Commission found that the English prison system had violated three Articles of the European Convention on Human

Rights. This ruling led to the revision and publication of Standing Orders on communications in June 1981.

26 Graham Zellick, 'Prison Rules', *Criminal Law Review*, 1981, p. 616.

27 Parole was introduced in England in 1967 partly as a device for reducing prison population size. The extent to which parole has this effect depends upon whether sentencers compensate for parole when determining sentence length. There has been no research on whether the 'penal credibility gap' influences sentencers in this way. In 1975, parole procedures were modified so as to increase the rate of parole. See generally, Howard League for Penal Reform, *Freedom On Licence, The Development of Parole and Proposals for Reform*, Sunbury: Quartermaine, 1981, esp. pp. 15–31. For estimates of the effect on prison population of various early release mechanisms, see NACRO, 'Attempts to reduce the prison population and their estimated effect'. Additional information submitted to the Home Affairs Committee, vol. 2, Minutes of Evidence, H.C. 412–2, 1981, pp. 275–6.

28 Johannes B. Feest, *Imprisonment and the Criminal Justice System in the Federal Republic of Germany*, University of Bremen, 1982, pp. 26–7.

29 Some prisoners serving longer terms are released under this scheme after completing one third of their sentence.

30 *Criminal Justice Act of 1960*, Section 2(1): 'The Minister may make rules providing for the temporary release, subject to such conditions (if any) as may be imposed in each particular case of persons serving a sentence of penal servitude or imprisonment'. While the total so released was 891 in 1980 and 441 in 1981, the number released at any one time is small, rarely exceeding ten. The practice of unplanned release is only resorted to when all institutions are full and, '. . . has been considered preferable to large-scale doubling or trebling of offenders in cells that were designed for one occupant only'. Personal communication from the Irish Department of Justice, 27/3/82; see *Annual Report on Prisons and Places of Detention for 1980*.

31 There have been seven amnesties of prisoners in France since 1945. When President Mitterand took office in 1981, he extended the amnesty to cover sentences of up to six months (previous amnesties had included sentences of up to three months), and released 7,000 persons. The French prison population fell by 28 per cent from 43,000 to 31,000 between April and September 1981. In Israel amnesties take three forms: Presidential amnesties (usually involves about 120 prisoners), special amnesties (e.g. in 1967 when 501 persons were released, and in 1982 when 440 persons were released; the prison administration wanted 800 but the police objected), and routine amnesties, available after half sentence is completed and have to be signed by Minister of Justice, usually involves 80–120 persons per year. Personal communication from Professor Menachem Amir of the Hebrew University of Jerusalem. See also Leslie Sebba 'Amnesty – A Quasi-Experiment', *British Journal of Criminology*, **19**, 1979, pp. 5–30.

32 Provision for early release was first made available under the Imprisonment (Temporary Provisions) Act of 1980, emergency legislation enacted during the Prison Officers' industrial dispute but was not brought into effect. In December 1981, a minister at the Home Office suggested that powers contained in the Criminal Justice Act of 1982 would not be used. H.C. Debs December 2 1981. The Michigan Prison Overcrowding Emergency Act of 1980 does appear to have succeeded in keeping the state prison population from rising. In 1981 Michigan was the only state prison system where the prison population fell. *Detroit Free Press*, 3 May 1982.

33 Fourth Report from the Home Affairs Committee, *The Prison Service*, House of Commons Paper 412–1, July 1981; para. 104 and the Government's Reply to the Fourth Report, Cmnd 8446, London: HMSO, December 1981, p. 20.

34 Andrew Ashworth, 'Reducing the Prison Population in the 1980s: The Need for Sentencing Reform', lecture to NACRO, 1982, draft pp. 17–21.

35 ibid., p. 14.

36 Reductions in sentence length may significantly reduce prison population. For example, the Home Office have calculated that if sentences of up to four years imposed on non-violent offenders had been halved, the effect would have been a reduction in total prison population size of about 20 per cent. Home Affairs Committee, vol. 2, Minutes of Evidence, H.C. 412–2, 1981, pp. 218–19.

37 Advisory Council on the Penal System, *Sentences of Imprisonment: A Review of*

Maximum Penalties, London: HMSO, 1978; see also Marjorie Jones, *Crime Punishment and the Press*, London: NACRO, 1980, pp. 9–20.

38   The partly suspended sentence, under Section 47 of the Criminal Law Act of 1977 came into operation on 29 March 1982. The Criminal Justice Act of 1982 attempts to restrict its use. See, D. A. Thomas, 'The Partly Suspended Sentence', *Criminal Law Review*, May 1982, pp. 288–95; and *R. v. Clarke*, *Criminal Law Review*, 1982, pp. 464–7.

39   In 1981, 13,600 young men were sentenced to detention centres. The minimum length of stay, with full remission was 6½ weeks for 14–16 year olds and eight weeks for 16–20 year olds. Under the provisions of the Criminal Justice Act of 1982 with remission of one-third for both age groups, the minimum sentence (making no allowance for time spent in custody or remand) becomes two weeks. The number of receptions into detention centres could by the mid-1980s increase to about 54,000 per year.

40   *Prison Statistics for 1981*, London: HMSO, 1982, p. 19.

41   The Magistrates' Courts Act 1980, Section 88 specifies conditions but these require to be extended and tightened. The Howe Committee on Fine Default observed: 'We are disturbed by indications that a number of people without the means to pay do, nevertheless, end up in prison for fine default'. *Fine Default*, Report of a NACRO Working Party, London: NACRO, 1981, p. 20. The report provides a comprehensive review of fine enforcement problems and possibilities. See also, P. Softley, *A Survey of Fine Enforcement*, Home Office Research Unit, London: HMSO, 1973.

42   See, Susan Fairhead and Tony F. Marshall, 'Dealing with the Petty Persistent Offender: an account of the current Home Office Research Unit Studies', in *The Petty Persistent Offender*, London: NACRO, 1979, pp. 1–9.

43   Andrew Ashworth, op. cit., note 34, p. 17. In 1981, 34 per cent of all persons received on sentence (excluding fine defaulters) were convicted of theft or related offences. *Prison Department Statistics, 1981*, 1982. Remarkably little research has been conducted on the composition of prison populations. There has been no general prison population census in England, and the only detailed study was carried out in 1972 and based upon a ten per cent sample in the South East Region. This research found that 30 per cent of the sample of sentenced adult men could be described as petty or minor offenders. See, 'A Survey of the South East Prison Population', *Home Office Research Unit Bulletin*, No. 5, 1978, pp. 12–24.

44   Stephen Shaw, *The People's Justice, A Major Poll of Public Attitudes on Crime and Punishment*, London: Prison Reform Trust, 1982, p. 18. While 47 per cent of the respondents favoured immediate imprisonment, seven per cent of those in favour of an alternative sentence advocated corporal punishment.

45   See, e.g. Elizabeth and James Vorenberg, 'Early Diversion from the Criminal Justice System', in *Prisoners in America*, ed. Lloyd Ohlin, New York: Prentice Hall, 1973. See also the extract from the statement by Daniel J. Freed to the Subcommittee of the Committee on the Judiciary of the House of Representatives in 1974, contained in *Diversion from Criminal Justice in an English Context*. Report of a NACRO Working Party, Chairman, Michael Zander, Chichester and London: Barry Rose, 1975, pp. 41–4.

46   *Report of Royal Commission on Criminal Procedure*, Chairman, Sir Cyril Philips, Cmnd 8092, London: HMSO, 1981, pp. 144–70.

47   *Justice, Breaking the Rules*, London: Justice, 1980.

48   Anthony Lester and Geoffrey Bird, *Race and the Law*, London: Penguin, 1972, pp. 98–120.

49   See, for example, David Tench, *Towards a Middle System of Law*, London: Consumers' Association, 1981.

50   See especially Louk Hulsman, 'Penal Reform in the Netherlands: Part 1, Bringing the Criminal Justice System Under Control', *Howard Journal*, vol. 20, 1981, pp. 150–9; and Part II in vol. 21, 1982, pp. 35–47; see also Nils Christie, 'Conflicts as property', *British Journal of Criminology*, **17**, 1977, pp. 1–15.

Hulsman was a central influence on the Council of Europe's comprehensive and far-reaching report on decriminalization. See European Committee on Crime Problems, *Report on Decriminalisation*, Strasbourg, Council of Europe, 1980. See also, Fifteenth Criminological Research Conference, *Sexual Behaviour and Attitudes and their implications for Criminal Law, Conclusions and Recommendations*, Strasbourg, 25 November 1982.

Glossary

Prison system: the personnel, bureaucratic structure and physical estate which constitute the structural apparatus of imprisonment, as well as the prison population. It is increasingly common for there to be a single national prison system. This is the case, for example, in Scandinavia and in several other West European countries. Elsewhere, other jurisdictional arrangements exist. In the United Kingdom there are separate prison systems for England and Wales, Scotland and Northern Ireland. In West Germany each state has its own prison system; this is the case for each province in Canada, but there is also a federal system, and in one province jails remain the responsibility of local government. A more complex pattern exists in the United States where there is a federal system, a separate state prison system within each state and, within most states, separate systems, often consisting of a single jail, for each unit of local government.

Prison systems vary in scope. In some instances, the system encompasses adult and youthful offenders. The English system, for example, includes youth custody and detention centre institutions, the latter holds youths as young as 14. In at least one American state, the prison system is responsible for all adult and juvenile penal institutions. Some prison systems have responsibilities which extend beyond custodial arrangements. In Sweden a single agency is responsible for prisons, probation services and parole operations. A similar bureaucratic pattern exists in some Australian states, and in a few jurisdictions in the United States. However, whatever the range of tasks, the organization is dominated by the business of incarceration.

Prison system administrators: persons responsible for setting policy and securing resources. Patterns of prison system administration vary according to size of the prison system, constitutional arrangements and bureaucratic traditions. In the United States, the state prison system head is appointed by the elected governor, often with legislative confirmation, is responsible for all aspects of the prison system including finance, and deals directly with the legislature to secure resources and support. In England, the head of the prison system is a senior administrative grade civil servant and appointed by the permanent-under-secretary of the Home Office, although nominally by the Home Secretary. The head of the English system chairs the Prisons Board and formulates policy along with other senior Home Office officials and government ministers.

Prison managers: prison governors (England) or wardens (USA) and other senior staff responsible for managing the institution. In very small prison systems, as with the local jail in the United States, the functions of management and administration are fused. On the other hand in large prison systems the gap between management and administration may be considerable.

Prison population size: the total average daily population of the prison system; or, for some prison systems, e.g. in the United States, it refers to the count at the end of the year or on another specified day.

Prison population rate: total prison population size as a rate per 100,000 inhabitants.

Custodial sentencing rate: total persons sentenced to immediate custody as a percentage of all persons sentenced (usually for indictable, penal code or serious offences).

Reported capacity: physical capacity as reported by the prison system, e.g. certified normal accommodation (England) and design or rated capacity (USA).

Measured capacity: capacity as defined by a physical measure, e.g. square feet.

Occupation factor: number of prisoners divided by reported capacity.

Bibliography

Abbott, Jack Henry, *In the Belly of the Beast: Letters from Prison*, New York: Vintage Books, 1982.

Abse, Leo, *Private Member*, London: McDonald, 1973.

Allen, Francis A., *The Borderland of Criminal Justice: Essays in Law and Criminology*, Chicago: University of Chicago Press, 1964.
'The Juvenile Court and the Limits of Juvenile Justice', *Wayne Law Review*, **11**, 1965, p. 685.

American Federation of State, County and Municipal Employees, *Deinstitutionalization: Out of Their Beds and Into the Street*, New York, 1975.

American Friends Service Committee, *Struggle for Justice*, New York: Hill and Wang, 1971.

Andersson, Jan and Solarz, Artur, *Drug Criminality and Drug Abuse in Sweden*, 1969–1981, Stockholm: The National Swedish Council for Crime Prevention, Report No. 10, 1982, pp. 35–44.

Ashworth, Andrew, 'Judicial Independence and Sentencing Reform', paper presented at the Cambridge Criminology Conference, July 1979.
'Reducing the Prison Population in the 1980s: The Need for Sentencing Reform', lecture to NACRO, 1982.

Bailey, W. C., 'Correctional Outcome: an evaluation of 100 Reports', *Journal of Criminal Law, Criminology and Police Science*, 1966: 57, 153–60.

Baldwin, John and McConville, Michael, *Negotiated Justice, Pressures to Plead Guilty*, London: Martin Robertson, 1977.
'Plea Bargaining and Plea Negotiation in England', *Law and Society*, **13**, 1979, pp. 287–307.

Bayley, David, *Forces of Order, Police Behaviour in Japan and the United States*, Los Angeles, California University Press, 1976.

Bentham, Jeremy, 'Panopticon or the Inspection House: Postscript Part II' 4, *Works*, 1843.

Beyleveld, Deryck, 'Deterrence Research as a Basis for Deterrence Policies', *Howard Journal*, **18**, 1979, pp. 135–49.

'Identifying, Explaining and Predicting Deterrence', *British Journal of Criminology*, **19**, 1979, pp. 205–24.

Bianchi, Herman, 'Social Control and Deviance in the Netherlands', in *Deviance and Control in Europe*, ed. H. Bianchi *et al.*, London: Wiley, 1975.

Biles, David and Mulligan, Glen, 'Mad or Bad? The Enduring Dilemma', *British Journal of Criminology*, **13**, pp. 275–9.

Bing, G. H. C., 'The International Penal and Penitentiary Congress, Berlin, 1935', *Howard Journal*, **IV**, 1935, pp. 195–8.

Black, Charles L., *Capital Punishment: The Inevitability of Caprice and Mistake*, New York: W. W. Norton, 1974.

Blau, Peter N. and Scott, W. Richard, *Formal Organisations: A Comparative Approach*, London: Routledge and Kegan Paul, 1963.

Blumberg, A. S., *Criminal Justice*, Chicago: Quadrangle Books, 1967.

Blumstein, Alfred and Cohen, Jacqueline, 'A Theory of the Stability of Punishment', *Journal of Criminal Law and Criminology*, **64**, 1973, pp. 198–207.

Blumstein, Alfred and Nagin, Daniel, 'Imprisonment as an Allocation Process', in *Prisons: Present and Possible*, ed. M. E. Wolfgang, Lexington, Mass; Lexington Books, 1979, pp. 169–200.

Blumstein, Alfred and Moitra, Soumyo, 'An Analysis of the Time Series of the Imprisonment Rate in the States of the United States: A Further Test of the Stability of Punishment Hypothesis', *Journal of Criminal Law and Criminology*, **70**, 1979, pp. 376–7.

'comment on Cahalan's article', *Crime and Delinquency*, January 1980, pp. 91–2.

Blumstein, Alfred, Cohen, Jacqueline and Goulding, William, *The Influence of Capacity on Prison Population: A Critical Review of Some Recent Evidence*, unpublished paper, 1982.

Bondesson, Ulla, *Fången i fångsamshället*, Malmo: P. A. Norstedt and Soners Forlag, 1974.

Bottomley, A. Keith, *Decisions in the Penal Process*, Oxford: Martin Robertson, 1973.

Bottoms, A. E., 'Reflections on the Renaissance of Dangerousness', *Howard Journal of Penology and Crime Prevention*, **16**, 1977, pp. 70–96.

'The Suspended Sentence in England, 1967–1978', *British Journal of Criminology*, **21**, 1981, pp. 1–26.

Bottoms, A. E. and McClintock, F. M., *Criminals Coming of Age: A Study of Institutional Adaptation in the Treatment of Adolescent Offenders*, London: Heinemann, 1973.

Bottoms, A. E. and McWilliams, William, 'A Non-Treatment Paradigm for Probation Practice', *British Journal of Social Work*, **9**, 1979, pp. 179–187.

Bottoms, A. E. and Preston, R. H., *The Coming Penal Crisis, A Criminological and Theological Exploration*, Edinburgh: Scottish Academic Press, 1980.

Bottoms, A. E. and Brownsword, Roger, 'The Dangerousness Debate After the Floud Report', *British Journal of Criminology*, **22**, 1982, pp. 229–54.

Boulding, K. E., 'Towards a General Theory of Growth', *Canadian Journal of Economics and Political Science*, **19**, 1953, pp. 326–40.

Bourke, Seán, *The Springing of George Blake*, London: Mayflower, 1971.

Box, Steven and Hale, Chris, 'Economic Crisis and the Rising Prisoner Population in England', *Crime and Social Justice*, **21**, 1982.

Boyle, Jimmy, *A Sense of Freedom*, London: Pan, 1977.

Brody, S. R., *The Effectiveness of Sentencing – a review of the literature.* Home Office Research Study No. 35, London: HMSO, 1976.

Brody, Stephen and Tarling, Roger, *Taking Offenders out of Circulation*, Research Study No. 64, London: HMSO, 1980.

Brydensholt, H. H., 'Crime Policy in Denmark', *Crime and Delinquency*, 1980, pp. 35–41.

Cahalan, Margaret, 'Trends in Incarceration in the United States since 1880', *Crime and Delinquency*, January 1980 pp. 9–41.

Caird, Rod, *A Good and Useful Life, Imprisonment in Britain Today*, London: Hart-Davis, MacGibbon, 1974.

Calvert, E. Roy and Calvert, Theodora, *The Lawbreaker*, London: George Routledge, 1933.

Caroll, Lewis, *Through the Looking Glass*, New York: Randolph House, 1946.

Christie, Nils, 'Conflicts as Property', *British Journal of Criminology*, **17**, 1977, pp. 1–15.
Limits to Pain, Oxford: Martin Robertson, 1982.

Churchill, Randolph S., *Winston S. Churchill*, Volume II, Companion, Part 2, 1907–1911, London: Heinemann, 1969.

Clemmer, Donald, *The Prison Community*, Boston: Christopher Publishing House, 1940.

Cloward, Richard A., 'Social Control in the Prison', in *Theoretical Studies: Social Organisation of the Prison*, eds. Richard A. Cloward *et al.*, New York: Social Science Research Council, pp. 20–48.

Cohen, Stanley, 'Prisons and the Future of Control Systems: From Concentration to Dispersal', in *Welfare in Action*, ed. M. Fitzgerald *et al.*, London: Routledge and Kegan Paul, 1977, pp. 217–28.

Cohen, Stanley and Taylor, Laurie, 'Psychological Survival: The Experience of Long-Term Imprisonment', Harmondsworth: Penguin, 1972.
Comment, 'Beyond the Ken of the Courts: A Critique of Judicial Refusal to Review the Complaints of Convicts', *Yale Law Journal*, **72**, 1963.

Cressey, Donald R., 'Prison Organisations', in *Handbook of Organisations*, ed. J. G. Marsh, Chicago: Rand McNally, 1975.

Crossman, Richard, *Diaries of a Cabinet Minister*, vol. 2, London: Hamish Hamilton and Jonathan Cape, 1976.

Davis, Kenneth Culp, *Discretionary Justice: A Preliminary Analysis*, Urbana: University of Illinois Press, 1971.

Dean, Malcolm, 'The News Media's Influence in Penal Policy', in *Penal Policy-Making in England*, ed. Nigel Walker, Cambridge: Institute of Criminology, 1977, pp. 25–36.

Dijk, J. J. M. van and Steinmetz, C. H. D., *The ROC Victim Surveys, 1974–1979*, The Hague: Ministry of Justice, 1980.

Dollard, J., *Caste and Class in a Southern Town*, New Haven: Yale University Press, 1937.

Downes, David, 'The Origins and Consequences of Dutch Penal Policy since 1945', *British Journal of Criminology*, 22, 1982, pp. 325–62.

Easton, Joseph W., *Stone Walls Not a Prison Make: The Anatomy of Planned Administrative Change*, Springfield, Illinois: Charles C. Thomas, 1962.

Eden, Colin and Fineman, Stephen, 'A Fitting Role', *Community Care*, 287, 1979, pp. 20–21.

Emery, F. E., *Freedom and Justice within Walls: The Bristol Prison Experiment*, London: Tavistock, 1970.

Evans, Peter, *Prison Crisis*, London: George Allen and Unwin, 1980.

Fairhead, Susan and Marshall, Tony F., 'Dealing with the Petty Persistent Offender: an account of the current Home Office Research Unit Studies', in *The Petty Persistent Offender*, London: NACRO 1979, pp. 1–9.

Farrington, David P. and Bennett, Trevor, 'Police Cautioning of Juveniles in London', *British Journal of Criminology*, 21, 1981, pp. 123–35.

Feest, Johannes B., *Imprisonment and the Criminal Justice System in the Federal Republic of Germany*, University of Bremen, 1982.

Fitzgerald, Mike, *Prisoners in Revolt*, Harmondsworth: Penguin, 1977.

Fitzgerald, Mike and Sim, Joe, *British Prisons*, Oxford: Blackwell, 1979.

Floud, Jean and Young, Warren, *Dangerousness and Criminal Justice*, London: Heinemann, 1981.

Folkard, M. S., Smith, D. E. and Smith, D. D., *IMPACT, Intensive Matched Probation and After-Care Treatment*, Home Office Research Unit Report No. 36, London: HMSO, 1976.

Foucault, Michel, *Discipline and Punish: The Birth of the Prison*, New York: Vintage Books, 1979.

Fox, Lionel W., *The English Prison and Borstal Systems*, London: Routledge and Kegan Paul, 1961.

Frankel, Marvin E., *Partisan Justice*, New York: Hill and Wang, 1980.

Freed, Daniel J., Statement to the Subcommittee of the Committee on the Judiciary of the House of Representatives in 1974, (extract), in *Diversion From Criminal Justice in an English Context.* Report of a NACRO Working Party, Chichester and London: Barry Rose, 1975, pp. 41–4.

Freeman, M. D. A. and Lyon, Christine M., 'The Imprisonment of Maintenance Defaulters', *Howard Journal*, **20**, 1981, pp. 15–28.

Fyffe, Andrew A., 'A Most Peculiar Absence of Monsters', *Prison Service Journal*, **27**, 1977, pp. 12–14.

Galligan, D. J., 'Guidelines and Just Deserts: A Critique of Recent Trends in Sentencing Reform'. *Criminal Law Review*, 1981, pp. 297–311.

Goring, Charles, *Statistical Study of the English Convict*, London: HMSO, 1913.

Grabosky, P. N., 'Rates of Imprisonment and Psychiatric Hospitalisation in the United States', *Social Indicators Research*, **7**, 1980, pp. 63–70.

Greenberg, David F., 'The Dynamics of Oscillatory Punishment Processes', *Journal of Criminal Law and Criminology*, **68**, 1977, pp. 643–51.
'Penal Sanctions in Poland: A Test of Alternative Models', *Social Problems*, **28**, 1980, pp. 194–204.

Greenberg, David F. and Humphries, Drew, 'The Cooption of Fixed Sentencing Reform', *Crime and Delinquency*, **26**, 1980, pp. 210–25.

Greenfeld, Lawrence A., 'Assessing Prison Environments: A Comparative Approach', unpublished paper, Washington D.C.: National Institute of Justice, 1981.

Guy, William A., *Public Health, A Popular Introduction to Sanitary Science*, London: Henry Renshaw, 1870.

Hamilton, V. L. and Rotkin, L., 'Interpreting the Eighth Amendment: Perceived Seriousness of Crime and Severity of Punishment', in H. A. Bedau and C. M. Pierie (eds.), *Capital Punishment in the United States*, New York: AMS Press, 1976.

Hart, Henry, M., 'The Aims of the Criminal Law', in *Crime, Law and Society*, eds. A. S. Goldstein and J. Goldstein, New York: Free Press, 1971, pp. 61–71.

Hirsch, Andrew von, *Doing Justice: The Choice of Punishments*, Report of the Committee for the Study of Incarceration, New York: Hill and Wang, 1976.

Hobhouse, Stephen and Brockway, A. Fenner (eds.), *English Prisons Today*, London: Longmans, Green & Co., 1922.

Hough, J. M. and Clarke, R. V. G., (eds.), introduction to *The Effectiveness of Policing*, Farnborough: Gower, 1980.

Hough, J. M. and Mayhew, Pat, *The British Crime Survey*, Home Office Research Study No. 76, London: HMSO, 1983.

Howard, John, *The State of the Prisons*, London: Dent, 1929.

Howard League for Penal Reform, *The Prisoner Population of the World*, London, 1936.

Losing Touch, Restrictions on Prisoners' Outside Contacts, Working Party Report, London, 1979.

Freedom on Licence, The Development of Parole and Proposals for Reform, Sunbury: Quartermaine, 1981.

Huber, Barbara, 'Safeguarding of Prisoners' Rights Under the New West German Prison Act', *South African Journal of Criminal Law and Criminology*, **2**, 1978, pp. 229–38.

Hulsman, L. H. C., 'The Evolution of Imprisonment in the Netherlands', *Revue de Droit pénal et de criminologie*, (Belgium), 57, 1977.

'The relative mildness of the Dutch criminal justice system: an attempt at analysis', in *Introduction to Dutch Law for Foreign Lawyers*, eds. D. C. Fokkema, W. Chorus, E. H. Hundius, *et al.*, Deventer: Kluwer, 1978, pp. 373–7.

'Penal Reform in the Netherlands: Part I, Bringing the Criminal Justice System Under Control', *Howard Journal*, vol. 20, 1981, pp. 150–9; and Part II in vol. 21, 1982, pp. 35–47.

Irwin, John, *The Felon*, Englewood Cliffs, N.J.: Prentice-Hall, 1970.

Prisons in Turmoil, Boston and Toronto: Little Brown, 1980.

Jackson, George, *Soledad Brother*, New York: Bantam Books, 1970.

Jacob, Herbert and Lineberry, Robert L., *Govermental Responses to Crime*, Executive Summary of Final Report to National Institute of Justice. Draft, January 1982.

Jacobs, James B., *Stateville, The Penitentiary in a Mass Society*, Chicago: University of Chicago Press, 1977.

Jacobs, James B. and Crotty, Norma Meacham, *Guard Unions and the Future of Prisons*, Cornell University: Institute of Public Employment, New York State School of Industrial and Labour Relations, 1978.

Jones, Marjorie, *Crime Punishment and the Press*, London: NACRO, 1980.

Justice, *Breaking the Rules*, London, 1980.

Kassebaum, Gene, Ward, David and Wilner, Daniel, *Prison Treatment and Parole Survival*, New York: John Wiley, 1971.

King, Michael, *The Framework of Criminal Justice*, London: Croom Helm, 1981.

King, Roy D. and Elliott, Kenneth W., *Albany: Birth of a Prison: End of an Era*, London: Routledge and Kegan Paul, 1978.

King, Roy D. and Morgan, Rod, *The Future of the Prison System*, Farnborough: Gower, 1980.

Krajick, Kevin, 'At Stateville, The Calm is Tense', *Corrective Magazine*, **6**, June 1980, pp. 8–10.

'The Boom Resumes', *Corrections Magazine*, **7**, 1981, pp. 16–20.

Land, Hilary, 'Detention Centres: the Experiment Which Could Not Fail', in *Change, Choice and Conflict in Social Policy*, ed. Phoebe Hall *et al.*, London: Heinemann, 1975, pp. 311–70.

Lerman, Paul, *Community Treatment and Social Control*, Chicago: University of Chicago Press, 1975.

Lester, Anthony and Bird, Geoffrey, *Race and the Law*, London: Penguin, 1972.

Lombrozo, Cesare, *L'uomo delinquente*, Milan, 1876.

Mannheim, Hermann, *Social Aspects of Crime in England Between the Wars*, London: George Allen and Unwin, 1940.

Marnell, Gunnar, 'Penal Reform: A Swedish Viewpoint', *Howard Journal*, **14**, 1974, pp. 8–21.

Martin, J. P., 'Jellicoe and After: Boards of Visitors into the Eighties', *Howard Journal of Penology and Crime Prevention*, **19**, 1980, pp. 85–101.

Martinson, Robert, 'What Works, – questions and answers about prison reform', *The Public Interest*, Spring 1974, pp. 22–54.

Mathieson, Thomas, *Across the Boundaries of Organisations: An Exploratory Study of Communication Patterns in the Penal Institutions*, Berkeley, California: Glendessary Press, 1971.
   The Politics of Abolition, Oxford: Martin Robertson, 1974.

Mayhew, Henry, *The Criminal Prisons of London and Scenes of Prison Life*, London: Griffin, Bohn, 1862.

Mayhew, Pat and Hough, Mike, 'The British Crime Survey', Home Office Research Planning Unit, *Research Bulletin*, No. 14, 1982, pp. 24–7.

McCleery, Richard H., 'Communication Patterns as Bases of Systems of Authority and Power', in *Theoretical Studies in Social Organisation of the Prison*, eds. Richard A. Cloward *et al.*, New York: Social Science Research Council, 1960, pp. 49–110.

McClintock, F. H. and Avison, N. Howard, *Crime in England and Wales*, London: Heinemann, 1968.

McConville, Seán, *A History of English Prison Administration*, Vol. I, 1750–1877, London: Routledge and Kegan Paul, 1981.

Miller, Walter B., 'Ideology and Criminal Justice Policy: Some Current Issues', *Journal of Criminal Law and Criminology*, **64**, 1973, pp. 141–62.

Moriarty, Michael, 'The Policy-Making Process: How it is seen from the Home Office', in *Penal Policy-Making in England*, ed. Nigel Walker, Cambridge: Institute of Criminology, 1977.

Morris, Norval, *The Future of Imprisonment*, Chicago: University of Chicago Press, 1974.

Morris, Pauline, *Prisoners and Their Families*, London: George Allen and Unwin, 1965.

Morris, Terence and Morris, Pauline, *Pentonville: A Sociological Study of an English Prison*, London: Routledge and Kegan Paul, 1963.

Murton, Tom and Hyams, Joe, *Accomplices to the Crime, The Arkansas Prison Scandal*, London: Michael Joseph, 1970.

NACRO, *Diversion From Criminal Justice in an English Context.* Report of a NACRO Working Party, Chairman, Michael Zander, Chichester and London: Barry Rose, 1975.

Fine Default, Report of a NACRO Working Party, Chairman, Lady Howe, London: NACRO, 1981.

New York Special Commission on Attica, *Attica, The Official Report of the New York State Special Commission on Attica*, New York: Bantam Books, 1972.

Note, '"Mastering" Intervention in Prisons', *Yale Law Journal*, **88**, 1979, pp. 1062–91.

Nuyten-Edelbroek, E. G. M. and Tigges, L. C. M., 'Early Intervention by a Probation Agency: A Netherlands Experiment', *Howard Journal*, **1**, 1980, pp. 42–51.

Oatham, E. and Simon, F., 'Are Suspended Sentences Working', *New Society*, **21**, 1972, pp. 233–5.

Ohlin, Lloyd E., 'Conflicting Interests in Correctional Objectives', in *Theoretical Studies in Social Organisation of the Prison*, eds. Richard A. Cloward *et al.*, New York: Social Science Research Council, 1960, pp. 111–29.

Packer, Herbert L., *The Limits of the Criminal Sanction*, Stanford: Stanford University Press, 1968.

Parent, Dale G., 'Minnesota's New Sentencing Guidelines Legislation', *Hennepin Lawyer*, Sept.–Oct., 1978, pp. 14–17.

Parliamentary All-Party Penal Affairs Group, *Too Many Prisoners, An Examination of Ways of Reducing the Prison Population*, Chichester and London: Barry Rose, 1980.

Still Too Many Prisoners, An Assessment of the Government's Response to the Report 'Too Many Prisoners' since June 1980, 1981.

Pease, Ken, 'Community Service and the Tariff', *Criminal Law Review*, 1978, pp. 269–75.

'The Size of the Prison Population', *British Journal of Criminology*, **21**, 1981, pp. 70–74.

Penrose, L. S., *Mental Disease and Crime: Outline of a Comparative Study of European Statistics. British Journal of Medical Psychology*, **18**, 1939, pp. 1–15.

Perrow, Charles, *Organisational Analysis: A Sociological View*, London: Tavistock, 1970.

Pugh, Ralph B., *Imprisonment in Medieval England*, Cambridge: Cambridge University Press, 1968.

Radzinowicz, Leon, *A History of English Criminal Law and its Adminis-*

tration, from 1750, Volume I, *The Movement for Reform*, London: Stevens and Stevens, 1948.

Radzinowicz, Leon and Hood, Roger, 'Judicial Discretion and Sentencing Standards: Victorian attempts to solve a perennial problem', *University of Pennysylvania Law Review*, **127**, 1979, pp. 1288–1349.

'Dangerousness and Criminal Justice: a few reflections', *Criminal Law Review*, 1981, pp. 756–61.

Ramsay, Malcolm, 'Two Centuries of Imprisonment', *Home Office Research Bulletin*, No. 14, 1982, pp. 45–7.

Robbins, Ira P., 'The Cry of Wolfish in the Federal Courts: The future of federal judicial intervention in prison administration', *Journal of Criminal Law and Criminology*, **71**, 1980, pp. 211–25.

'Legal Aspects of Prison Riots', *Harvard Civil Rights Civil Liberties Review*, **16**, 1982, pp. 769–72.

Robbins, Ira P. and Buser, Michael B., 'Punitive Conditions of Prison Confinement: An Analysis of *Pugh* v. *Locke* and Federal Court Supervision of State Penal Administration Under the Eighth Amendment, *Standard Law Review*, **29**, 1977, pp. 893–930.

Robison, J. and Smith, G., 'The Effectiveness of Correctional Program', *Crime and Delinquency*, **17**, 1971, pp. 67.

Rose, Gordon, *The Struggle for Penal Reform, the Howard League and its Predecessors*, London: Stevens & Sons, 1961.

Rothman, David J., *The Discovery of the Asylum, Social Order and Disorder in the New Republic*, Boston and Toronto: Little Brown, 1971.

Ruck, S. K. (ed.), *Paterson on Prisons*, London: Frederick Muller, 1951.

Rusche, George and Kirchheimer, Otto, *Punishment and Social Structure*, New York: Russell and Russell, 1939.

Rutherford, Andrew, 'The California Protection Subsidy Scheme', *British Journal of Criminology*, **12**, 1972, pp. 186–8.

'Formal Bargaining in the Prison: In Search of a New Organisational Model', *Yale Review of Law and Social Action*, **2**, 1971, pp. 5–12.

'The Dissolution of the Training Schools in Massachusetts', Columbus, Ohio: Academy for Contemporary Problems, 1974.

'Decarceration of Young Offenders in Massachusetts', in N. Tutt (ed.), *Alternative Strategies for Coping with Crime*, Oxford: Blackwell, 1978, pp. 103–19.

Rutherford, Andrew *et al.*, *Prison Population and Policy Choices* [see under United States Department of Justice].

Sachs, Albie, *Justice in South Africa*, Berkeley and Los Angeles: University of California, 1973.

Scheff, Tom J., 'Control over policy by attendants in a mental hospital', *Journal of Health and Human Behaviour*, **2**, 1961, pp. 93–105.

Scull, Andrew, *Decarceration: Community Treatment and the Deviant: a Radical View*, Englewood Cliffs: Prentice-Hall, 1977.

Sebba, Leslie, 'Some Explorations in the Scaling of Penalties', *Journal of Research in Crime and Delinquency*, 1978, pp. 247–65.

Shaw, Stephen, *Paying the Penalty: An Analysis of the Cost of Penal Sanctions*, London: NACRO, 1980.

Sherman, Michael and Hawkins, Gordon, *Imprisonment in America; Choosing the Future*, Chicago: University of Chicago Press, 1981.

Smith, Polly D., 'It Can Happen Here: Reflections on the Dutch System'. *Prison Journal*, **58**, 1978, pp. 31–7.

Smith, Robert L., *A Quiet Revolution*, Washington D.C.: U.S. Department of Health, Education and Welfare, 1971.

Sparks, R., Genn, H. G. and Dodd, D. J., *Surveying Victims*, Chichester: Wiley, 1977.

Steenhuis, Dato W., Tigges, L. C. M. and Essers, J. J. A., 'The Penal Climate in the Netherlands: Sunny or Cloudy', *British Journal of Criminology*, **23**, 1983, pp. 1–16.

Sutherland, Edwin H., 'The Decreasing Prison Population of England', *Journal of Criminal Law and Criminology*, **24**, 1934, pp. 880–900.

Tarling, Roger, *Sentencing Practice in Magistrates' Courts*, Home Office Research Unit Study No. 56, London: HMSO, 1979.
'Unemployment and Crime', *Home Office Research Unit Bulletin*, No. 14, 1982, pp. 28–33.

Tench, David, *Towards a Middle System of Law*, London: Consumers' Association, 1981.

Thomas, D. A., 'The Partly Suspended Sentence', *Criminal Law Review*, May 1982, pp. 288–95.

Thomas J. E. and Pooley, R., *The Exploding Prison*, London: Junction Books, 1980.

Tomasic, Roman and Dobison, Ian, *The Failure of Imprisonment, An Australian Perspective*, Sydney: George Allen and Unwin, 1979.

Tulkens, Hans, *Some Developments in Penal Policy and Practice in Holland*, London: NACRO, 1979.

Ward, David A., 'Inmate Rights and Prison Reform in Sweden and Denmark', *Journal of Criminal Law and Criminology and Police Science*, **63**, 1972, pp. 240–55.
'Sweden: The Middle Way to Prison Reform?', in *Prisons: Present and Possible*, ed. Marvin E. Wolfgang, Lexington, Massachusetts: Lexington, 1979, pp. 89–167.

Ward, David A. and Schmidt, Annesley K., 'Last-Resort Prisons for Habitual and Dangerous Offenders: Some Second Thoughts about Alcatraz', in *Confinement in Maximum Custody*, eds. David A. Ward and Kenneth F. Schoen, Lexington, Massachusetts: Lexington, 1981, pp. 61–8.

Webb, Sidney and Beatrice, *English Prisons Under Local Government*,
    London: Longmans, Green & Co., 1922.
Wicker, Tom, *A Time To Die*, New York: Ballantine Books, 1976.
Wildeblood, Peter, *Against the Law*, Harmondsworth: Penguin, 1957.
Wilkins, Geoff, *Making Them Pay*, London: NACRO, 1979.
Wilson, Harold, *The Labour Government 1964–1970, A Personal Record*,
    London: Nicolson and Weidenfeld, 1971.
Wilson, James Q., *Thinking About Crime*, New York: Basic Books, 1975.
Wright, Martin, *Making Good: Prisons, Punishment and Beyond*, London:
    Burnett, 1982.
Yeager, M. G., 'Unemployment and Imprisonment', *Journal of Criminal
    Law and Criminology*, **70**, 1979, pp. 586–8.
Zander, Michael, 'Operation of the Bail Act in London Magistrates'
    Courts', *New Law Journal*, **129**, 1979, pp. 108–11.
Zellick, Graham, 'The Prison Rules and the Court', *Criminal Law Review*,
    1981, pp. 602–16.
    'The Prison Rules and the Courts, A Postscript', *Criminal Law Review*,
    Sept. 1982, pp. 575–6.
Zimring, Franklin E. and Hawkins, Gordon J., *Deterrence: The Legal
    Threat in Crime Control*, Chicago: University of Chicago Press, 1973.

Home Office
Prisons and Borstals, England and Wales, London: HMSO, 1960.
Report of the Working Party on Communications, Prison Department,
    1964.
The Regime for Long-Term Prisoners in Conditions of Maximum Security,
    Advisory Council on the Penal System, Chairman of sub-committee,
    Professor Leon Radzinowicz, London: HMSO, 1968.
Young Adult Offenders, report of the Advisory Council on the Penal
    System, Chairman, Sir Kenneth Younger, London: HMSO, 1974.
A Review of Criminal Justice Policy 1976, London: HMSO, 1977.
*Report of an Inquiry by the Chief Inspector of the Prison Service into the
    Causes and Circumstances of the Events at H.M. Prison, Hull During
    the Period 31st August to 3rd September 1976*, London: HMSO, 1977.
Sentences of Imprisonment: A Review of Maximum Penalties, Report of
    the Advisory Council on the Penal System, Chairman, Lady Serotta,
    London: HMSO, 1978.
Report on Judicial Studies and Information, Report of Working Party,
    Chairman, Lord Justice Bridge, London: HMSO, 1978.
Evidence submitted to the Inquiry into the United Kingdom Prison Services
    (May Committee), vols. 1 and 2, *Evidence by the Home Office, the
    Scottish Home and Health Department and the Northern Ireland Office*.
    Vol. 3, *Evidence by H.M. Treasury, the Civil Service Department and
    the Central Policy Review Staff*, London: HMSO, 1979.

Home Office Statistical Bulletin, *Changes in the Prison Population during the Industrial Action by the POA*, London: Home Office issue 12, 1981.

Working Party Report on Categorisation, Prison Department, 1981.

H.M. Chief Inspector of Prisons, report on *Gartree Prison*, 1981.

H.M. Chief Inspector of Prisons, report on *Gloucester Prison*, London: Home Office, 1982.

H.M. Chief Inspector of Prisons, report on *Leeds Prison*, London: Home Office, 1982.

Parliamentary Papers

Report of the Departmental Committee on Prisons, Chairman, Herbert Gladstone, C7702, LVI, 1. London: HMSO, 1895.

Report of the Committee Appointed to Inquire into the Pay and Conditions of Service at the Prisons and Borstals in England and Scotland and at Broadmoor Lunatic Asylum, Chairman, The Earl of Stanhope, Cmnd 1959, London: HMSO, 1923.

Report on the Circumstances Connected with the Recent Disorder at Dartmoor Convict Prison, Chairman, Herbert du Parcq KC, Cmnd 4010, London: HMSO, 1932.

Penal Practice in a Changing Society, Aspects of Future Development (England and Wales), Cmnd 645, London: HMSO, 1959.

Report of the Committee on Homosexual Offences and Prostitution. Chairman, Sir John Wolfenden, Cmnd 247, London: HMSO, 1957.

Report of the Inquiry into Prison Escapes and Security (Mountbatten Report), Cmnd 3175, London: HMSO, 1966.

Eleventh Report from the Estimates Committee, together with minutes of evidence taken before the sub-committee on Social Affairs, *Prisons, Borstals and Detention Centres*, H.C. 599, 1967.

Fifteenth Report of the Expenditure Committee, *The Reduction of Pressure on the Prison System*, 662–1, (Report), 662–2 (Evidence), London: HMSO, 1978.

Report of the Inquiry into the United Kingdom Prison Services, Chairman, Mr Justice May, Cmnd 7673, London: HMSO, 1979.

The Reduction of Pressure on the Prison System, Observations on the Fifteenth Report from the Expenditure Committee, Cmnd 7948, London: HMSO, 1980.

The Government's Reply to the Fourth Report from the Home Affairs Committee, Cmnd 8446, London: HMSO, 1981.

Report of Royal Commission on Criminal Procedure, Chairman, Sir Cyril Philips, Cmnd 8092, London: HMSO, 1981.

Report of an Inquiry into the Brixton Disorders, 10–12 April, 1981, (Scarman Report), Cmnd 8427, London: HMSO, 1981.

Fourth Report from the Home Affairs Committee, *The Prison Service*, House of Commons Paper 412–1 (Report), 412–2 (Evidence), 1981.

Statement on the background, circumstances and action taken subsequently relative to the disturbance in 'D' wing at H.M. Prison, Wormwood Scrubs on 31 August 1979; together with the Report on an Inquiry by the Regional Director of the South East Region of the Prison Department. H.C. 198, London: HMSO, 1982.

Report of Her Majesty's Chief Inspector of Prisons for England and Wales, 1981. Cmnd 8532, London: HMSO, 1982.

Report of the Work of the Prison Department, 1981, Cmnd 8543, London: HMSO, 1982.

Prison Statistics, England and Wales, 1981, Cmnd 8654, London: HMSO, 1982.

Criminal Statistics, England and Wales, 1981, Cmnd 8668, London: HMSO, 1982.

Report of Her Majesty's Chief Inspector of Prisons for England and Wales, 1982, H.C. 260, London: HMSO, 1983.

United States Department of Justice

President's Commission on Law Enforcement and Administration of Justice, Task Force Report, *Corrections*, Washington Government Printing Office, 1967.

National Advisory Commission on Criminal Justice Standards and Goals, *A National Strategy to Reduce Crime*, Washington D.C.: Government Printing Office, 1973.

National Institute of Law Enforcement and Criminal Justice, *Prison Population and Policy Choices*, Volume 1, Preliminary Report to Congress; Volume 2, Technical Appendix. Washington D.C.: Government Printing Office, 1977.

National Institute of Justice, *American Prisons and Jails*, Vol. 1, *Summary and Policy Implications of a National Study*; Vol. 2, *Population Trends and Projections*; Vol. 3, *Conditions and Costs of Confinement*; Vol. 4, *Supplementary Report – Case Studies of New Legislation Covering Sentencing and Release*; Vol. 5, *Supplementary Report – Adult Pre-Release Facilities*; Washington D.C.: Government Printing Office, 1981.

Attorney-General's Task Force on Violent Crime, Final Report, Chairman, Griffin Bell, Washington D.C.: Government Printing Office, 1981.

Index